Janey

A LITTLE PLANE IN A BIG WAR

Janey

A LITTLE PLANE IN A BIG WAR

Alfred W. Schultz

with Kirk Neff

SOUTHFARM PRESS, *Publisher*
Middletown, Connecticut

SOUTHFARM PRESS, PUBLISHER
Publishing imprint of Haan Graphic Publishing Services, Ltd.
P.O. Box 1296, Middletown, Connecticut 06457

ISBN: 0-913337-31-5

Library of Congress Cataloging-in-Publication Data

Schultz, Alfred W., 1920-
    Janey : a little plane in a big war / by Alfred W. Schultz, with
Kirk Neff.
      p.   cm.
    ISBN 0-913337-31-5 (hardcover)
    1. Schultz, Alfred W., 1920-   . 2. World War, 1939-1945--Aerial
operations, American. 3. World War, 1939-1945--Personal narratives,
American. 4. Military reconnaissance. 5. Military surveillance.
6. Air pilots, Military--United States--Biography. I. Neff, Kirk,
1950-   . II. Title.
D790.S3375 1998
940.54'4973--dc21
                                    98-12934
                                    CIP

Attention: Schools/Businesses/Veterans Organizations
Southfarm Press books are available at quantity discounts with
bulk purchase for educational, business, or sales promotion use.
For information, please write to Special Sales Department at our
address shown above.

Printed in The United States of America

Second Printing

*T*O THE FLESH-AND-BLOOD JANEY
—*JANE WILLIS REESE*—
WHO WAITED FOR ME, MARRIED ME
AND BECAME MY BEST FRIEND

Group photo of pilots and mechanics in front of *Janey* on the flight deck of LST 906 in the harbor at Naples, Italy. Photo was taken the day before the August 15, 1944, invasion of southern France. *Top row, left to right:* **Alfred W. Schultz, W. H. "Fred" Boucher, Edwin "Irv" Rosner, Hubert A. Boone, W. A. "Bill" Richards, Robert N. Peterson, Arlie E. Schumacher, Warren T. Reis.** *Bottom row, left to right:* **Theodore J. Royston, David P. Guthrie, William K. Baker, George W. Desrassers, John E. Samsa, Wesley W. Kelly.** —*National Archives*

ACKNOWLEDGMENTS

Ken Wakefield, author of *The Fighting Grasshoppers,* encouraged me to record my adventures. He used my stories and pictures in his book.

John Hoover first translated my oral stories into the printed word in 1987. Kirk Neff expanded them and began submitting the material to publishers.

My family gave me much advice and many hours of help to turn out the initial 548-page story, which was subsequently reduced to this 288-page, action-packed adventure.

—Alfred W. Schultz

INTRODUCTION

Rise before dawn. Drink what could be your last cup of coffee. Spin the prop of your linen-and-plywood L-4B Piper Cub. Then climb into the cockpit and fly toward German lines. Above 800 feet, you're easy prey for the lurking ME-109s and FW-190s, but almost out of range of small-arms fire. Below 800 feet you're safer from the marauding Luftwaffe bandits, but a slow, easy target for any rifleman. There's a price on your head, and every German wants to collect it. This was the reality of Alfred W. Schultz's morning schedule during World War II.

Schultzie, also nicknamed "Dutch," flew his Army-issue Piper Cub named for his college sweetheart, Jane Reese, over every battle the Third Infantry Division fought during World War II. Schultz and *Janey* flew all the way from Casablanca to Berchtesgaden, despite daily attention from German troopers, AA gunners, and bandits in the sky.

To the dogface soldiers on the ground, the L-4B artillery spotter plane was a guardian angel. While a Cub was in the air, the Germans dared not fire a shot or make a move. To do so would have given away their position, risking retaliation from the American guns. The little Cubs were such annoyances that any German fighter pilot, AA gunner, or foot soldier who downed a Cub was rewarded with a six-day furlough.

Schultz and *Janey* also provided a bird's-eye view of the battlefields for several commanding officers. Generals Patton, Truscott, and "Iron Mike" O'Daniel were regular *Janey* passengers. On one trip, Schultzie, *Janey*, and General Patton almost bit the dust when they were attacked by a German sky bandit. Iron Mike O'Daniel directed the breakout from Anzio and the breaching of the Siegfried Line from tree-top heights at near-stall speeds while sitting in *Janey*'s rear seat.

As General Walter T. Kerwin, Jr. (Ret.) recently wrote, "Schultz tells *Janey*'s story with humor and clarity. Schultz's daily grind was at one moment humorous and the next moment life-threatening, but always interesting. Flying in his Piper Cub, *Janey*, Schultz saw more of World War II than anybody else in the Third Infantry Division. He enjoyed badgering the Germans—and *Janey* became a legend."

—Kirk Neff

Shown sitting on a downed ME 109 in Africa and enjoying victory toasts made in Austria, Chuck Croal's mechanical skills made Alfred W. Schultz's Piper Cub *Janey* start easily. —*Charles Croal*

1 • BOMB THE SHEEP

"Schultz, go out and bomb the sheep," Captain Brenton Devol ordered.

Even though it was a chicken detail, as a 22-year-old second lieutenant in the Third Infantry Division, I was bound to do my duty. We had a war to fight and couldn't let a bunch of damn sheep get in our way. We had already lost Round One against Rommel and his *Africa Corps* at Kasserine Pass, and on this early spring day in 1943, I relished the chance to play even a small role in preparing for Round Two.

Janey, the olive-drab U.S. Army-issue Piper Cub that I had named after my college sweetheart, started on the first spin of her propeller, and Captain Nelson, the artillery observer, and I were soon cruising above the Moroccan countryside in search of sheep.

Round Two was not going to be easy. Rommel had absolutely humiliated our men at the Kasserine Pass in February and had bragged that in the upcoming engagement he would give us an inferiority complex. In preparation for Round Two, General George S. Patton was preaching his blood-and-guts sermons to instill fighting spirit into young men raised in the Christian tradition of love thy neighbor. To instill discipline into those dispirited troops, he ordered that officers wear ties and that all soldiers be clean-shaven and wear helmets at all times, even while in the latrines.

General Lucian Truscott, Jr., the newly-appointed commander of the Third Infantry Division, a unit in Patton's newly -forming Seventh Army, had vowed to personally avenge the defeat American soldiers had suffered in their first engagement with the Germans and to restore the reputation of America's fighting men and the confidence of our British allies.

Acting as General Dwight Eisenhower's eyes and ears, Truscott had personally observed the battle of the Kasserine Pass, and after reporting on the rout of untried American troops, had asked Eisenhower for command of a full infantry division, the dream of any fighting general.

Truscott, not a West Pointer but a schoolmaster who had been commissioned as a reserve cavalry officer in 1917, had risen steadily through the ranks in the peacetime Army after World War I. During the invasion of Morocco's Port Lyautey (now Kenitra) in 1942, General Truscott had commanded a regimental combat team, and now he wanted a full infantry division and a chance to prove that Rommel and the *Africa Corps* were not invincible.

Eisenhower made Truscott's dream come true. He gave him the Third Infantry Division, a proud old regular Army division that had earned the name "The Rock of the Marne" for its heroic and distinguished service against the Germans in World War I. A majority of the officers and men of the Third Division were seasoned veterans with many years of service and a sense of pride in their unit. In addition to being well-trained in military tradition and procedure, General Truscott also demanded that his men be physically fit as well. He expected them to out-march, out-shoot and out-fight the best Germany had to offer. Round Two would be their test.

The new general instituted forced marches that became known as the "Truscott Trot." All soldiers, from high-ranking officers down to lowly cooks and clerks, mastered the technique. They marched at the speed of 5 mph the first hour, 4 mph for the second and third hours, then maintained a speed of 3.5 mph for the remainder of the march. After marching 30 miles through swamps, tidewater flats, and sand dunes, the troops would fire their weapons, and fire them fast. General Truscott had seen heavy casualties at Kasserine Pass that had resulted from the lack of covering fire, and he didn't want it to happen again. Ammunition was not a problem with the American Army. Workers back home would supply all the weapons and ammunition the troops could ever use, and the secret of success was to be: *Fire your weapon!*

"The more you fire, the safer you and your buddies will be," battle-wise veterans of the Kasserine disaster assured the new men. Everyone grew accustomed to the smoke and kick and noise of their weapons, the ache of strained muscles, the agony of blistered feet. They drilled and marched and fired their weapons day and night, in fair weather and in muck. The Truscott Trot turned out to be both their pride and their curse. Those who wore the blue-and-white shoulder patch of the Third Infantry Division became the "Walking Pride of Uncle Sam" to General Truscott and the "Blue and White Devils" to the Germans who faced them.

After his men had mastered small-arms firing, General Truscott instituted combined-weapons drills. "Big Bangers," the 155mm howitzers that could reach the reverse sides of hills, were fired by the Division's Ninth Field Artillery Battalion in concert with the rifles of the infantry dogfaces. Instead of firing their rifles out to sea, they now fired them into the pastures along the Atlantic Ocean. This artillery range, allotted to the Allies by the Sultan of Morocco, was his contribution to the Allied effort.

The sultan had provided only one parcel of land, and it happened to be the local pasture land. Generations of Berber shepherds had grazed their sheep and goats on that land, and despite pleas, bargains, bribes and threats from the Senegalese troops, who were assigned by the Free French to keep the target area clear, the shepherds continued to graze their flocks on the artillery range. The Third Infantry Division needed desperately to plan and coordinate infantry, tank, and artillery exercises for their upcoming combat with the *Africa Corps.*

They couldn't afford the repeated disruptions and the loss of training time that resulted whenever a shepherd decided to graze his flocks on the firing range.

The Ninth Field Artillery Battalion Commander, Major Christopher Coyne, wanted the range cleared without endangering the lives of the Berbers or their animals, so he decided that *Janey* and I could provide a little friendly persuasion from the air. Chasing sheep had not been part of my flight training at Fort Sill, but I was confident that *Janey* and I could fulfill our mission. We would locate the wayward herds of sheep and bravely shoo them out of the line of fire.

Captain Nelson, trained to spot enemy artillery from the air, spotted the intruders right away. Flocks of white sheep and goats dotted the target area where the Big Bangers' 155mm practice shells were aimed. Nelson tapped my shoulder and shouted into his microphone, "Let's clear the area!"

I started *Janey* in low-level runs at the flocks of sheep, and Nelson and I enjoyed watching the animals scatter below us. The shepherds, however, didn't share our joy. They shook their angry fists at us and spat Moroccan epithets into the air, undoubtedly commenting on our ancestry.

Undeterred, I expertly maneuvered *Janey* into several low-level swoops, daring to go lower and lower. Each time around, the shepherds punched the air with their fists and shouted. When the artillery field was almost clear, Nelson told me to make one more dive and then we'd call it quits. At the critical point of the last, and lowest, dive, one of the shepherds launched his only available antiaircraft missile, his staff.

A loud WHAP resounded through the airframe. *Janey* shuddered, hesitated, then lurched groundward. The shepherd had scored a direct hit on the leading edge of *Janey*'s right wing. My heart jumped past my throat and sweat flooded my palms. I had only a millisecond to prevent a collision with the North African desert, yet a thousand clear thoughts raced through my mind. The split-second loss of forward speed, the trembling of *Janey*'s airframe, and the ground rushing toward the windscreen combined to make the engine's response to my throttle command seem like an eternity.

As *Janey* fought to regain the required altitude and airspeed, Nelson shouted Cease-fire! into his microphone while tapping my shoulder to indicate a return to base, a retreat from combat with this particular enraged shepherd. *Janey* had received her first combat wound before the factory paint had been scorched from her exhaust ports. The deep diagonal gash in the leading edge of her right wing, the exposed bright aluminum edge and interior ribs, and the torn and ragged fabric whipping in the wind combined to make a ghastly sight. I took *Janey* to an altitude beyond the range of the shepherds' staffs and headed her back to our base in the Sultan's cork forest. Luckily, the wound was close to the tip of the wing and did not damage the junction where a support strut from the airframe joined the wing. *Janey*'s mechanic, T-3 Charles Croal, would be able to have her flying again in four or five days.

Janey was a Piper Cub, built in Pennsylvania, disassembled, and shipped to Morocco in pieces. To the Army Air Force, Piper Cubs like *Janey* were O-59s; to the Army, they were L-4Bs. During large-scale maneuvers in 1941, the small observation cubs had been dubbed "grasshoppers" by General Innis Swift, and the dogfaces in their foxholes referred to them as "our Cubs" or "our guardian angels." Air Force enlisted personnel, however, referred to the Piper-Cub fleet derogatorily as the "putt-putt air force," and in song the Cub pilots themselves glorified their flying machines as the "Maytag Messerschmitts." The Moroccan shepherds, too, probably had a special name or two for us, after we scattered their sheep and goats over the rolling pastures.

2 • *ARRIVING IN AFRICA*

Tugboats nudged the troop ship against a Casablanca pier on a cloudless December afternoon in 1942. The blazing sun and the multicolored robes and turbans of the dock workers left little doubt that we were in Africa. As the workers scurried and sweated below us, we soldiers lined up in spit-and-polish formations on deck. To our dismay, no military band greeted us with the expected pomp and circumstance, but a far worse circumstance assaulted our egos: No Army trucks were anywhere in sight. Not even one! We were a motorized unit, and somebody had misplaced our transportation. We would have to walk the three miles to our bivouac area.

Units of enlisted men that debarked ahead of us marched off with rifles and duffel bags slung over their shoulders. But our equipment was different. We officers had .45 pistols instead of rifles, over-the-shoulder musette bags instead of duffel bags, and Val-Pacs, which resembled modern-day carry-on suit bags. The pistols were easier to carry than rifles, but our Val-Pacs were too cumbersome to sling over the shoulder like duffel bags. They had to be carried by the handle, a particular inconvenience when marching a long distance.

We marched in columns, by fours and eights. The troops walked and I kept pace by trotting along beside them, often catching up when the columns halted for a rest. I marched alongside men who averaged 5-feet-10 to 6-feet tall, so at 5 feet, 5 inches, I had to dogtrot to keep up with their normal stride.

Private First Class Homer K. Crow, gung-ho and proud of it, suggested we sing to remind the French that we had arrived to repay our debt to Lafayette, but after a few butchered choruses of "I'm a Yankee Doodle Dandy," it was apparent that the cause of camaraderie might be better served if we just counted cadence. The wary natives along the way greeted us with blank stares. To them, we were just another occupying nation in a long series of occupying nations. The Vichy French and the Germans had abandoned Morocco to us, and perhaps victory would come easy; but as we marched through the streets of Casablanca's European quarter, Frenchmen did not come out to kiss us and maidens did not bedeck us with garlands of flowers.

We marched for hours through Morocco's blazing sun to our bivouac area, a campsite on a barren hill. Parked there amid the splotchy patches of dry grass were our trucks, the ones that should have been waiting for us back at the dock. Much needed latrine flies were being set up. Latrine flies were six-foot-high walls of canvas that hid from public view men responding to nature's call.

Latrines always came first. Next came lister bags, barrel-shaped canvas bags filled with drinking water. Like thirsty camels at a waterhole, we crowded around the multiple spigots of the lister bags for our first drink of Moroccan water. A Texan in our midst took a sip and announced, "It'll do, I reckon, but it don't taste like Texas water. Back home, the water tastes like cherry wine." The Moroccan water had been made safe for our consumption by lacing it with a massive dose of chlorine.

Men fresh from training maneuvers in the Southwest compared Morocco's terrain to that of Nevada and New Mexico. When somebody mentioned poisonous snakes, one guy informed us that it wasn't the snakes that posed a serious problem but the scorpions that nestled in your shoes during the night.

We made camp, which called for posting a guard, digging drainage ditches, erecting a flagpole, and establishing "officer country" near the Command Post Headquarters tent. We ate cold C-rations for supper and prepared for the night.

My assigned patch of ground for sleeping was sparsely covered with dry grass. It seemed to need only a minimum of stone clearing, so I spread my blankets on the ground, deciding to sleep on top of them fully clothed and wearing my boots so they couldn't be invaded by scorpions.

As the sun sank below the horizon, it immediately took all its heat with it, just as suddenly as if a furnace had shut down. I was ready for sleep, but soon I was awake, shivering and sweeping away the North African desert gravel from under my makeshift bed. This time, I spread the blankets over me, but even for an old Boy Scout, my first night in Morocco was a cold night on hard ground.

At dawn we gathered around the cook fires for hot coffee. We ate our breakfast C-rations *froid*, French for cold, because the stoves had not yet been offloaded. By now water was in short supply too.

We arrived at the sultan's cork forest in midafternoon. That night I slept in a tent with four blankets under me and my boots beside me. I had accepted the inevitability of scorpions and the necessity of a morning boot shakeout.

The most significant thing about this day for me was meeting T-3 Chuck Croal, the mechanic who would later care for my plane.

One day Croal and I, anxious to get some flight time, went to see the Third Division Artillery Air Officer, who was second in command of the Third Division's artillery pilots. His name was Captain Devol, and he had been part of the Division's initial invasion of Morocco at Fedala, a coastal city between Casablanca and Rabat. With three other L-4Bs, he had taken off from the deck of the Navy carrier U.S.S. *Ranger* from 60 miles at sea. Flying through several miles of inaccurate Navy antiaircraft fire, the planes crash-landed on the beach. Only two of the planes survived and in December of 1942, when I arrived in Africa, they represented the entire Third Division Air Section.

Devol explained that our chances of flying right away were slim. "With several pilots and only two planes, plus lots of brass wanting to fly, flight training will have to wait until the Air Force, which is in charge of dispensing aircraft, receives more planes."

Devol said we were welcome to hang around his airfield until our plane arrived, but he firmly reminded us that we needed Major Christopher C. Coyne's permission to do so. Coyne was first in command of the Ninth Field Artillery Battalion.

We scheduled one day a week for each battalion air section to visit the Third Division Artillery (DIVARTY) airstrip, hoping to gain flight time and to possibly fly a mission. The Air Force, which was responsible for the drawing of Army pilots' flight pay, required four hours of flying in a 30-day pay period. Devol wanted to make certain we all received our qualifying time.

I reported to Major Coyne the status of our flying potential, and he sent me to report those facts to Captain Shaunessey at Headquarters Battery. Until my plane came in, I would perform the duties of a battery officer.

As a lieutenant who stood 5-foot-5 and weighed 145 pounds, I was not the most awe-inspiring of soldiers. In fact, in order to pass my 1940 ROTC exam to become an officer, I had chinned myself and hung by my chin for ten minutes at a time for two weeks prior to my actual physical exam to meet the minimum five-foot-six requirement for an officer. But after passing the exam, I had retreated to my original five-five.

One of my first assignments was to accompany our mess sergeant to the closest village to find fresh food to supplement our meager, boring C-rations. French was the local tongue in and around Rabat, so I stuck a copy of the GI's French handbook in my back pocket and off we went. Our search was futile. Other units had already been to the village and gotten all the good stuff. The black-market pipeline was just beginning to trickle with sought-after goods. The local Arab and French merchants were eager for our business and encouraged us to keep in contact with them. If we wanted oranges and eggs, for example, they could get them for us—for a price. For three eggs or oranges, they charged 100 units of the legal currency, invasion francs. We decided we didn't want eggs or oranges that badly.

On the way back to our cork-forest camp we decided to check out the French air base at Port Lyautey. As we cruised up and down the runways of this ghost base, we detected no sign of any French military presence other than several damaged and abandoned French aircraft and vehicles.

In one corner of the field adjacent to a wide canal were dozens of 1920s-era seaplanes with wings drooping and fabric hanging loose and flapping in the wind.

Scavengers had cannibalized the planes so completely that nothing of value remained to be salvaged. But the paved runway was intact. It was about 1,000 meters long and would make a perfect field for practicing wheel landings. I reported the information to Devol, who decided that he and I would fly over it the next day to inspect it more completely.

Once in the air, Devol allowed me to take the controls, insuring that the flight would count toward my flight time. I approached the field at about 500 feet and we spent nearly an hour surveying the base and the surrounding countryside. It was evident that the cache of antique seaplanes had been deliberately discarded in the marsh. The grass surrounding the planes made a smooth, uninterrupted green carpet. If recent traffic had been through it, a telltale path would have shown clearly. The circumstances at Lyautey remained a mystery, but as we flew low over the site we saw that all metal had been stripped away from the wooden frames. Only rotting wood and painted strips of fabric remained.

Captain Devol located the cleanest taxiway for me to make a wheel landing. I ran the entire strip tail high and we checked the condition of the pavement. It was good, so I came in for a regular three-point landing.

We spent more than an hour walking the tarmac and talking about the possibilities. The landing strips, though cluttered with debris, showed no surface damage. Once they were cleaned up, they would serve as perfect strips to practice landings and takeoffs.

3 • *THE BLIVETS*

Finally the long wait was over. Devol sent word to the Ninth FA Battalion that my Piper Cub was here and being assembled at the Casablanca Airport. Corporal Croal, my mechanic, and I went to pick her up. I felt like a kid getting his first car when I saw the little olive-drab plane sitting on the runway. Croal eagerly opened her up and checked all her parts, while I sat in the pilot's seat, fretting about getting her into the air.

"She looks good," Croal beamed, as he closed her up.

I signed the requisition form, got the documentation, and the plane was mine. Twenty minutes later I landed the plane on the cork-forest airstrip and pulled her under the trees. Chuck and I showed off our new plane to all onlookers and admirers, including the constant stream of Arabs who hid behind the trees trying to sell us eggs, oranges, laundry services, or their virgin sisters.

"Now, Schultz, you need to christen her," Croal said with as much excitement as if it were his plane.

"*Janey*, after my college sweetheart," I announced.

The next day Croal inspected the cowling that covered the engine, making sure it was free of grease and that the paint was dry. Then in careful, even lettering he painted *J-a-n-e-y* across it at a jaunty angle.

My orders were to practice flying. Croal and I worked out procedures for gassing and maintaining the airplane, but there was not yet a clear understanding of the role my plane and I were to play. Major Coyne, the battalion commander, decided to fly over and check the camouflage of our area in the cork forest. General Truscott had returned from the Kasserine Pass debacle, having learned that all vehicles, guns and other equipment should be widely dispersed and hidden under trees or camouflage nets. Major Coyne had never before been in a light plane like *Janey*, so after we went over the principles and procedures of Piper Cubs, I flew him up over the battalion area. It was *Janey*'s and my first important flight together.

Coyne spotted several problems that would betray our position to an airborne enemy. Sunlight flashed off mess kits hanging on tent ropes. Our vehicles' windshields were lying flat, so they reflected the sun. Worn paths were evident between the trees, indicating that a large number of men was moving about.

To prove how easily the enemy could spot us and our equipment, the major decided to set up a fake enemy attack using flour bombs. Kitchen workers filled small cloth bags with white flour and, without any announcement, Major Coyne and I flew over and dropped the bags on poorly-camouflaged targets. The flour bombs were wide of their targets and didn't explode with the big white puffs we had anticipated. The bags, made of squares of sheeting sewn together, were too strong and didn't break when they hit the ground. Flour bombing was a failure, so the next idea was to use condom bombs.

The Army had issued rolls and rolls of condoms, and we filled hundreds of them with water. *Janey* and I took up an observer, who dropped the tiny bombs, which we called blivets, on any troops or equipment we could spot below us. The observer sat in the back seat holding the condoms in his helmet. The condom bombardment worked pretty well when we could get the blivets out of the airplane intact. The troops had overfilled them, and the slightest fingernail pressure ruptured the thin skin and caused the blivets to explode inside the plane, showering both passenger and pilot. The floor of the small plane sloshed with water. Although it was effective, we disliked bombing ourselves with blivets, so we called a stop to that action.

Finally we were issued camouflage nets, and the troops

were busied with interweaving the nets with strips of burlap, greatly improving our camouflage efforts.

Our guns were not yet ready to do any actual firing, so there was nothing for an observation plane like *Janey* to observe. I was so anxious to fly, however, that I became a chauffeur for a few of the battalion officers who had learned that they could fly from our cork-forest base to Rabat or even up to our rifle range at Port Lyautey. By doing so the officers not only saved time, they avoided the putrid smells of North Africa—the sheep and donkeys, the unwashed Arabs themselves, and even the sweet, pungent methane odor generated by the burning charcoal that powered the French buses. Americans had learned that out of respect for the native Arab troops and the local population, we had to be courteous and follow the slow traffic flow, which meant that travel by land involved continual delays, while swallowing the ever-present brown dust created by dry, powdered manure.

The number of higher-ranking officers who asked for flights in *Janey* grew. If *Janey* and I weren't needed at Battalion HQ, I would oblige and be off flying. I soon became a taxi driver, flying officers who ranked me by insignia or duty assignment on 10-to-15 minute flights.

Shuttling officers in *Janey* was a pleasant job in one respect because it enabled me to build up flying time and see more and more of the country. Yet, in another respect, I was getting into trouble. An officer who out-ranked me would order me to fly him somewhere. Then an officer with an even higher rank would say, "Hey, Schultz, I told you I was going to do such-and-such and you were gone. Where were you?"

The lack of dispatching authority even affected my relationship with Captain Devol. One time he came over to inspect my installation and I was off playing chauffeur for a first lieutenant. Devol roundly chewed me out for being away when I was supposed to be on duty awaiting inspection. After that, Captain Shaunessey became my dispatcher, and officers could no longer pull rank with me and *Janey*.

4 • RACES WITH SUNSETS

Cut the power at 100 feet. Turn 90 degrees right or left, then try to land on a designated spot on the runway. Do it again at 200 feet, then at 500 feet, and once again at 50 feet. Then you will get the feel of the plane.

We practiced on the long, abandoned airstrip at Port Lyautey. The Navy PBYs that landed on Port Lyautey's canal did not interfere with our practice. There were many of us in observation Cubs, learning the desert terrain and flying conditions. It wasn't long, however, until the Navy's presence became so pervasive that whenever Cub pilots approached the airbase, they were given a red light to warn them off the field, the field that had once been their private playground. And the Air Force was moving in too. They would land their big C-47 transports and other craft, so it became obvious that the Army Piper Cub pilots' easy access to the landing strip was soon to end.

Rather than give up that practice area, I approached the ranking Navy man on the field and asked if we could use some of the macadam taxistrips for spot landing drills and simulated road landings. But it was apparent that the lack of radio contact made our use of what was now their field impractical and downright dangerous to our small planes, as well as the large craft of the Navy and Air Force. The Navy needed a base for its antisubmarine patrols and the Air Force needed an emergency landing field for its supply convoys. A practice field for Army Piper Cubs was low priority.

The Navy pilots were friendly, though, and when they dis-covered that the Third Division had an officers' club, they sug-gested exchanges of rations and beverages. The Navy had better food than a combat division, and Navy pilots could get hold of hard liquor, sometimes from the medicinal stocks on board ships. I immediately approached the director of our officers' club, and a deal was made to admit Navy officers in exchange for their superior rations and beverages.

Pilots are pilots the world over, and it wasn't long before I was exchanging flying time with Navy pilots. They would get four hours' flying in *Janey* and I would fly an anti-submarine patrol with them.

The first Navy pilot to get the afternoon off was Lieutenant Dick Rath, and he was eager to follow through with our agree-ment. I reported to my unit that I was going to the new Navy air base to hunt for parts, but as I flew *Janey* toward Port Lyautey, I began to worry. Would the plan be as easy to imple-ment in daylight as it had been to plan at night over a drink in the officers' club? Dick was waiting on the taxiway as I landed. He had cleared everything with his control officer, so without even needing to cut *Janey*'s engine, we were off.

It was an excellent day for flying. The weather was clear and the sun as usual was beating unmercifully on the dry, yellow grass trying to grow in the reddish-brown desert soil. The wadi beds were clearly defined by the bands of green grass and scrub. Wadis were the North African river valleys, bone-dry except during the rainy season. They looked identical to the dry creeks in the California desert. The countryside from the air resembled western Nebraska.

Flying through desert thermals is not violent but is less smooth than flying in the predawn air. Dick handled *Janey*'s con-trols until we could see the low brown mud huts outside Fez through the shimmering heat waves. The huts seemed to spring from nowhere and form orderly rows. Closer to Fez, we began to see stark white avant-garde French architecture and stately government buildings, one of them the Moorish palace of the sultans with its splendid formal gardens.

The French airport where we landed was primitive. Senegalese troops, handsome in their bright red and gold uniforms, served all policing functions and were constantly in sight. An airport official offered us a jeep and a driver to give us a tour of the Old Palace grounds. Because this was my second tour, I recognized the casual treatment the guide was giving to historical facts. It was more entertainment than history.

Finding fuel for our return trip posed a problem. I anticipated that headwinds during the return flight might require extra fuel, and if we waited too long we might run out of daylight. During winter in Morocco, the sun goes down quickly and darkness falls fast. I asked our driver if he could spare some gasoline for the plane, but his spare can was empty and the gas depot was five miles away.

I was ready to stretch the safety factor and wait for our driver to make a run to his depot for gas when a GI supply truck rolled by. Luckily they had plenty of gas to spare. I poured about 7 gallons into *Janey* while Dick watched the agonizingly-slow process of filtering gas through a chamois skin. When we took off, barely three hours of daylight were left.

The tailwind that had blown us 3,000 feet "uphill" and eastward toward Fez had not changed velocity or direction. Even though the elevation of the land dropped 3,000 feet as we ran west to Port Lyautey, the 100 miles of ground distance was slow going. *Janey* could maintain a 65 mph air speed, but now she had to fight a 20 mph headwind as well as the thermals that rose suddenly out of the trackless miles of yellow-beige semi-desert. I had not planned to race the setting sun nor had I expected such a turbulent ride.

The ocean skyline was bisecting the setting sun when *Janey*'s wheels finally touched the tarmac at Port Lyautey airfield. It was too late to make it back to my home base in the cork forest, but I was happy to be stranded there rather than in Fez.

The very next day I went sub hunting. German subs were reported to be lurking in the Atlantic Ocean off the Straits of

Gibraltar, ready to pounce on the Allied convoys that were supplying our coming fight against Rommel and his *Africa Corps*. I sat in the copilot's seat of the Navy PBY, with Dick at the controls.

Taking off from the water was a new experience for me. Once the PBY was airborne and out of sight of the coast, however, life got boring. My sub hunt was six hours of nothing but empty Mediterranean. The PBY's controls were stiff and the constant roar of the twin engines made *Janey* sound like a glider in comparison. We saw no Nazi subs.

Landing on the water was as much a thrill as taking off had been. Dick signed the six hours into my logbook to mark the event, but I preferred flying my "Maytag Messerschmitt" and being the "eyes and ears" for the artillery.

Commander Phil Harrison, U.S. Navy, was to attend a conference in Oran, and *Janey* and I were the chosen pair to make sure he arrived on time. This would be my first flight to Oran, and to add spice to the flight, I was to land at the French Naval base on the eastern edge of Oran Bay. The map markings indicated it was a seaplane base, so I would have a good airstrip to land *Janey* on, and if luck was with me, I might be able to trade with the French for parts, supplies and special amenities to spice up our Spartan lifestyle in the sultan's cork forest.

The flight would be simple. Eight hours, based on zero winds, and fifteen hours of daylight. Assuming three gas stops at one hour each, we would have four hours of light to offset any headwinds we might experience. With a dawn departure it promised to be a long but pleasant trip.

Commander Harrison and I were up and away at first light, heading east to the pass between the Rif mountains, which ran parallel to the Mediterranean Sea, and the Middle Atlas Mountains, which ran in a southwesterly direction somewhat parallel to the Atlantic. After Meknès, it would be possible to follow the Steel Beam, the railroad tracks, to our destination. The cool sea air was giving us a tailwind as we started to climb to the 5,000-

foot altitude we would need to safely clear the pass at Fez.

Less than 100 air miles from our base in the cork forest, the French-controlled airport at Fez was marked on the map as a major facility, and it was our first refueling stop. We made such good time it appeared that we might make Oujda by mid-morning. The landing at Fez was smooth, and though the air was thin, the nighttime humidity gave it body. U.S. troops had several installations on the field, so I merely taxied over to the closest group and asked for assistance. The sight of the commander in his Navy Whites gave a lot of impact to my requests. The airport flak wagon crew filtered *Janey*'s gas efficiently, and we were ready to fly on in less than half an hour. With a light heart and the luxury of using up far more runway than *Janey* was used to, we were soon airborne again and following the Steel Beam toward our next gas stop.

East of Fez, the pass broadened into a wide valley of steppes and mesas, colorless and gray, with occasional dark splotches of scrub growth. A thin dust cloud in the distance turned out to be a small flock of sheep being herded to another, perhaps grayer, pasture. The steady drone of *Janey*'s engine was our assurance that all was going well and we were drawing closer to our destination. We were making good groundspeed past the map check points, but as I approached Taza, it was apparent that either the barometer had changed or I would have to climb to 6,000 feet in order to clear the pass with safety. Gas consumption was less than I had expected, so rather than stop at Taza, I decided to press on for another hour and land at one of the new airstrips being built in preparation for our Allied offensive against Rommel.

With an hour's worth of gas left in the tank, I landed at a field about 75 miles short of Oujda. Again, refueling was prompt. The Navy uniform worked wonders and Commander Harrison was enjoying his visits with the foot soldiers.

The infantry radio had been taken out of *Janey* for this flight in order to accommodate the commander's luggage, and the radio would not have been of any use with the Air Force system and frequencies anyway. Therefore, instead of hailing the control platform, I signaled them by flying a standard civilian pattern, and as I passed the control platform, they gave me a red light. Why? I wondered. There were no other aircraft in sight.

So I landed anyway. The bright yellow jeep of the field control officer was soon racing toward me as I taxied to the gas pumps. His gestures left no doubt about the words being shouted at our deafened ears. The white Navy uniform did the job again, I thought, because the situation cooled down. Immediately, however, an Air Force major took me aside and gave me the facts of life: I was never to land at an Air Force combat airport without establishing radio contact first. It was hard to believe we were on the same side fighting the same enemy. To add insult to injury, the airport's enlisted men refused to chamois the gas for *Janey,* so I began filtering and filling the plane myself. The Air Force crew used fuel pumps and other modern fueling techniques on their planes. When the Navy commander saw me at work, he called the Air Force major, who ordered the crew to do the work. Oujda had cost us two hours just to get gassed.

L-pilots in the Air Force were often pilots who had washed out of basic training or regular pilots doing penance for some infraction and were, therefore, regarded as just one step above latrine orderly. To the Air Force, the L on my wings branded me as a misfit and a bustout.

Desert-temperature C-rations are not that bad when you haven't been invited to dinner, so the commander and I ate our C-ration in the plane watching the Steel Beam snake below. Smart money said refuel again before Oran, so this time, to give the Navy commander a new experience, I made a road landing in a traffic pause between Army convoy units. After filling *Janey* with gas and relieving ourselves of excess internal water, we were ready to go again, and traffic was stopped for our takeoff.

Two thousand feet was the approach altitude for a survey of the harbor. In the absence of radio contact, I had to rely on the height-judging tricks I'd learned at Fort Sill. If you can cover a truck with your thumb at arm's length, you are about 1,000 feet high. If you can cover the same truck with your little finger, your altitude is around 1,500 feet. That system gave an approximation, but I soon discovered that I would need a more exact calculation to safely deliver my passenger to Oran. Barrage balloons ringed the harbor. The balloons were fastened to ships and buoys in an irregular pattern at staggered heights to discourage any visits the Luftwaffe may have planned.

As I flew above the forest of barrage balloons looking for the French air base, I had the worrisome feeling that my map was in error. I turned east past the Bay of Oran until the tidal flats and beaches became rocky cliffs. It was obvious that we had somehow missed our field and must turn back.

Heading west into the setting sun, now only two fingers above the horizon, I started to feel panic. We would soon run out of daylight and we had not yet located the seaplane base. My next pass over the east shore of the bay was just a few hundred feet above the balloons. Below us, we spotted French seaplanes on two paved ramps leading to the bay. The ramps appeared to be the length of two football fields. Instead of landing at what I had assumed was an air base, I was expected to land on a glorified boat ramp. This clearly was a marginal field in the best of times, but now I would have to fly between the balloons as well. Landing here would have been difficult in full daylight, with a chart of balloon locations and thick morning air. But now the air was thin, the sun was rapidly setting, and to frustrate my attempts to establish reference points, some balloons were being towed into new positions.

I made a second and then a third pass, each time getting lower until *Janey* was just above the highest balloon, and by dead reckoning I felt we were 600 feet above the water. I motioned to Commander Harrison that I would make a try and he gave me the OK sign.

I went to the middle of the bay and started shoreward, lining up on a distant smokestack. As my descent took us below the first balloon, more giant balloons seemed to come rushing at us from every direction. I was forced to make two quick turns, and then I lost my reference point, the smokestack. Jamming *Janey*'s throttle to full power, I climbed above the balloons, looked back, and saw a big smile on Harrison's face. We now had one finger of sun on the horizon.

On our search east I had seen a motor-pool parking lot filled with trucks randomly spaced. It had a clear, double-wide central drive. I flew over it again and decided it was wide enough and long enough, so I revved my engine to attract attention. Personnel on the ground read my mind. The men moved aside and without difficulty I set *Janey* down just as the sun bisected the horizon. The double tap on my shoulder was all the reward I needed from my passenger, but the real reward was being alive.

I had landed in the Ninth Infantry Division motor-pool area, so there was an immediate common bond. The Ninth was a Regular Army division, and members of peacetime Regular Army Divisions were a society unto themselves, always eager to hear information on their buddies. After going through the inevitable "Did you know so-and-so?" and "Whatever happened to what's-his-name?," I gassed and secured *Janey* for the night with the help of motor-pool personnel.

By 10:00 a.m. *Janey* and I were flying high on our way home. Without stretching the parameters of my mission too far, I felt I could gas up at Sidi-bel-Abbès, headquarters of the French Foreign Legion. By doing so, I would avoid another hostile Air Force reception at Oujda. The Free French Army had established an L squadron on the air field there, and they might have plane parts to swap or sell. Actually I wanted to make a pilgrimage to the home of *Beau Geste*. While growing up in Iowa I had spent many a dime to see the French Foreign Legion in action at afternoon movie matinees.

I left Oran following the Steel Beam until I was above the road junction that led to Sidi. It was a clear route, and within minutes I could see the big fortress town across the monotonous expanse of desert landscape. As I approached the nondescript buildings of Sidi from the air, I began to realize that much of the charm and mystery of this town had been planted in my mind by Hollywood. Favorable winds had helped and I was landing just about lunch time. The arrival of a foreign plane of like breed was cause for an outpouring of genuine comradeship. Instead of C-ration a lá can, lunch was a French modification of American rations, topped off with a good French wine.

There were a couple of pilots at Sidi-bel-Abbès with whom I had shared common time at Fort Sill, so we compared notes and flying tales. By midafternoon I was fully provisioned with choice bottles of wine and special hellos for Captain Devol and several others in our unit. I bid adieu to my French hosts and soon *Janey* and I were airborne over the desert again.

The Steel Beam in the distance was like an old friend, for now, at least until I was through the Middle Atlas mountains at Fez, I had a reliable guide below me. I was bypassing Oujda and had at least another hour of gas and four hours of daylight. I spotted a convoy on the road below me. *Janey* and I circled the area, and when I saw the troops' welcoming waves, I was confident that it was a good landing place. I could get *Janey*'s gas from an Army truck.

The convoy was parked for the night, waiting for a section that was overdue. The captain asked me to fly him back to check on the wayward trucks. It was the perfect way to earn my keep. Back we went, and soon we discovered the missing section just getting underway. I let the captain use a message drop that I kept stored in *Janey*, and he dropped a message on the road ahead of the column of trucks. We understood from their frantic hand waving that one of the drivers had dozed off and got his vehicle stuck in a ditch.

After sharing C-rations and a bottle of French wine with my new friends, I was airborne again. The higher altitude here required a long takeoff run, but with a clear road I was off and headed toward home base. I had completed a four-day trip in three days and was returning with presents.

There was no festive air to my homecoming. Two pilots

and one of our hard-to-replace planes had been lost when a Cub had spun out of fleecy white clouds the previous day. Observation pilots enjoyed what we called cloud busting. The Piper Cubs were not equipped with the instruments needed for non-visual flight. Deprived of visual reference points, a pilot could easily become disoriented and go into vertigo; he would then start to panic, over-control the aircraft and start it into a spin. If the pilot had the presence of mind to let go of the controls, a Piper Cub would level itself out, given sufficient altitude. Apparently something had gone wrong yesterday, and from that day on, cloud busting was forbidden. The prohibition on cloud busting was fine with me.

All usable parts from the lost plane had to be salvaged, and it was my duty to salvage them. First I had to help separate the parts from the pilots. I took two enlisted men with me to accomplish the unpleasant task. The worst part was moving the pilot's head, which was impaled on the knobbed control lever protruding from the instrument panel.

5 · *BRASS AND BRANDY*

The flight with Commander Harrison to Oran set the pattern for the next phase of my flying career. Instead of shuttling first lieutenants and captains on short hops, *Janey* and I were flying majors, lieutenant colonels and full colonels on their missions to such distant cities as Taza, Oran, Algiers and Sidi-bel-Abbès.

Those special mission flights were often delayed because of the animosity of the Air Force personnel toward us. The Army Air Force had become a separate body prior to World War II and was busy developing its own identity. Our planes, although they had once been part of the Air Force, were now under U.S. Army jurisdiction and not responsible to the Air Force.

In addition to the wound still present between the Air Force and the Army, we were not operating on the same radio bands and had to rely on prearranged signals, a primitive inefficiency the Air Force despised. Piper Cub pilots would circle the tower of an Air Force base, indicating they wanted to land, and would hold up until they received a green light from the tower. A red light indicated they could not land, and the Cub pilots would wiggle their wings to indicate they got the message. We seldom received a green light.

Our planes could not make Oran, a major command station, without refueling, and the Air Force's Oujda base was halfway between Oran and Casablanca. The Air Force control tower at Oujda usually ignored us. They gave us neither a green light to land nor a red light to beware of incoming airplanes. I would have to keep circling the field to find an opening in which I could inject myself, hoping that the ass-chewing from the field lieutenant and from whoever was in command of the tower on a given day was worth the risk that I had taken.

If a lieutenant colonel or full colonel was my passenger, I felt secure that his rank would relieve me of responsibility for sneaking into the Air Force's private territory. Unfortunately, this wasn't true when I was returning without my passenger and had to stop for gas.

Janey's gas had to be filtered directly into the tank through a chamois to ensure that no impurities got into the fuel line. Air Force enlisted personnel despised the technique because it meant standing up on a box or stepladder and pouring gas from a 5-gallon can a half-gallon at a time through a funnel and waiting for it to filter through the chamois. It took fifteen or twenty minutes to pour in 12 to 14 gallons, and it was hot and dirty work. The Air Force airplane engines had their own complicated filtration system; *Janey* and other Piper Cubs just like her had a plain old carburetor just like a Model A Ford. The gas went directly from the tank by gravity to the carburetor and was not force-fed.

Even though Cub pilots held rank over the enlisted crew, often they would rather gas the airplanes themselves than endure the sour looks and gripes from the ground crews. It was standard procedure that we all carried a funnel and a chamois with us, and it was standard procedure that we would use them.

I could not fly into the Air Force's Oujda field, get gas and be on my way in half an hour. Even with a full colonel on board, it would take two to three hours by the time the tower had reluctantly and grudgingly found out that we were not the enemy, then allowed us to refuel and proceed with our mission.

During these ferry trips I became acquainted with several high-ranking officers in the Third Division. I knew Captain Devol and how he responded to the unpredictable flying conditions. Because we had no long-distance radios and there was no weather forecasting available to us, we could only fly contact missions in which we had constant visual observation of the ground. During these flights, Captain Devol allowed us to use our own judgment if the weather looked bad. I often remembered the old adage back at Fort Sill: There are old pilots and there are bold pilots, but there are no old, bold pilots.

Devol had faith in the judgment of his "old" pilots, and we were already losing airplanes through the errors and dumb flying tricks of "bold" pilots who tried to come in without any lights or too late in the afternoon. As darkness fell, pilots lost their depth perception and broke landing gear, banged up props, or worse, totally washed out airplanes, so Devol was tolerant of setbacks if we felt the weather looked bad and we wanted to hang back.

Flight instructors at Fort Sill had taught us to constantly read the ground and look for little signs. We could tell by the dust streams behind vehicles what the wind might be doing; a flag flying straight meant 25-mph winds; the air sock at an airport is designed and built to fly straight out at 25 mph. Whenever we were up against 25-mph winds, we had to nearly double our flight time. Many nights we were forced to camp out along the roadside or in any place we could land, because we knew that we would be arriving at our home base too late. Camping out meant sleeping under the wing or cramped inside the plane and shivering through the cold desert night. The Army didn't issue sleeping bags in those days, and Cubs had limited space, making it difficult to take along a blanket.

The Atlas Mountains proved to be a formidable obstacle for *Janey*. It was necessary to fly through or around the mountains, which formed a blockade for the weather systems coming from the Atlantic Ocean down into the drier desert region. Cloud banks and mist formed on the mountainside and were difficult to fly through. *Janey* didn't have the capacity to fly over the Atlas Mountains, which were about 14,000 feet at the highest peak. There were also strong downdrafts where the dry North African desert air encountered the moisture-laden air from the Atlantic. When the mist and clouds were hanging on the Atlas Mountains, it was hard to fly through the valleys because we lacked the necessary instruments. It took great quantities of gas to climb to an altitude sufficient to clear the peaks, and it was too great a distance to fly around them. Since it could take another hour's flying time and we were apt to hit all kinds of cross drafts and unsettled weather, it was best to play it safe if the mountains were clouded in.

At Fort Sill, it was part of pilot training to always be on the lookout for a place to make an emergency landing; therefore, I was aware of every flat piece of ground that could possibly be used for a landing strip in an emergency. I had also marked on my maps the locations of all the new fighter fields as they were being developed for the final move to purge North Africa of Rommel and his *Africa Corps*.

A British Hurricane base caught my eye. I had always wanted to examine the British Spitfire and Hawker Hurricane. Their silhouettes were clear from the air, and I was eager to inspect them up close.

Flying back from a mission one day, I spotted a bevy of Hurricanes that had just moved into the neighborhood. The weather was iffy at the time, so I decided to land at the British airbase. The airstrip was empty but had an elevated 10-foot platform. I got neither a red nor a green light, but I came in anyway, landed and taxied over to their line of planes. Pretty soon a couple of men came out of one of the huts and directed me to park beside one of the Hurricanes and near a fuel lorry.

"What can we do for you, mate?" they wanted to know, obviously delighted to see a little Piper Cub like *Janey*.

"I need some gas. I was trying to get to the Atlas Mountains, but it looks like there might be some headwinds up ahead," I said, building my excuse for stopping. I brought out the funnel and the chamois skin. "It's best to chamois all the gas because clean gas is my best insurance against engine failure."

"We insist upon filling her up, sir," one friendly chap said, reaching for the funnel.

"Thanks! It has to be done in the evening so that condensation doesn't get in the tank," I replied. While they poured and strained the gas, we chatted. "Is there any chance that I can get something to eat and a place to stay?"

"Of course, sir," they replied. By that time, a couple of their flying sergeants had arrived on the scene. In the Royal Air Force, Hurricanes were flown by sergeants as well as lieutenants. The gas crew finished gassing *Janey* and tied her down with sandbags and ropes for the night. The flying sergeants escorted me to the mess tent, where we shared a pleasant evening meal of lamb stew heavy with potatoes, and delicious bread.

The British base had recently been activated by leapfrogging over from Egypt, south of Rommel's bastions near the Mediterranean coast. The British were coming in for a fight, expecting that Rommel would be resupplied and would counterattack at his discretion. We had no idea how long Rommel was going to hold out, and the Allies did not realize that the Germans had made a decision to withdraw.

During dinner they grumbled about their supply corps.

"They didn't bring us any beer, they didn't bring us any bully beef, but they gave us plenty of boots," they complained.

"Like the ones you're wearing?" I asked. At the time, the American combat boots were basic ankle-high work shoes worn with canvas leggings. They were neither stylish nor comfortable. The British battle dress boots were rakish and sturdy, much better designed for the rigors for combat than even our paratrooper boots.

"Yes, if you want boots, we've got boots." Luckily I had some invasion francs with me and was able to buy myself a pair of those rakish British boots.

I next enjoyed the hospitality of a unique American Air Force unit that treated me like a long-lost brother instead of a leper. It started one evening when I realized I couldn't make Oujda. Fog was hanging low over the Atlas Mountains, so I decided to land *Janey* before I got into a bad weather system. The horizon of sand and scrub growth revealed an intriguing spot for an overnight stay. A squadron of P-40 Warhawks was perched on the sand. They were some of the meanest-looking fighter aircraft of World War II, and I wanted to see them up close.

They were even meaner-looking when I landed beside them. A sneering shark's mouth, bright red and full of long pointed teeth, had been painted on the nose of each P-40. The propeller hubs were painted with a serpentine spiral. An enemy pilot would not want to see one of those fighters on his tail. The spinning spiral on the hub would give the impression of a drill bit or corkscrew ready to bore through him, and the menacing shark teeth would trigger primal fears.

As I rolled *Janey* past the Warhawks, black ground crewmen grabbed *Janey*'s wings and helped me taxi her over. Other black ground crewmen came out immediately, bringing sandbags to tie *Janey* down for the night. They were aware of the bad weather to the west and knew that I'd be staying the night.

I had landed on an Air Force base manned entirely by black fighter pilots and ground crew. It was a segregated squadron, and they had given me the green landing light promptly. There was no ass-chewing at all; instead, I was treated like a brother. I was ushered to the officers' mess where they fed me even though I had arrived after regular evening mess hours.

The U.S. military was not integrated or even desegregated during World War II. Blacks were in separate units, some were in combat units. Like all pilots, those men could someday tell their grandchildren that they had flown or serviced these fierce warbirds.

Not long after that, I became a sometime bootlegger. I had first met Lieutenant Hicks when we were crossing the ocean to become part of the War. He knew me well because I had been master of ceremonies for the ship's talent show. Hicks was the type of man who had the instincts of a river-boat gambler. He was now Captain Hicks and an aide to General Truscott, Commander of the Third Division. Hicks had heard that there was apple brandy available somewhere near the Oujda air base, and the Third Division staff wanted it checked out. He and I flew to Taza, which took one full tank of gas. We had to refuel at Oujda in order to get back, and while I was refueling, he went to a Quartermaster depot beside the Oujda airbase. He came back in the supply depot jeep with four cases of apple brandy from Spanish Morocco.

Loading the brandy presented two challenges. One, avoiding the watchful eyes of the officers in the tower, and two, stashing the bottles around inside *Janey* while maintaining a weight balance. We devised an elaborate plan.

The jeep drove off with its cargo of booze. I headed *Janey* down the taxiway as if we were taking off, but I stopped at the end. The jeep came back onto the airbase sort of cross-country to make it look like it was a last-minute thought. It raced toward us at full speed, the top bouncing and the windshield rattling, as though something was amiss. The driver parked on the opposite side of *Janey* and we transferred the cargo out of view of the spies in the tower. We nestled the straw-wrapped bottles all up and down *Janey*'s floor boards, leaving barely enough room for the rudder pedals to move.

Hicks and I made it back to base safely with all but two bottles of the brandy intact. Those two bottles had been broken in the wild ride in the jeep, and some of the bottles had leaked from the corks. *Janey* stank for days, but we had successfully completed the first of many brandy runs.

Subsequently, we streamlined our booze running. After the second trip, it was decided that I could go alone and bring back nearly twice as much. We packed the bottles in ammunition cases instead of peasant baskets. But the secret was too good to keep. The Air Force personnel at Oujda smelled a rat and figured out what we were doing. The control tower wanted a cut, so we gave one bottle to the man who gassed *Janey* and one bottle to the control tower crew.

Captain Hicks and I decided we wanted finer stuff yet, so we planned a trip into Spanish Morocco. We were promised some really fine brandy and liqueur if we went in directly, and Hicks's Army connection from our Quartermaster Corps made the arrangements. Even though our Navy PBYs were overflying Spanish Morocco during anti-submarine patrols and several planes had landed there, Spanish Morocco was neutral territory. We had to be discreet.

The Air Force found out all the way up the ladder about the Army's bootlegging trade, and they decided to get some for themselves. They sent an unarmed American B-25 bomber into Spanish Morocco to pick up a whole plane load of brandy and liqueurs. The plane crashed on a mountainside in Spanish Morocco, causing a major diplomatic incident.

On a similar mission, the U.S. Army's Third Infantry nearly lost a plane and pilot when making a short-distance ice cream run sanctioned by the commander of the Ninth Field Artillery Battalion. Staff Sergeant Joe "Hook" Casanova was always on the lookout for that special item that might add some variety to our standard government food ration. If he was on the trail of a choice item, his trips were often far-ranging, usually adventurous, and sometimes legendary.

Tabarqa was a seaside village that had an ice-cream factory, and ice cream was just the pièce de résistance Casanova sought to build his reputation. Transporting this precious commodity in the midday heat of June by jeep over 60-plus miles of twisting and turning North African roads would be a challenge. Casanova claimed it took him over three hours to make the whole trip, bucking traffic and not being slowed by MPs. If the MPs directed traffic, it could take four to five hours, he said, making soup of the ice cream.

Undaunted by the logistical obstacles, his discovery was discussed at all command levels. Ice cream was declared a number-one priority, and Coyne and I went out the next day on a reconnaissance flight. The airfield at Tabarqa was miles from town, down hidden trails that would take hours to negotiate, but the beach was broad and I decided to use it as my airstrip. The sand was hard-packed and we headed home with the good news. Our unit's airstrip was only 25 minutes from the beach at Tabarqa.

There were five basic feeding units in our combat Battalion, so after melding the officers' mess into the five basic units, we computed the load factor based on ten marmite cans of ice cream. Marmite cans were heavily-insulated steel containers designed to withstand the rigors of rough handling and deliver warm meals to front-line troops. Now we would use marmite cans to deliver cold ice-cream treats in the desert.

After careful calculations, it was determined that ten marmite cans were the equivalent of my flying a 280-pound passenger. That calculation was on the ragged edge of safety, but with a long takeoff run down the beach, the radio taken out, and a minimum amount of gas in *Janey's* tank, it could be done. Next we had to fine-tune our logistics. The milk products, sugar, and other ingredients would be delivered to the factory, then the ice-cream makers would give us a pickup day and time.

At 5 o'clock two days later, Operation IC would commence. *Janey* and I would be on the Tabarqa beach at ten minutes to 5. Casanova and his crew of sergeants with overnight passes would transport the ice cream from the factory to the beach, and they'd clear the beach of bathers. By 5 o'clock, *Janey* and I would be airborne for the 25-minute trip back to base. Five jeeps would be waiting at the battalion airstrip to pick up their ration of ice cream and speed it to their battery mess lines by 5:30.

The takeoff went according to plan, but we had miscalculated either the weight of the ice cream or the headwind velocity. I ran out of cleared beach before *Janey* was light on her wheels and ready to lift off. To avoid the sunbathers on the uncleared section of beach, I veered toward the ocean, and as I pulled back on the stick to become airborne, one of *Janey's* wheels slightly kissed a wavelet.

The difference between life and death is sometimes measured in fractions of inches. It seemed like *Janey* hit a brick wall, but the stagger was only momentary, and *Janey* lurched into the air, on her way with the precious cargo.

Although the marmite cans didn't keep the cream frozen solid, it was the best thing we had tasted in months. If there had been a medal for ice cream, we would have awarded it to

Coyne for authorizing this feat of military ingenuity and logistical coordination.

By dawn of the next day, disaster had struck, and the medic from C Battery was searching frantically for spare bivouac toilet paper, flour for parching, cheese and any other "hinder binder." Three of Battery C's gun crews had the trots. They had detected a slight salty taste in their last can of ice cream and now decided that some of the saltwater brine used to keep the marmite cans cold had leaked through the seal on the lid, or maybe some Vichy Frenchman had struck a low blow for the Axis.

Janey had completed another successful mission, but it was never to be duplicated. Too many men had been put out of action by a bad or sabotaged marmite can of ice cream.

My bootlegging runs ended, too, when the Third's Regimental Combat Team was ordered into Tunisia. We were moving in stages for the final pincer movement to cut off and annihilate Rommel's *Africa Corps*. My days of recreational flying were over. The atmosphere of the war had changed. *Janey* and I were now leapfrogging battalion commanders and infantry regimental commanders up ahead of their troops.

Our first contact with the enemy was near the port of Arzew, east of Oran. Our first and only fire mission of the African campaign was shelling the entrenched position of the German observers on Hill 609. The Germans had used the hill's vantage point to direct deadly 88 fire down the valley and prevent reinforcements from coming up to close the jaws of the pincers. After several German units had escaped our trap, the Germans on Hill 609 were ordered, or scheduled, to surrender.

This was a harbinger of things to come. The Germans were masters at finding great defensive positions, extracting a ghastly toll of lives, and then peacefully surrendering. The surrender of the Germans in Tunisia left us all stunned. We had been spoiling for a fight, but now it was over and we had more war booty than anyone could imagine because we had not destroyed German equipment on the ground, as we would in later battles. The

Luftwaffe flying out of Sicily and the few remaining fields in North Africa had denied our Air Force the complete air dominance that we would achieve later on.

We were now newly-unbloodied Americans with a sort of victory on our hands, but we soon realized that North Africa might have been a different story. In the front armor plate of the German tanks, we saw the gouges where our 37mm anti-tank rounds had hit them and just ricocheted off. Their gas tanks were dry due to the Allied bombing of German supply ships, and they had been denied a role in the final battle. We didn't know at the time that the Allies had broken the German code and lay in wait for German ships crossing the Mediterranean.

Even though we had captured German tanks, we were denied the most-prized individual item of booty, the German semiautomatic pistol—the Luger. The German Luger has a little steel plate on one side about the size of a postage stamp, and from that plate projects a tiny stem of steel that locks the trigger into place. Surrendering Germans had completely nullified both the practical and collector value of these Lugers by throwing the little plates away. We had hundreds of Lugers that would not fire, but the Germans had not disarmed other items in their inventory. The inexperience of our handling those captured weapons cost us hundreds of casualties. Our troops would pick up German 20mm antiaircraft cannon rounds that looked like our .50-caliber slugs, but as they handled this ammunition, the charge on the projectile would explode and our soldiers would lose a hand or an eye. Inexperience with the German potato-masher grenade cost many lives. Every day officers received safety reports to read to the troops warning of some newly-discovered hazard. Because of these bitter experiences, new recruits in later campaigns were afraid to handle German equipment, thus preventing many casualties. German ingenuity had devised clever booby traps and terrorizing weapons. One was the flare pistol, which shot a shell that left no visible stream of powder or smoke but screamed like an incoming artillery round. The first time troops heard the flare round, they would drop to the ground, trembling because they thought a real shell was heading straight for them.

The German shoebox mines, however, were not an imagined hazard, and they blew off many American legs. In the latter days of the campaign, the Germans had planted thousands of those mines. Shoebox mines were not made of metal but of wood so that mine detectors couldn't detect them. The only way to find a suspected mine was to poke a hole in the ground with a bayonet—carefully! The planting of booby traps and mines, especially those shoebox mines, was one of the most heinous of war crimes.

Janey's and my sightseeing days passed quickly, and when we regrouped, General Truscott resumed drilling the troops in the Truscott Trot. Although we had seen no protracted action, we guessed something big was ahead.

Captain Brenton Devol, the first Third Division Artillery air officer with his L-4B *Kathy*, named for his wife. Devol took off from the aircraft carrier USS *Ranger* to open the invasion of Casablanca, Morocco on November 9, 1942. Note the circle around the identification star and the lack of white side bars on either side of the star.

6 · *DEEP PURPLE*

Captain Devol approached me with a special request when I returned from flying a general on what turned out to be a sightseeing tour of Cape Bon. A group of diehard Nazis was disregarding the official surrender and had nearly nailed us with their 20mms. Luckily, I was able to dive *Janey* behind a low hill and hedgehop inland beyond their range. If we had flown the short route the general had suggested, cutting over the bay at Bizerte, we would have been fish food.

I was having nightmares, reliving the millisecond that *Janey*'s wheels kissed the water as I flew my cargo of ice cream from Tabarqa. Therefore, when Devol asked me to volunteer to fly *Janey* off a 200-foot-long by 16-foot-wide deck built on an LST for the invasion of Sicily, I was not enthusiastic.

"Fly off of an LST and direct Naval gunfire? No!" I said, "I am not volunteering for that!" I later lived to regret that off-hand remark and the green-eyed monster it created.

An LST (Landing Ship Tank) was a large flat-bottomed ship about the length of a football field with two vertical swinging doors in the bow. Once the ship was grounded on the invasion beach, the doors opened and an interior ramp extended shoreward, allowing tanks, trucks and artillery pieces to drive onto the beach, ready for combat.

Sicily was the first major Allied amphibious attack on what Churchill called the "soft underbelly of Europe." Once we hit the beaches, we were there to stay. Pre-invasion shelling of suspected enemy defense positions and the ability to give the assault troops covering fire were vital to the success of the landing. The Navy had patrol planes, but they couldn't go slow enough to spot small concealed ground targets and direct fire in close support of infantry. Navy gunfire is rapid, accurate and can reach far inland to destroy enemy troop concentrations and supply routes. The problem was how to shut off the firing as our ground troops advanced. Each combat team would be in direct radio contact with the Navy command ship to ensure that gunfire could be lifted if it began to endanger the assaulting troops. Once inland, normal artillery control could be exercised with forward ground observers. The situation required an innovation that would give the army its own baby aircraft carrier to launch its own artillery-spotting planes.

Lieutenant Bill Cumming accepted Devol's risky assignment of taking off in his Piper Cub from a small narrow runway constructed on an LST. He would be the first wave to hit the beach. *Janey* and I would be in the third wave. Her wings were removed and lashed to the sides of a 2½-ton cargo truck. Her fuselage was rolled tail first into the truck's steel bed. With our gear and tools wedged in around her, *Janey* was a neat package. Our LST would carry 155mm howitzers, ammunition, light tanks, and small patrol elements of the Third Division reconnaissance troop. If all went according to plan, we would use a floating pontoon between the LST and the beach and land with dry feet.

We had no way of knowing what awaited us on the beach—possibly Tiger tanks like those the Germans had left behind after surrendering in North Africa. They were bigger and tougher looking than anything we had and our 1942-style antitank guns only pockmarked their steel flanks. We were relying on the bazooka, our infantry's new rocket-propelled antitank projectile, which had not been tried on a moving Tiger in combat.

Waiting for embarkation day created an unsettling combination of fear and misgivings about the fight ahead. Yellow dung-laced dust swirled in the hot dry air as we drove through the bombed-out port city of Bizerte in Tunisia. Once our truck arrived at the dock, however, the Navy took charge and quickly loaded us up, and the ship moved swiftly away from the dock. A fresh cool breeze welcomed us over the water as the sun set behind the low mountains surrounding Lac Bizerte. Purple shadows rose from the ground and began to hide the rugged details of the desert landscape. The words and music of the popular song "Deep Purple" crowded out the apprehension that had been my subconscious companion for many days.

About midnight a lone German raider flew over dropping flares, bathing Lac Bizerte with a silver light. On the LST we felt naked in the glow of the swinging flares. The Navy withheld fire to avoid detection and, as the plane's engine faded, a sigh of relief accompanied our prayers of thanksgiving.

An early-morning raid the next day by a single Luftwaffe Dornier bomber did little more than chip paint from the sides of two ships and provide our antiaircraft gun crews with practice. The tension of waiting for action broke as we watched the black puffs of ack-ack in the sky chase the raider off.

A hot dry wind from the desert raised a small chop on the harbor waters of Lac Bizerte as we hoisted anchor and slowly moved toward the channel leading to the Mediterranean and Sicily. The midday sun was torrid and bright in the clear blue sky. *Janey* and I had recently flown over Lac Bizerte with Navy engineers to pinpoint the location of dozens of German and Italian ships our Air Force had sunk in the harbor and along the narrow channel that led to the sea. Now we passed over those jagged wrecks, leaving the harbor behind us as we met the gentle swells of the Mediterranean, saying farewell to Africa.

As darkness fell, I stood on the fantail of the LST and watched the fluorescence churned by our wake. The gentle chop on the lake that had sent us from the harbor grew to a heavy swell as the full force of the wind-driven sea tried to control our flat-bottomed boat. It was a long and sleepless night.

Man-made flashes of lightning and rolls of thunder announced the dawn as pre-invasion Naval gunfire gave notice to all that the battle had been joined. We were not receiving answering fire from the shore. Through a half-light we could see the land mass and the outline of the ships heading toward the shadow of the distant shore. Firing halted momentarily, the silence broken only by the throb of our engines as we moved shoreward. The rattle of small arms could be heard in snatches, and it sounded like ours. We had lucked out. The Italians on the beach had been caught unaware.

The H-Hour (hour of invasion) crackle of gunfire from the beach was drowned out by the roar and whine of landing-craft engines as they formed a second wave to rush toward the beach. We were part of the third wave, and the large docking pontoon had been lowered so it could be pushed up onto the sand for a dry landing. The opposition was fading into the hills, leaving the beaches free from concentrated small-arms fire and from the deadly mortar fire.

German ME-109s and Stukas dived from above to strafe and drop their shrieking bombs before disappearing over the low hills surrounding the beachhead. We chased them with black balls of antiaircraft bursts and streams of multicolored tracer dots.

By H-Hour plus two, *Janey*'s truck rolled onto the beach. I selected a site close to the beach road where we could reattach her wings. It was out of the traffic pattern so we wouldn't interfere with movement on the beach and from where we could push *Janey* to the road for takeoff.

The rolling thunder of 40mm antiaircraft guns and the rattle of the .50-caliber flak wagons heralded the approach of another flight of enemy planes. They left a trail of exploding gas drums and plumes of dense black smoke that polluted the sky above the beachhead. Silver barrage balloons were being hoisted, giving the beach an eerie circus-like appearance. The balloons floated lazily above us to discourage the Luftwaffe from making low-level strafing passes.

The tide was going out, leaving still-loaded ships stranded on sand flats, adding to the congestion in the already-crowded landing area. The beach was in chaos. Many vehicles had come ashore with fully-inflated tires in direct disregard of orders; lower tire pressure doubles traction in sand. That carelessness was enough to light the already-short fuses of several beach officers, and they didn't hesitate to physically rough up any drivers who hesitated to deflate their truck tires.

On the sea side of the coastal road, the Beach Party maintained absolute control, and the roadway was controlled by our Division MPs. Traffic had to move and those men had been selected for their size and ability to make sure it did. When they said move, everybody from private to sergeant moved.

Initially I had no doubt that when it was time to fly off the beach the road would be cleared, yet with the mounting confusion caused by the bomb damage, doubts were stirring. I wished I stood 6-foot-6, tall enough to intimidate the Beach Party boys, most of whom were big, solid midwesterners of Scandinavian or Celtic stock.

Corporal Bill Collins, driver of the 2½-ton truck loaned to us for the invasion, was anxious to get off the beach, and by midmorning we had unloaded *Janey* and he was gone. *Janey's* parts were stashed between hastily unloaded gas cans and C-ration boxes. My job was to make her flyable and wait for notice of a mission. Then while in flight, I would pick a field appropriate for the assembly of our second plane. It sounded simple, but as the day passed and no observer with a mission appeared, I became concerned. I was within 100 feet of where I was supposed to be. Where was my observer?

Croal, who had joined me, took everything as a matter of course and suggested we build a shelter of ration cases, get some straw from a nearby shepherd's shack, and settle in for some much-needed sleep. Soon it would be too dark to fly, so we moved on his idea and built a wall 2 feet high and two ration-cases wide, enclosing an area about 6 feet square. The spasmodic popping of ammunition fires on the beach was dying down and the black smoke and dust began thinning as we lay on our blankets, cradled in the straw. Gazing skyward into the stars, we speculated that only a direct hit would harm us, for the multiple layers of C-ration cans would deflect any bomb shrapnel that might rake the beach.

We were rehashing the day's events when the sound of seaward firing rolled toward us and every gun in the area responded by sending bits of burning steel skyward. It was beautiful and terrible all at once. Planes were shooting flares and dropping paratroopers—German or American, we could not be sure which.

Cease-fire! shouts echoed up and down the beach. Croal and I stayed low behind our C-ration wall, for by now the Navy was shooting at the parachutes as they floated down and the 20mms from the Navy ships were raking our beach area. Bullets pinged as they struck the trucks and boxes on the beach. Shouts for medics came from right and left.

When at last the firing stopped, a semblance of order was restored and supplies continued to move over the beach, guided by the hooded red flashlights and shouts of the Beach Party. We discovered that we had disrupted the landing of the American 82nd Airborne Division, whose planes unfortunately arrived moments after a flight of German raiders had finished their bomb runs. The Navy boys, thinking they were a second flight of German raiders, shot first and asked questions later.

Croal's idea of building a C-ration case fort had saved our skins, but now we were feeling the tiny nibbles of new friends from the straw. Dawn revealed that we were providing a home for a colony of red fleas.

7 · *THE RED MENACE*

Collins stood peering down into our C-ration case revetments, a canteen cup of steaming coffee in his hand.

"Well, you made it," he said with a broad smile on his ruddy English face. "When all the shooting started down here, we thought you two were goners." The guns of the Ninth Field Artillery Battalion were parked in a grove about a mile above the beach. From Collins's description, last night's shooting frenzy that greeted the intended landing of the 82nd Airborne had been a real SNAFU (Situation Normal All Fouled Up).

Croal and I were tantalized by the smell of Collins's coffee. Our mouths were bitter and dry from the dust and sand that permeated the air. The pall of dust blocked the sunrise, but once we saw the fleas, Croal and I erupted from our fort in paroxysms of scratching. Every fold of cloth that touched our skin felt like sandpaper.

"You guys take this; I'll find some cups and be back," Collins offered. With that he disappeared down the beach, and Croal and I were left to scratching places normally left untouched in public. Thus began D-day plus one. Collins shortly returned with two cups of that wonderful hot, brown liquid.

"Lieutenant," Collins said. "The word is that you are to stay put. They will send an observer when they need you. In the meantime, I'm to get water and go back to the hills." Traffic on the road was already moving at breakneck speed because everyone wanted to be clear of the beach. Unless we missed our guess, the Luftwaffe would be paying us a morning call.

The green-eyed monster churned within me. I hadn't been too smart. I'd played it safe and not volunteered like Cumming had. He was now safe, uninfested and would get the coveted Distinguished Service Cross, the second-highest award for valor. I, on the other hand, was sitting in the hot seat, breathing suffocating dust, and scratching myself raw.

In my musette bag, which I had packed inside *Janey*, were two cans of bug powder, along with my shaving gear and toothbrush. Croal and I took a swim, cleaned our teeth in salt water, and then dusted our clothes to rout those little red devils. Yet, life is rarely that simple.

Other men had apparently slept in the same straw because the swim detail was large until a burly and authoritative MP rousted us out of the water and informed us that a war was still going on. Nobody wore rank while swimming and I was damn glad, for the chewing-out was resounding and it was obvious that the MP didn't have fleas. Had I been 8 inches taller and wearing rank insignia, I might have registered some objections.

I had carried those cans of bug powder since they had been issued in Casablanca and only dusted around my ankles for sand fleas. Now the powder really had to go to work. As we dressed, Croal and I shook copious amounts of the bug powder in all the seams of our clothes, hoping to rid them of the pests.

As it turned out, our beach area was lucky. The 45th Division sector got more air attention than we did. A Stuka dive bomber hit an ammunition ship, setting it afire and disgorging a deadly hot steel spray skyward like Independence Day fireworks, punctuated by flames and smoke in dense clouds of black and then again in wispy, white clouds belching upward.

The Germans had counterattacked the 45th with tanks, penetrated the initial advanced position and had moved within two blocks of the landing area. This unexpected action caused some concern, for in the Third Division sector the Italian shore garrisons were surrendering in such numbers that containing the prisoners was a problem.

Our guns were still in a trail position. The self-propelled

guns of the Second Armored Division had been withdrawn as their units were being consolidated to advance to the west against very scattered Italian opposition. Yet, on our right flank, German tanks were in danger of overrunning the beach. Soon the Luftwaffe came at us again with whistling bombs that sent chills of terror down our spines. Barrage balloons kept the fighters above 200 feet and our antiaircraft gunners, both the 40mm and the .50-caliber, gave good account of themselves. However, the hit-and-run raids of the ME-109s and Stukas drove us frantic.

In the late 1930s and early 1940s, Italy held many world airspeed records, and therefore, we had assumed Italy would play a leadership role in fighter aircraft. Italian fighter-bombers, however, appeared only in limited numbers, dropping their bombs and escaping over the hills.

Janey was covered with a thick film of road dust and, although I had draped the white recognition stars on her wings and sides with green camouflage burlap, I feared her shape would draw enemy fire. I stayed close by, but when I heard the deep roar of the German planes or the high pitch of the Italian planes, I ran for cover some distance from *Janey*.

My impatience to get in the air and off the beach ended when Second Lieutenant Ed Hill hailed us from the road, shouting above the throb and moan of the truck engines and clanking steel of tank treads, "We've got a mission. I'll lead you to the Ninth's emplacement."

After both of us pleaded with the burly MPs, they finally stopped traffic long enough for us to push *Janey* onto the road. Off we flew, with the fleas as passengers.

8 · *THE TRUSCOTT PACE*

According to the grapevine, General Truscott had developed a new march: a pace. He paced back and forth in the olive grove, stewing because the Third Division was being held in reserve to assist the 45th in case the Germans broke through. Fortunately, the 45th held.

There were two reasons why Truscott and his Trotters were still on the leash. The sector in which we had landed, Licata, was defended by Italians, not by Germans, and the large number of Italians that were surrendering to us actually clogged our roads, creating traffic and logistical problems. The 45th, which landed on our right at Gela, hit a hornet's nest known as the Hermann Goering Panzer Division. The elite unit was named to honor Hitler's number two man—and those tankers were determined to hold Goering's banner high. Lieutenant General George S. Patton, in command of the invasion, wanted to play it safe and keep the Third in reserve until the German counterattack had been turned back.

Truscott finally convinced Patton that the Third should be allowed to send armed patrols toward Agrigento, in southern Sicily. As the Second Armored charged along the coast road, the Third started toward Agrigento on the inland roads that lead through the mountains of the Sicilian interior. Our armed patrols fanned out, and behind the patrols moved companies of infantry, in a leapfrogging fashion, without committing the main force of the Third Division, in compliance with Patton's order.

The hilltop town of Agrigento proved to be a formidable

roadblock. The Third Division launched its first battalion-sized attack force of the war, and after bitter fighting against loyal and committed Fascist troops, we captured Agrigento. The Truscott Trot training began to pay off. As soon as we cleared Agrigento, the dogfaces began completing unbelievable daily marches, forcing the Italian retreat into a rout.

On the trip to Palermo, *Janey*'s radio wouldn't transmit. Ed Hill and I both felt the information we had was urgent, so I made an emergency landing on a curved hillside field that paralleled a tree-canopied road. Once down, I knew getting airborne again with a passenger would be impossible, so Ed hiked to the road to hail a radio car and relay his information to our HQ.

As I rested in the shade of a tree, I realized that Ed Hill was an excellent observer. He had good eyes and a strong stomach. He had the ability to withstand the bobbing, weaving, diving and turning that made up my irregular flight pattern when firing a mission. He had a 360-degree swivel joint in his neck so he could constantly study the skies above and the ground below.

As I sat in the orchard waiting for Ed's signal that he had made contact, an Italian farmer came through the trees pushing a donkey cart piled high with a cargo of fuzzy, bumpy, pear-shaped fruit. When he saw me standing by a tree, he smiled broadly and pointed to the fruit hanging on the tree and said, "*Bueno, bueno, bueno.*" I nodded, feigning understanding.

To convince me, he reached up and picked two fruits. He bit the small end off one and squeezed its main body in the palm of his hand while sucking on the exposed end. When he finished, he put his right thumb to his right cheek and twisted his hand, saying, "*Moto bueno.*" He handed the second fruit to me and I ate it the way he had demonstrated. He had it right—it was *moto bueno.* Now I knew two new Italian words and the delightful taste of fresh figs.

A high sign from Ed told me that he was all set, and I propped the plane. Once *Janey*'s engine purred, I used the entire field to gather enough airspeed to rise through the vagrant wind currents and light warm air to soar out of the narrow valley.

On an observation flight in *Janey* late the next afternoon, 40 miles south of Palermo, Ed and I directed the fire for our ground troops. We hit the jackpot with one lucky shot. Immediately after impact, a huge cloud of black smoke boiled over the crest of the hill and continued to erupt, shooting tongues of yellow flames skyward, backlighting the billowing smoke. To an artilleryman, black smoke is beautiful because it indicates you have hit pay dirt—an oil fire.

We had suspected there were Italian guns on the reverse side of a hill, near what our 1883-vintage contour maps indicated might be a cliff. Ed called fire control for a high trajectory ranging round, since we were within the parameters of high trajectory horizontal distance. We directed the fire for all four guns of A Battery, and thick smoke and flames continued to belch, obliterating the setting sun. We spread the shells in a circle around the first shot and soon the whole battalion joined in the cannonade. As our unit continued lobbing shells through the swirling smoke, we could see giant geysers of orange sparks attempting to delay the gathering dusk. We knew we had a great target and subjected the area to interdicting fire, the artillery term for periodic shelling, all night. By morning the Italians and Germans had completely abandoned their burning supply dump, which must have been a major ammo, gasoline, food and clothing depot.

Our troops moved rapidly along the road to Palermo until they reached the line just outside the city where the combat team had been ordered to halt and wait for the Second Armored. General Truscott again asked for armed patrols to feel out the enemy. Third Division patrols began reconnoitering and soon were in Palermo guarding the streets when the Second Armored tanks clanked in.

The Third Division was ordered to bypass Palermo to the east. As often happened in a rapidly moving situation with radio communication restricted, I had not received the message. As I landed on the debris-littered, smoke-shrouded Palermo Airport, I sent for my ground crew, thereby moving onto the Palermo

Airport. Gathering darkness ended flying for the day, and my ground crew arrived and started to set up camp. We began exploring the abandoned enemy airplanes, many of which were still smoldering. The Air Force ground crews were still hours away when a Second Armored Division tank group raced toward my camp with sirens blaring.

Already a few young Italian boys and girls were begging food. Not knowing what to expect, I ran them off. The ragged, hungry children touched our hearts, but we didn't dare feed them. To do so might have brought the whole community, and we were not capable of handling a situation of that magnitude. We soon learned how badly the children wanted food. A few of the little girls lifted their dresses, pointed between their legs and chanted, "*Una can, una can.*" They were about the age of my young sisters back in Iowa, but they were starving and desperate to sell themselves for a can of C-rations.

"Get those girls out of here!" I ordered, without realizing that I had made such a moral statement. The fellows from the Third Division, because they were Regular Army soldiers, accepted the order I had given without any hesitation. The children ran off down the road, and I forgot the matter. As darkness oozed from the ground, it cast a purple haze over the surrounding hills. We congregated under the wings of our planes and ate cold C-rations, our standard fare. We dared not tempt fate by starting a fire, which might silhouette us and attract a sniper.

The tankers were heating their C-rations on the exhaust manifold of their tanks' engines. I could hear snatches of them grumbling about something but didn't understand what it was about. They had had a hot supper, so I was unconcerned about their grumblings. I went to sleep. In the morning when I woke up, Sergeant Bellili was standing over me.

"Schultzie, you really caused us some trouble, and I don't know how you're going to get us out of it," Bellili said. "But you've got to do something."

My mind went blank. I had no idea what I'd done wrong.

"A bunch of us came down last night to keep this situation quiet," he continued, "but we can't hold it for another day. It's up to you. You've got to get it figured out," he insisted. "You gave orders to the tankers and they don't like it."

It seems that I had spoiled the tankers' hopes of having some fun with the little girls. The tankers didn't have to obey the orders of an infantry lieutenant, but I had interfered with their plans by running the girls off, and their resentment was brewing. During the night, I had heard someone mumble, "Who does he think he is, Jesus Christ?" Now I realized the grumbling had been about me. Because the tankers would have put out their own perimeter guard, there must have been some shoving matches with our perimeter guard during the night. It was obvious that Bellili had brought down some fellows from the Battalion to reinforce our guard detachment.

I decided I'd go to Captain Devol and explain the situation to him, then ask if I could withdraw from the airstrip. There was no sense in being part of a fight between the tankers and the Third Division over the orders of a naive lieutenant. I borrowed the weapons carrier Bellili had used to bring the extra guys and went to see Devol.

"Schultzie," Devol said. "I want you to take Schumacher and Croal and three other men and go back to those cracked-up planes to see what can be salvaged and see if we can get a couple of 'em flying. We've been pulled out of the line, so fix up what you can. It may be some time before we get replacements and parts."

We had left the landing area at Licata with eight airplanes flying, but by the time we got to Palermo, there were only four. We lost them through pilot error and poor landing conditions, not enemy action.

"Don't fly anything back that's not safe, but we can't guard them forever," Devol insisted. "Stay till they're fixed or junked, but bring in as many as you can." The damaged planes were a burden because crews had to guard them from souvenir hunters. Although the Italians had been very generous in giving us melons and tomatoes, they begged for our food, and if anything was left loose, it disappeared quickly.

Happy that I didn't need to explain last night's problem to Devol, I returned to the Palermo airport. Bill Shaw flew *Janey* back to the DIVARTY airstrip. Schumacher was in charge of the mechanics on my detail. Croal and the other men went along as helpers and guards. We were off on a salvaging mission.

Four Piper Cubs were in unflyable condition, having been cracked up on three different airstrips because pilots overshot the fields. To stop, the pilots had stomped on the brakes, standing the planes on their noses or tearing up wing tips doing ground loops, which in some situations are good maneuvers to save an aircraft from total destruction and the crews from serious injury.

The first plane was hopeless. The second wasn't much better, and the third was a tragedy. Schumacher and I decided the first one looked pretty good after seeing the fourth. We decided to rebuild two planes out of the four.

Devol scrounged us a 2½-ton truck to transport the salvaged parts, and it arrived with blankets and a Command Post tent, providing us with a little luxury in terms of sleeping. We could even read at night. He also sent along better rations with instructions, "Take your time, but bring them back."

"I told you guys that I liked my job in Division Motor Pool," the truck driver said when he arrived. I could hardly believe what I was seeing—Collins was the truck driver. "Don't hassle me. I won't join the artillery. You guys get too close." It was good to see him again, especially since he brought with him an accurate, up-to-date map of the current geographic situation.

Plane number one was fairly easy to repair after we cleaned her up. We replaced the shock cords, straightened the rods in the sprung landing gear, cleared the packed dirt out of the engine, added a few quick patches to cover the ripped fabric, and gave her a new prop, and she was flyable. When I flew her back to base, a band should have greeted my landing.

The second airplane took us a lot longer, for we had to straighten the struts, and that meant straightening them gradually. We never got them completely straight, but they fit. That airplane would never again fly true, but it would fly.

All we left behind for the Italians was one badly bent-up airframe and two wings to be burned. We salvaged a tailfin, a rudder, an elevator and an elevator mechanism, landing gear, one engine, and some Plexiglas. Two of the four planes were ready to fly, but they looked like they had a skin disease. Wherever we straightened aluminum struts we painted them with a dull red patching dope to give warning that the parts were not full strength.

The salvaging detail had given us a few days respite from the Army routine and a new awareness of our place in Third Infantry Division. Friendly waves came from passing GIs. "Hey lieutenant? Were you the fellow that cracked up in the woods? Or were you hit when that ME chased you?" Real concern for our safety had crept into the dogfaces' conversations. They called us their putt-putt Air Force.

When I took the last repaired plane back to the Air Section, I learned there would no longer be separate battalion airstrips. The fighting along the north coast of Sicily required safe airstrips within easy wire links to Artillery HQs. They would be difficult to find along the narrow ledge of the rugged coastal plain. Mother Nature now dictated our modus operandi.

The 45th Division had performed a difficult job in cutting north through the center of Sicily, from Gela to San Stefano. The Third now passed through the 45th to hasten the drive to Messina, hoping to trap the German Army before it could escape into Italy across the narrow Strait of Messina.

9 · *BLOOD AND GUTS*

Generals George S. Patton and Bernard L. Montgomery were racing to Messina. Subsequent history has shown that, because of the terrain, we advanced on a German timetable. The race between Montgomery and Patton was not really a race under Allied control. It was more like a sporting event created and promoted by the Press.

Though the Germans were pulling out, they held the high ground looking down our throats, and we were meeting heavy resistance. They were experts at placing concealed machine guns and mortars and at developing fields of fire. With their antitank guns, the enemy made us pay dearly for each foot we advanced.

The ancient Sicilian coastal roads on which the Germans retreated were built on the sides of cliffs. In order to isolate the fighting and destroy equipment, the Navy's big guns and Air Force bombers were blowing up the bridges along the route. While the Germans were retreating, it became fair game to blow a bridge, blow out the side of a road, or shoot above the roadway and start a landslide. When our troops got there, however, and needed the road to advance, they inherited the problem the bombardment had created for the Germans. Our combat engineers would try to rebuild the roads while under enemy fire, and they suffered tremendous casualties.

Despite the obvious dangers, we sent our Cubs behind German lines by going out to sea to get direct observation into the concealed mountain valleys and drop high trajectory artillery fire on German gun positions. We often fired smoke shells to screen the Corps of Engineers and give them time to rebuild the roads. Sometimes our men threw a Bailey Bridge over the bridge abutments they had blown up only a few hours before.

In order to avoid the heavy casualties caused by attacking entrenched German positions on narrow mountain roads, Patton decided on an amphibious landing several miles behind the German lines. The Third Infantry spearheaded this end-run attack, and the little "grasshoppers" like *Janey* were expected to provide observation for artillery fire in support of the infantry.

On a hot day in August 1943, we were flying next to an evacuation hospital. Locating military installations near a hospital was not a generally-accepted procedure, but a dry mountain river delta provided the only level ground within miles and it abutted the hospital. We could not use the road because that would interrupt traffic moving to and from the front.

The hospital occupied the high bank of the river and was bounded on the inland side by the coastal railroad. Immediately to the east of the river we were firing a smoke mission to screen our pontoon bridgehead as the engineers built a full-service river crossing to move in heavy artillery for support of troops on our beachhead—the Germans' 170mm gun out-ranged our 155mm Long Tom by 3,000 yards, even when we fired it with a super-charge.

The valley and broad riverbed resounded with the sounds of war. The Germans were sending their shells against our infantry three miles farther east. About three miles beyond the river, a peninsula projected into the sea and on the east shore the Third Division held a beachhead.

We were flying missions in rotation, and *Janey* and I were the next up. I heard sirens on the road and assumed a new tank battalion needed a clear road. Through the road dust I could see Devol talking to someone, and he motioned for me to come to his Command Post. I started *Janey*'s engine and taxied up to him to find out who my observer would be.

I instantly recognized him. He was tall, slender and ramrod-erect, dressed nattily in a custom-tailored uniform, with a lacquered helmet and boots polished to a high gloss. Two ivory-handled Colt revolvers rode on the custom leather gun belt. It was Lieutenant General George S. Patton himself.

If I hadn't been terrified, I would've enjoyed the spectacle. Generals always filled me with awe, but I was especially nervous when I learned old Blood and Guts was to be my passenger. We had heard stories of what happened when Patton spotted officers not wearing their proper uniforms and of the resultant cash fines, ass-chewings and the reprimands for not wearing helmets, neckties, leggings, and not tucking pant legs neatly into boot tops.

I was hardly in uniform at all that day. No tie, shirt collar unbuttoned, English boots, and instead of the standard-issue web belt and GI holster, I wore my .45 automatic in a Moroccan leather shoulder holster that I'd purchased from an Arab peddler just outside a Rabat sporting house. I cringed as I thought of all the non-regulation items on my person and in my plane.

Patton briskly strode to *Janey* and got in.

"I want to look at the beachhead," he said as he locked the seat belt. He put on the radio headphones, checked the mike, and gave me a thumbs-up signal. Off we went. I checked the magnetos and we took off over the beach and out to sea, to gain altitude.

General Patton studied his map board and motioned me eastward. He wanted to fly behind the peninsula to observe the beachhead and see how he could assist in making the link despite the blown bridge. This involved flying about three miles along the coast, within range of German 20mm flak wagons. To minimize this risk, I went a mile seaward before climbing, then turned east to the beachhead and warily approached beached landing craft at about 600 feet. I still was more terrified of Patton than of German fire.

We were flying with only the bottom half of the side doors mounted and the wind rushing in made conversation between us impossible. We communicated by hand signals. He tapped me on the shoulder to get my attention. He motioned for me to make several passes over the beachhead to observe the smoke, the fire, the positions of our troops, and the effects of the incoming land-based artillery firing, the most accurate fire for that kind of close-support mission.

The end run must have made the Germans nervous, for while we were still over the beachhead, some of their scarce dive bombers arrived to strafe the American positions. I'm not sure whether they were Stukas or Focke-Wulf 190s because we didn't stick around for a second look. One of them spotted us, pulled out of his bomb-release dive, and rose toward us with what looked like Christmas-tree lights twinkling on his wings.

I pulled *Janey* into a stall, and she lost lift from one wing. It dipped earthward, and as *Janey* began swishing back and forth in a spin, I plunged toward the sea. Getting down to the deck, a few feet above sea level, was our only salvation.

The bandit had missed on his first pass. If my irregular fall had fooled him into thinking we'd been hit, he might not come back, because *Janey* would head home before our fighters, flying top cover, attacked him. Grasshoppers loved to see those Air Force planes hovering above!

My hours of extra practice doing spins paid off. As the wing dipped, I made a single-revolution spin, regaining full control just before we might have corkscrewed into the Mediterranean. I flew seaward and westward toward our lines, dusting the waves with the throttle full open, pressed to the stops. I soon got *Janey* down to about 10 feet over the water, so that the shore was eye level, and we scooted over the sea.

Our attacker did not pursue. He might have been low on ammunition after strafing the beach or at the stretch end of his fuel. The Luftwaffe had to fly a couple hundred miles from mainland Italian bases, lessening the length of time the German planes could be over the Sicilian battlefields. After I caught my breath, I realized I had forgotten my fear of the General.

I kept *Janey*'s throttle jammed forward, going like hell for our lines while still keeping a safe distance from the shoreline. The Germans still held more than three miles of beach, and I wanted to be certain their flak wagons weren't waiting when I turned shoreward. I continued westward a couple of minutes to get past the German-held shoreline and turned inland to locate the hospital and river delta.

Patton had been a good passenger despite the attention from the German plane, the dive to the deck, and my obvious lack of a proper uniform. "Nice flight, lieutenant," was all he said. I uttered a silent prayer of thanks. The flight was over and there were no holes in *Janey*, me, and especially not in Patton.

I was promoted to first lieutenant the next day. Was my promotion a result of the flight with Patton, or coincidence?

We joined with the beachhead and within a few days were at the Strait of Messina, looking across a narrow strip of water to Italy. The night before, we won the race to Messina. First we established a new airstrip on the beach. Beside it lay a large, low barn. Men from our Air Section inspected the barn for enemy troops and found it to be filled with crates of Italian carbines, sacks of sugar, and cans of strawberry and other red fruit preserves. We filed this information away for future use, but only after liberating several cans of preserves and sacks of sugar.

Two days after the fighting on Sicily ended, I was assigned temporary duty at Patton's headquarters in Palermo. Since it was a temporary duty assignment, I could take Croal and my crew.

I felt a great comradeship with the Third Division and our Air Section. No one any longer doubted what L-pilots were about. The front-line troops had seen us chased by ME-109s, surrounded by black antiaircraft bursts and trailed by white tracers from German machine guns. Dogfaces waved respectfully to us as they marched by our airstrips, and they eagerly helped us to gas up and move our planes. The forward units told stories of our exploits, some real and some imagined. But whenever we were in the air, the Germans hesitated to fire their big guns and mortars, which saved the GIs' lives when advancing or withdrawing. We discovered or luckily guessed at hidden German gun locations and smothered them with whistling shards of steel and billowing smoke.

10 · *PALERMO*

General Patton's Headquarters was located on an estate near the Palermo Airport. I couldn't use that airport, but close by stood a walled race track being used as a ration depot. It had a hard-surfaced parking area that made a great landing strip.

An all-black unit manned the installation. At this time the Army was still run by sergeants. Croal approached Master Sergeant Herbert Jackson, who was in charge of the enlisted complement of the supply depot, about sharing guard duty and space inside the wall. Jackson immediately expressed a desire to see Palermo from the air. I was a trader, so we were off and running. After a couple of informational flights around the harbor area for Jackson and his friends to check camouflage, the deal was closed. Croal and I had established both a friendship and trade partnership with Jackson. The depot guard would allow my plane within its perimeter and my ground crew could eat at their mess and sleep in their buildings. Our trump cards were new, greasy, Italian carbines, still in wooden cases, under our squad tent.

I traded airplane rides for cases of boned turkey, pineapple juice, orange juice and other such delicacies. They were welcome treats after months of C-rations, and they were valuable trade commodities almost anywhere.

Soon a small-statured black soldier, who seemed to be the chief negotiator, approached Croal with an offer he could not refuse: "You get me a few long rides for my ladies and I will deliver groceries to your doorstep!"

Devol had established a policy in North Africa that any booty obtained through special requisition channels was to be shared equally by everybody in the Air Section. Croal and I kept our part of the bargain and yet Croal must have gained twenty pounds in three weeks' duty in Palermo, due to the groceries delivered on our doorstep.

I reported daily to Patton's headquarters in full and proper uniform, tie straight, and my Government-Issue boots shining. I cached my British battle dress boots and my Moroccan-made shoulder holster for future use, and I wore my .45 in a standard-issue web belt with GI holster. The gunbelt was uncomfortable in the close confines of *Janey*'s cockpit, but I didn't want Patton to think I was testing to see how far I could go with uniform modification

I stayed in the junior officer's quarters on the estate and had the use of a motor-pool jeep and driver. Croal and the crew had the use of a ¾-ton truck for fun and games in Palermo. Days went by sometimes without a flight for *Janey* and me. It was the old Army game of hurry-up-and-wait, and I stood by to respond to Patton's bidding, like a chauffeur.

General Patton was deeply concerned for the wounded soldiers, and on several occasions *Janey* and I flew him to the evacuation airstrips where he would meet and talk with the wounded men as they were loaded onto C-47 transports headed for hospitals in Africa and then home. On one of those flights, I approached an evacuation field, circled twice and got neither a red nor a green light from the tower—the same routine that the Air Force had often given me in North Africa. I observed that there were no fighter planes coming in, only one or two fighters taxiing toward the runway. As I landed *Janey*, a yellow jeep raced toward us with an Air Force lieutenant waving his cap. I pulled off the runway and started to taxi to the line of C-47s. The lieutenant pulled along side *Janey* in his jeep and proceeded to chew me out over the roar of the engine. He had no idea I was carrying a three-star general, General Patton to boot. Patton took offense at the verbal abuse and shouted, "STOP!"

I stopped. As the lieutenant approached us, I cut *Janey's* engine, fearful he would run into the propeller in his agitated state. He was shouting wildly and gesturing for me to get the hell out of there because it was a combat field. Just then, the flight of fighter planes roared past, giving us all a dust bath as they took off. Patton slowly stepped out of the plane and strode over to the yellow jeep, standing ramrod erect in full-dress regalia. I couldn't hear his words, but the lieutenant became very subdued. Patton drove off in the jeep to visit the wounded soldiers, and the lieutenant helped me push *Janey* farther off the runway. Patton strolled down the line of stretchers, shaking hands, and speaking with the soldiers being evacuated.

A few days later, Private Harold Stein, Devol's jeep driver, arrived with a message that Devol wanted to see me as soon as possible. I suggested to Patton's headquarters that *Janey* might need a new magneto and received permission to fly back to home base for the vital part. When I landed I found out why Devol's request was not the thing to go through wire, over air waves or to write down.

"On behalf of our Air Section, Stein is negotiating a deal with the Navy. We're to send a truck to the barn in Messina that we liberated and still guard. We'll trade some of the sugar, jam, and carbines for cots, hams, and cases of Coke. Stein has done well, for you know the Italian carbines are nearly worthless to us since we're combat troops. The only weapons that have good cash or trade value up front are German Lugers, P-38s and Schmeisser machine pistols. The hams will be a welcome replacement for our K- and C-rations. The Cokes will be a pleasant alternative to the packets of sticky lemonade powder or instant coffee in the combat rations. The cots will be sheer luxury compared to blankets spread out on rocky ground.

"I want somebody to be on hand so that if a whistle blows we can get our truck out with or without our trade items," Devol continued. "The Third Division MPs are our guys and willing to forget minor matters for trade goods or airplane rides. Stein is a charming scrounger. He is vital to our operation, but he requires help." Devol wanted me to volunteer, and I jumped at the chance.

Although I enjoyed respect as a fighting member of the Division, Devol suspected I liked to wear funny hats and enjoyed play acting. The next day I visited the base post exchange and bought quartermaster collar insignia and majors' oak leaves. In case anything serious happened during the swap, I would be a major in the Division's Quartermaster Battalion.

Everything went like clockwork. The truck drove out of Palermo and back to the Third Division airstrip loaded with tents covering the goodies below. Croal and I celebrated by each drinking a whole bottle of Coke instead of splitting it with somebody. Then I went back to being a lieutenant, keeping the major insignia for a future opportunity.

Even though we'd been discreet, the results of our coup could not be kept secret from the organization of Staff Sergeant Joe "Hook" Casanova, the logistics genius who had organized Operation Ice Cream in North Africa. Hook, skilled at exploiting Army supply Snafus, such as issuing bales of woolen blankets in midsummer and a bountiful supply of mosquito nets in midwinter, made a specialty of pirating edible goodies from the Higher Headquarters' ration supply. He had established a never-fail reputation.

Hook learned that hams and Cokes were being passed around our Air Section, so he came looking for me and Croal. Always direct, Hook wasted no time. "Schultz, I understand you can get your hands on hams, and you didn't call me. I'm the man to get you the maximum benefit. Let's see what we can work out."

Before I could answer, Croal walked under the lean-to beside the truck with Master Sergeant Brown and asked me, "Lieutenant, do you want some more coffee?"

Croal later said Hook's jaw dropped a foot. But I was not a stickler for military protocol. From that day forward Croal and I were on Hook's team.

The next afternoon, *Janey* and I flew Patton to an evacuation field in the western part of Sicily. I was careful not to raise the ire of the Air Force so I made several circles of the field, making certain there were no planes in motion as I landed near the line of C-47s marked with large white circles surrounding bright red crosses. My landing caused little commotion as I parked beside the larger planes like a little chick beside a mother hen. Dozens of C-47s were lined up and stretchers were being placed on board. Patton walked down the line, shaking hands with the individual soldiers and exchanging a few words with them. When he returned to the plane to start back to Palermo, he took a map from his pocket.

"Do you think we can make this German glider field and still have enough gas to get back to Palermo?" he asked. He wanted to stop and look at a few of the abandoned German gliders, for he had understood that some of them were in nearly-flyable condition. I calculated the distance, flying time and fuel level.

"We have enough gas for the trip, but because it's midafternoon, we'll have to limit our time at the glider field," I explained. "It will be about 40 minutes flying time to the field, and 40 minutes back to Palermo, so we will have an hour and a half or two hours to explore the German glider field."

"Let's go," he said.

Those gliders were not like the throwaway gliders that the Allies later used in Market Garden. They were gliders that the Germans actually used to ferry troops, and had also been designed to bring back wounded. They were big enough to carry 30 to 40 shock troops to a battle and perhaps an equal number of wounded back.

The Germans had built the glider field on a large plain that had once been a lake bottom. It was obvious that the Air Force had bombed the field on many occasions because the runways had the expected number of craters. As we flew low over the field, we could see that some of the gliders were still in pretty fair condition, especially the ones back in the trees.

We landed, and because there were no troops on the field, I stood close by *Janey* while Patton went off by himself to examine the gliders. Sicily was well secured at that time, and we felt no threat from the few shepherds and their sheep that were nearby, but I didn't want to turn my back and discover that *Janey*'s tires had been stripped and her gas tank drained.

The gliders were basically skeletons now, and the fabric on them was ripped and slashed. Nothing usable was left on the planes. The Germans, presumably, had taken the instrument panels, and the tires had either been salvaged by the Germans or stolen by the Italians. After looking at several gliders, Patton returned to *Janey* and instructed me to fly along the lake bed a little farther to see if we could find any that were in better condition.

While we were up, I put in a radio check to his HQ and got no response. I cautioned him that we only had about 60 to 90 minutes' worth of daylight left, but we landed and he went off to look at another cluster of gliders.

Again I stood by *Janey,* and when Patton returned, we took off again. I put in another radio check to his HQ, and, again, got no response. As we climbed higher, he saw one more cluster of airplanes close to the woods he wanted to examine.

"We don't have much time left," I warned as we landed. "I can't get into Palermo and there's not an opening between here and Palermo, unless we go along the side of the road we used during the invasion." Yet, he was determined to look at one more group of gliders. I cautioned him again that we were very close to being out of daylight.

"I will be right back," he said. But when he started going from plane to plane to plane again, I knew there was no way we could safely land at Palermo, even though it was still light out.

"General, there's no way we can make it back to Palermo," I said when he returned.

"We'll go up and radio back where we are," he said confidently, "and they will send a car." We made one more short flight. I took *Janey* up to 2,500 feet, which is fairly high for an

L-4B. I still couldn't establish radio contact and was increasingly concerned about saving gas, so I pointed down to suggest we land right where we were. He nodded.

The abandoned field seemed safe enough. I landed, taxied *Janey* over by the woods and parked her near a small road. Patton said he had told his staff that he might stop by this field. He thought they might drive by to look for him. We settled in for the night. I had nothing to eat in the plane and neither did he. We had a canteen full of water stashed in the plane, but after my experience in North Africa and Sicily, water discipline was no problem. We were not big water drinkers, so we'd survive.

We decided to survive in some degree of comfort. I dug the knife out of *Janey*'s first-aid kit and we cut a couple of swatches out of one of the gliders to make ground cloths and a couple more swatches for blankets. We folded up the fabric and bedded down for the night. We were in a forested area, so it was easy to get comfortable on a mattress of dry leaves, and because it was the dry season, there were not many bugs.

I wondered at his equanimity over this small overnight interlude and his almost-deliberate ignoring of my warnings about our flying time. Perhaps he needed a respite from being always in charge of personnel and from the momentous decisions a general must make. Was Patton playing old-fashioned hooky? If so, I can't say I blame him for wanting a break.

We gazed at the stars and talked about light-plane flying. Patton had been one of the big boosters of sport aviation, and he told me how proud he was of the way it had developed. Artillery aviation had come along much as he had anticipated, but he lamented the fact that it was so late in starting, and that a special-use plane had not been built that was an equal to the German Fiesler Storch. He explained to me how tightness in appropriations had delayed the development of a small artillery-spotting and liaison plane; nevertheless, he felt that the L-4B was doing an admirable job.

Patton spoke of the difficulties he had had with the Air Force during the time that he was promoting small planes and how the Air Force didn't want to release any aviation to the Army. He outlined the ongoing conflicts with the Air Force and the changes needed to solve those problems.

He was interested in the history of the German gliders parked all around us. He conjectured on what the gliders might have been used for, how they could be used with different tow planes, and what role they might play in various military operations.

Finally, we dozed off. I think the General went to sleep first. I felt duty-bound to guard him, even though I felt no threat from the local residents. I had my GI .45, and he had his ivory-handled Colt Peacemakers. I figured we could hold off a large number of sheep if we had to.

At the first light of dawn, we were ready to return to Palermo. It was apparent that Patton knew how to fly a Cub just as well as I did. From his position in the observer's seat, he held the duplicate set of brakes and the throttle for me as I propped the airplane.

By that time in my flying career, I had developed strong shoulder muscles and could prop *Janey* by myself from behind the propeller. I would wedge my right foot under the tire to brace myself, reach over to the throttle, prop the engine, then while keeping my right foot under the tire, I would reach in and catch the throttle. Because Croal had so lovingly tuned *Janey*'s engine, it was easy to prop her by myself, but it was even easier with Patton on the brakes and throttle.

The dawn air was smooth and still as we started back toward the sunrise. Flying toward Palermo, I at last made radio contact. When we arrived, several staff cars were waiting for him. I imagine that some of his staff had been ready to push any number of panic buttons. There was also the fallout from the slapping incident.

Almost everyone had heard of the slapping incident by then, but I was unaware that there was going to be a public apology. The slapping incident was nothing until the Press reported it. Most of us shared Patton's attitude toward battle fatigue. Everybody had battle fatigue, so we felt that if a soldier was copping out on battle fatigue, he was copping out on battle. Yet, the Press seemed to change the issue from a soldier's copping out to an abusive general slapping a sick soldier.

About a week after the slapping incident, *Janey* and I flew Patton to a war room. Like many other war rooms, it was just a couple of command tents in a barbed-wire enclosure made to look like a stockade for enemy POWs or an MP stockade holding soldiers who had been arrested. Nobody would easily recognize it for what it was. On this particular day, Patton took me into the war room with him and allowed me to see the model of the Salerno invasion. Now I knew what was next, and he knew that I knew.

Soon after that, I reported to Patton that Captain Devol needed me and *Janey* for the first days of the invasion because Devol's replacement pilots had not arrived as scheduled. "Good spirit," Patton replied. "Go on back."

Battlefield meeting on Sicily next to a new Army L-5 aircraft. *Left:* **an unknown photographer.** *Center:* **British Field Marshall Bernard Montgomery.** *Right:* **General George S. Patton, Commander of American forces in Sicily.** *—Charles Croal*

11 · *THE DUEL*

The 36th Infantry Division, a Texas National Guard Unit, and two divisions from the British Eighth Army were meeting stiff German resistance on the Salerno beachhead. The battle-hardened Third Infantry Division and several attached units, after three weeks' rest at the end of the Sicilian campaign, were called in to bolster the beachhead. I volunteered to leave the comforts of Palermo, and perhaps the patronage of General Patton, to rejoin the Third on the beachhead.

The Italian Army's surrender in September of 1943 only served to strengthen the Germans' resolve. They had salvaged most of their troops and equipment from Sicily and were ready to fight. The euphoria we enjoyed after the fall of Sicily vanished as we started on the road to Rome. It would be a gauntlet of death, not a parade route.

We were short-handed. The Division's replacement pilots and planes had not arrived, but the shortage of planes and pilots didn't worry the planning brass, for the Grasshoppers were still a novelty with an Infantry operation. We had not proven ourselves as vital members of the Infantry team as we began the fighting on mainland Italy.

The new battlefields were a boost to the pilots' morale. Compared to the short gully-pocked fields we landed on and took off from in Sicily, the gently sloping fields south of Naples were much safer. The smooth, rolling countryside was lush with vegetation that provided cover for our planes and a soft landing surface. At last I was able to land and take off into the wind, with slight crosswinds present only on rare occasions. This was especially helpful when a heavy-weight battalion commander wanted to examine the terrain ahead from *Janey*'s rear seat.

The dawn-to-dusk air-cover patrol Devol had initiated in Sicily now became our daily routine. The early morning haze could conceal many things from air observers, but the muzzle blast of a large artillery piece was plainly visible, betraying the enemy's position. Our presence in the area discouraged the German gunners, and though it didn't eliminate their harassing fire, we held it to a minimum. German prisoners reported that if a fighter pilot, antiaircraft gunner, or infantryman knocked out an observation plane, he was awarded a special furlough, so *Janey* and all the other Cubs were fair game.

We always flew erratic patterns and stayed close to the ground to hide the location of our airstrip from enemy observation. I constantly feared enemy gunners might be letting me pass, hoping that I would become overconfident and fly within easy range of their 20mm flak wagons or along a predictable flight line so a salvo of black antiaircraft bursts would either shred me or scare me to death.

I liked to fly, especially from large fields. Anyone who wanted to fly in *Janey*'s rear seat and had a reasonable reason was my man. The more I could get the feel of the seat in my hard ass, the better pilot I would be. It was self-preservation, yet it built a host of friends throughout the Division and a nickname I liked, Schultzie.

The master mechanics at Fort Sill drilled us in common-sense routines that would enable us to minimize the loss of life and planes to mechanical failure. Flying, itself, has many dangers, but they can be controlled. "Take care of your plane and it will take care of you," was a theme expressed over and over. It only took a couple of minutes to check the strut connections, the oil level, and a quick look would reveal any water or sediment in the carburetor bowl. Croal and my trusted crew chief, Sergeant Arlie Schumacher, didn't object to my micro-managing their efforts in the care of *Janey*; instead, it gave the two men a feeling of pride to maintain the plane in first-class condition.

A verbal report after landing was fun for the ground crew and a great tension reliever for me. The after-flight action details gave Schumacher, Croal and other ground-crew members a feel for the terrain ahead and how the day's action was going.

After the action report, the discussion turned to how the engine sounded at the cruise rpms, a direct reflection on Schumacher's and Chuck's ability to perform their jobs. Both men took great pride in the fact that *Janey* was an easy starter and always started on the first spin. *Janey*'s ease in starting was commented on by everybody on the field. A slow starter, on the other hand, brought hoots of derision from ground crews. The pilot would always have a small tinge of uncertainty when his engine required coaxing to run.

I routinely gave *Janey*'s fuselage a quick check for holes, even though most of the time when the plane was hit by groundfire I would hear a faint *ping*. But many times the engine drowned out the sound. Possibly it wasn't groundfire at all, but merely a small stone kicked up by the tires.

Antiaircraft fire was a different story. If it was within a city block, I was scared out of my wits and was certain that the rending sound and violent buffeting caused by the blast had destroyed the entire plane. I was often disappointed to find not a mark on *Janey* from the AA burst, and if someone else hadn't observed the encounter, I was accused of bucking for a Section Eight, which is Army jargon for a mental-disability discharge.

The dreaded Fiesler Storch, the German counterpart to our L-4Bs, never appeared in southern Italy. We Cub pilots had spent hours in plane identification class at Fort Sill trying to recognize it from any angle, for it was our natural enemy. Twice as fast as our Cubs, the Storch could fly at low speeds, and it could land and take off on the most primitive of airfields. The Storch even came with a rear-mounted machine gun.

The 441st, our Division AA battalion, was always active driving off other airborne menaces. The Messerschmitt 109s, Focke-Wulf 190s and the siren-carrying Stuka dive bombers were frequently evident over the battlefield as we moved on Naples. The 441st AA crews had a good success record in knocking them down, but the bombers kept coming. Their strafing attacks were heralded by the pop-pop of the 40mm AA guns, the crack-crack and the black smudges of their air bursts, plus the chunk-chunk of the .50-caliber two- and four-barrel guns on our AA wagons.

Those sounds froze my blood. I immediately looked for a depression in the ground or the cover of a hill or forest where *Janey* and I might become invisible.

On my second flight on a clear September day, as I was heading back from a completed mission, flying low beside a supply convoy, white tracer bullets streaked in past me. Had some green replacement opened fire on me, or was this a hungry Messerschmitt 109? The roaring of his engine and the turbulence of his slipstream left no doubt. It was an ME-109, and he was turning in front of me.

Obviously he was not interested in the convoy below. He wanted my L-4B for a quick snack and that special furlough given as a reward for the downing of an air observation plane. A sergeant in the supply convoy, the legendary Joe "Hook" Casanova, had a front-row seat at this particular air show. Here is his version of the proceedings:

> It was always so nice and quiet when our little Cubs were up there, buzzing away, putt-putt-putt-putt. There was no goddamn Kraut artillery coming in, there were no 88s blowing our heads off, no mortars. I could lay my head down on the ground and rest. I knew I could get a couple hours of sleep as long as I saw a Cub up there. A Cub pilot was an angel, as far as we were concerned.
>
> That day we were going up the road. I had a load of rations to drop off to the front-line troops, and I told Reb, my driver, "Something's going to happen." I uncovered the .50-caliber that was on

the ring mount of my truck.

Then I heard this son-of-a-bitch ME-109 coming out of the sun. The way ME-109s screamed was sort of like a siren. You could hear them long before you could see them.

"Pull the truck to the side," I told Reb.

The sun was behind us, and I had a tarp over the rear. There was no way I could get a shot at the damn 109. I wanted to get the truck off the road, because I knew the son-of-a-bitch was going to start strafing.

Then another came down out of the sun. The first 109 came after us, making a strafing run at the vehicles on the road. There were several other trucks besides mine on the road, ammo trucks and ration trucks that had just come from the ration depot, and we were all heading for the forward positions.

While the first 109 made a strafing pass at us, the second one went after the poor little Cub. I was laying on the ground watching the 109, and he went after that Cub, guns blazing.

When I knew I wasn't in trouble anymore I stood up. Once we got off the road, I wasn't worried about the 109 that was strafing. He might have gone up the road a little bit, or he might have gone back. The last time I saw him he was strafing while heading away, but the other bastard was still hot after the Cub. I could see that 109's tracers and it looked like they were going right through the Cub, right through the wings.

The 109 couldn't turn sharply enough to come directly back at me, for we were in a box canyon. Yet because he didn't climb out of the potential range of our flak wagons, I knew for sure that I was his quarry.

Unfortunately for our advance, we had been stalled in this location for several days. Fortunately for me, I had flown this path several times and I knew that a low hill with a depressing air current was close to the end of the canyon. If I could zigzag while diving to increase my airspeed, and then do a tight 180-degree turn just off the face of the hill, perhaps I could evade him and gain enough time for our flak wagons to discourage him. It was worth a try. I didn't have too many choices.

One look told me he was close behind me, and I was still a considerable distance from my hillside. But it was now or never. I banked and dived as steeply as possible and it felt good. Practice was paying off: I was sitting not slipping in the seat. I held the turn to 270 degrees and when I was below tree level I allowed myself another look up, for the ground seemed only inches away. He was past me and my extra degrees of turn had enticed him lower than his prudent flight pattern allowed. He was now flying toward the side of the canyon and could suffer the downdraft of the hill.

Hook continues the story from his ringside seat:

> We were 100 yards away at the most. As soon as the 109 made the first pass, the Cub pilot must have seen what was going on because I bet the 109 wasn't 25 feet above the Cub. And then the 109 turned and came back again, screaming out of the sun.
>
> By this time, the Cub pilot was zigzagging, first a square, then he was working on a triangle. The more he zigged and zagged, the lower he came toward the treetops, and so did the ME-109 each time it came around to make another firing pass at the Cub. He was staying in the sun so the Cub couldn't see him, and he was coming out of the sun every time he made a pass. The ME-109 was bound and determined to get that Cub.
>
> Then the Cub was coming one way, and the

ME-109 was coming from another direction, at an angle, and I don't think the Cub pilot could see him. From where I was, it looked like the Cub went into a bunch of trees, like there was a hollow. We were thinking that he was going to get down in there to hide.

And then the Cub came up, over the tree-tops. The 109's four guns were still blowing. Tracers were streaking, and you could see fire on the wings as the goddamn ME-109 overshot the Cub and hit that wall. It popped like a balloon.

And then we didn't see the Cub. When I saw the fire and I didn't see the Cub anymore, I figured that, sure as hell, the 109 got him. Then all of a sudden, about 15 seconds later, we saw the little Cub come out of the trees, over the treetops.

Then it was celebration time, just like the Fourth of July, like raising the flag in Berlin. Everybody was clapping, hollering, throwing their helmets in the air. We were so damn happy that the Cub didn't get knocked out, you could hear the hollering way off in the distance. We were in a little pocket right at the foothills, and the echo, it came all the way back.

"Listen to them SOBs," I told Reb.

"He did a pretty good job," Reb said.

"Let's find out from Devol who the pilot was." Then the Cub hovered over the Messerschmitt, over the fire. The whole side of the hill was burning. There was no way the ME-109 pilot could have got out of there.

I didn't see the actual crash, but as I rose above the masking of the trees, I saw smoke. As I passed over the supply convoy, infantrymen were waving wildly and flashing V signs. In the tradition of the WW I movies that had held me transfixed as a boy, I flew beside the crash site.

It was not a good landing. Buck fever had set in and my legs were trembling. I had that dryness of the throat that comes from relief when the worst is over. Word had spread that an ME-109 was down, and BA of the Cub Air Force was to get the credit. I was BA, the only one flying at the time. *Janey* had made her mark.

Immediately, I wanted Devol or someone to put me down for a medal, but actually, it wasn't worth an air medal. The first step was five enemy planes to become an Ace. Well, I had 20 percent, but medals don't come easy in an infantry division. A certain amount of daily heroism comes with the territory. To the credit of the system, the rules are firm. The Third Division was the most decorated Division in Europe, but it was tough and thorough in giving its rewards.

12 · *THE SPY*

As we inched our way up that narrow valley east of Naples, slugging our way to the old capital of Caserta, we were treated each evening to a beautiful pyrotechnic display as the Germans bombed the ships in our newly-acquired supply port, Naples Harbor. The Navy Seabees and the Army engineers had done an outstanding job of clearing the debris and rubble from the harbor, so a steady supply of war materiel could reach mainland Italy. Having Naples Harbor under our control gave us a deep-water harbor for unloading and a good road network leading from Naples to Rome, which combined would insure a reliable supply of ammunition and fuel as we marched to liberate Rome.

After a morning flight, as we were describing the Germans' gun emplacements and marking the situation map, Devol took me aside.

"Schultz, I've got a mission for you. A fellow from the British Eighth Army will be here soon. He's part of the Royal Air Force Intelligence Corps. I want you to fly him to the Foggia area in eastern Italy. You'll be gone a couple of days. The British are just starting to attack a German air base there, and it seems there's some special item over there that they want to get at before it gets looted or picked up by souvenir hunters."

I replied, "Will I be flying without the radio so we can carry a bag or two?" Weight was a real problem during landings and takeoffs due to the soft, wet fields. A soft field softened our landings, but it made takeoffs sluggish and we required more room to get enough lift.

"Wait till the British officer comes," Devol answered. "Let's see how much stuff he has and what he thinks the duration of the trip will be."

I talked to Croal about taking the radio set out and hiding it somewhere safe. *Janey*'s radio was valuable. It was in good shape and it worked well, so I didn't want it to get lost in an equipment shuffle or be requisitioned by another crew. In addition to being jittery when another pilot flew *Janey*, I was beginning to develop a personal attachment to her equipment. I particularly hated to have the radio taken out for fear that any jostling would throw it out of kilter, and I didn't want to have it act up again as it had with Patton in Sicily, or have the batteries fade when I was in a perfect position to direct artillery fire.

Devol was waiting when Captain Jim Robertson of the Royal Air Force drove onto our field. I feared Robertson would be one of those 6-foot-plus, 200-pound Scotsmen we had encountered in North Africa. A big passenger like that made our Cubs grunt and groan just getting off the ground. To my great relief, however, Robertson could have passed for an overweight jockey.

It became clear that we would be gone for perhaps two or three days, depending on how fast the British were able to clear the runways of enemy troops. The Germans were defending the base and torching the unflyable planes. A special unit of elite British troops was leapfrogging ahead, trying to punch its own hole through the German lines in an effort to acquire the secret item before the Germans destroyed it or the Italians stole it.

Robertson wouldn't say exactly what "it" was, but he was very anxious to stow his gear and be underway. Our first step was to remove *Janey*'s radio. It would improve her handling characteristics; however, since we might have to land and refuel en route, we had to carry a full 5-gallon gas can. The fuel would add extra weight, and unfortunately the only place to carry it was in the tail section. That would definitely affect *Janey*'s handling. I would have to readjust all my piloting habits and instincts. I made sure that all our equipment was strapped in and clear of the elevator and rudder cables.

"I'm Jim," was his first instruction after we had made all our travel preparations. "And for this trip remember that, and I'll call you Schultz like everybody else does."

That was fine with me. As a first lieutenant, I still felt a certain awe of captains, and whenever I made captain, I hoped to be addressed by that title. But since Jim and I would be camping out together for several days, it was nice to know that we would be on a first-name basis.

We had a long airstrip, and the heavy takeoff went well. We flew east, away from the sun, at altitudes ranging from 400 to 800 feet, if we saw British vehicles below us. Eight hundred feet is considered above the range of most ground fire, but within easy range of the wily ME-109s if they were lurking behind our lines for targets of opportunity. Whenever I saw regular Allied military traffic, I dropped down low to 400 or 500 feet, assuming that our Allied comrades in arms would retaliate against any ground-based threat to *Janey*. But whenever I flew over country of undetermined ownership, I would climb above 800 feet and keep my eyes skinned for bandits.

We flew without any attention from the Luftwaffe or any *pings* from small-arms fire for about an hour before spotting a large British compound and motor park. We landed, got a briefing on the latest ground action, and filled up with British petrol. Then we took off for Foggia. We saw an occasional shell burst to the north as we neared the east coast of Italy, but we were not fully aware of the developments on the ground.

Foggia wasn't like any airfield I had ever seen. It was a large, flat, dry bed from a prehistoric lake. Dozens of landing areas and runways had been marked and graded on the firm soil. Some of the runways were thousands of yards long with aircraft dispersal areas that branched hundreds of feet from the runway. The Bren gun carriers, low-slung half-tracked armored vehicles with a machine gun mounted on the front, had done a good job of punching their way through the southern end of the German defense. Jim decided we'd camp out with a Bren carrier crew for the night and start our flight forward in the morning.

Dining on beef and biscuits and listening to the thick British accents, I learned why they had asked for an American plane. The British were flying Taylorcrafts, or L-2s, but due to a supply snafu involving the Taylor Aircraft Company and Air Force Procurement, they were rapidly running out of parts. Although they were supposed to have several L-2s in the theater, only one or two were flyable, so they requested an American plane for this mission.

Some of my British comrades had been at Dunkirk, and most had been in North Africa under Montgomery and had the swagger that came from fighting against the Desert Fox. Even though I was the only Yank among them, they made me feel so comfortable I hated to turn in for the night.

Dawn and the sound of distant small-arms fire brought me back to reality and I asked, "How soon should we start, Captain Robertson?"

"Jim! It's Jim!" he reminded me vociferously. "Remember, Schultz, we're going to be together for some time. Let's forget the captain stuff. First we'll have tea, then we'll go up and take a look."

We breakfasted on tea and kippers and hardtack, and the sun was well above the horizon before we took off. The sound of gunfire was dying away, indicating that the Bren carrier crews were making progress. We flew toward the rattle of small-arms fire and up one of the runways, then started circling the different plane emplacements. The planes had been widely dispersed over a large area. Many aircraft, though not flyable, had survived the attention of U.S. Air Force bombers. Stukas, Heinkels, Dorniers, and Junkers trimotors that had survived the wrath of the American raiders had been torched. It appeared someone had taken an ax or a big can opener to many of the wings. We were not sure if it was the Germans or Italians, but someone was obviously draining the fuel from each plane.

The farther north we flew, the better the condition of the enemy planes, but as we drew closer, we saw Italian civilians darting from cover and chopping at the wings of the planes. We buzzed them, but to no avail. They continued hacking.

Jim was ready to panic, so we landed on one of the taxiways and ran toward the Italians. Instead of dispersing, they just stood there awe-struck, not knowing what to think. To help them make up their minds, Jim drew his Webley revolver and I drew my .45.

"No! No!" Jim shouted harshly, but the Italians just smiled and continued chopping at the wings to drain out what little fuel remained in the tanks. There was no way to communicate with them. Their priority was scavenging fuel, possibly to sell on the black market, and they were unconcerned about the ongoing battle and indifferent to the needs of the Allies.

Jim's panic turned to relief, however, when he realized that the Italians were not venturing into the planes' cockpits. The planes had been in German possession not more than a few hours ago; they may have even flown the bombing raid on Naples Harbor the previous night. After venturing into one of the cockpits, Jim came out smiling from ear to ear. He wrote a note and told me to take it to the last Bren carrier crew we had seen. I hated to leave him there alone, but following his instructions, *Janey* and I took off.

I landed *Janey* next to a couple of parked Bren carriers and handed the note to one of the troopers. Its contents had an immediate effect, for soon the Bren carriers were racing up the field. I got *Janey* airborne and dropped a purple smoke flare to mark Jim's location.

When I landed, Jim was ecstatic. He had found the "it" he was searching for—a radio control box of some sort in the Heinkel's cockpit. He took several photographs of the bomb rack configurations under the wings, and after a thorough examination of the Heinkel, he climbed into *Janey* with the black box cradled in his lap. We fast-taxied down to another group of Heinkels that were being worked over by the Italians. We spotted the same bomb rack configuration under the wings. Jim climbed into the cockpit of another Heinkel, and in a short while he shouted from the window, "I've got another one!"

This time he took more care in disconnecting the box. Fortunately, the planes hadn't been booby-trapped, but Jim was in a hurry and he didn't have enough time to be as careful as he should have been. It was obvious that he wanted to deliver those boxes somewhere, and soon. He climbed into *Janey* with another black box and off we went to search for more. We located another plane with the same bomb racks and he removed a third black box. As we waited for a Bren carrier to come and take the black boxes, Jim revealed to me the purpose of his mission.

The Germans had a new weapon, a radio-guided missile. Two of them had scored direct hits on freighters during recent raids, and the Allies were desperate to find out what type of radio equipment had guided the missiles. With those black boxes in our possession, there was a chance to discover how to jam the missiles' radio signals.

I stood by *Janey* as Jim continued his search for more black boxes and took more pictures. The sound of gunfire continued to fade, and about noon Jim returned, pleased with the morning's events. He had placed several black boxes in the Bren carrier. We brewed some of his tea, snacked on hardtack, then flew forward, where we saw the Bren carriers actually engage in combat with the enemy.

Enemy mortar shells were still landing and some of the German planes that had been torched by throwing incendiary grenades into the cockpits were still smoldering. The Germans were leaving the airbase in haste. They had managed to destroy only sixty or seventy planes out of about 200. Although the British had no artillery with them, the fast little low-slung Bren carriers were taking on the role usually reserved for tanks.

The Italian civilians kept busy, chopping into the wings of unburned planes and draining out the last few quarts of gasoline, oblivious to the battle raging just north of them. We tried to fly above the fighting and look ahead, but the black puffs of German ack-ack smoke convinced us that although the Germans were on the run, they were still annoyed with the Cub Air Force. Jim indicated that we had gathered enough information and that it would now be impossible to find a German plane completely intact. We flew back to the camp where we had spent the previous evening.

Bully beef was the bill of fare that night. The Australian corned beef was a regular item on the British menu. For an American soldier surviving on C-ration vegetable stew, beans and franks, and American-style corned beef hash, bully beef was a gastronomic delight, especially when washed down by steaming pots of freshly-brewed tea. Even in the field, the British maintained a separate officers' mess. Glasses of brandy were routinely served after the evening meal.

Jim arranged for all the black boxes except one to be transported back to Naples via jeep on the next supply run. The next morning we packed the one remaining black box into *Janey* and took off. The roads below us were crowded with our military traffic, so there was no need to worry about pockets of enemy resistance. We followed the same route back at 400 to 500 feet and landed at the Naples Airport, where Jim and I said farewell.

The mission had been a welcome relief from the tedium of camp life. I had gained valuable flying experience in fast taxiing for hundreds of yards at a time. And I had been able to see up close and on my terms the dreaded bomber aircraft of the Luftwaffe. By evening I presented a load of bully beef to Devol, and *Janey* and I rejoined the Blue and White Devils in the drive to Caserta.

The Naples Harbor was now safe from the German bombers that had been based at Foggia; and now the Germans would have to sweat. Control of Foggia gave us a base with long enough runways for the P-38 raiders, a base from which bombers could easily reach Romanian oil fields, a base for tactical bombers, and most importantly, a base from which our long-range bombers could hit all of Germany from the south. With the black boxes in our possession, maybe we could outwit the German smart bombs.

13 · *THE ALBATROSS*

When I first flew toward the Mignano Valley, on the last day of October in 1943, I reported seeing a small snow-capped peak at the north end of the valley. Snow seemed impossible, but after several other missions reported seeing the same phenomenon, Devol learned the official version. It was the Abbey of Monte Cassino. "Aren't any of you Catholics?" he asked. "That's the home monastery of the Benedictine Order."

Captain Devol, always ready to provide spirited discussion and humor, took a flight to check it out for himself. Back on the ground, he called his pilots and observers together and in a very serious tone stated, "I'm sending you all in relay flights to the Air Force eye clinic in Naples. You can't tell a white building from snow. What are we going to do come winter?"

We cheered at the idea of going to Naples and enjoying the creature comforts and diversions that "garritroopers" took for granted. If what looked like a snow-capped peak was actually a building, it had to be one of the wonders of the architectural world.

None of us in early November of 1943 wanted to get much closer to verify Devol's information or marvel at the size, grace and beauty of the monastery. Our five worst enemies would be waiting on that mountain, eager to nab *Janey* or another Cub as a trophy. Each predator had its favorite zone but wouldn't hesitate to intrude on another predator's territory, or even to cooperate, so they might together devour *Janey* or a sister Cub while it took off, flew a mission, or landed.

Enemy number one lurked from zero to 1,000 feet. There, .30-caliber groundfire could riddle *Janey's* flimsy linen, wood and aluminum frame full of holes. Predator number two, from zero to 3,000 feet, was the 20mm flak wagons that could chew a Cub into rags and kindling. Above 1,000 feet, predator number three, the omnipresent 88s, waited to blast *Janey* into fine particles of ash. The dreaded ME-109s and FW-190s were predators four and five, and they were everywhere, ready to sneak from below or pounce out of the clouds. And, to add to the peril, unpredictable updrafts and downdrafts in the vicinity of the Abbey made flying there a constant test of a pilot's responses.

The mountain range that separates eastern and western Italy provided enemy aircraft protection from early radar detection. The winding valleys between the millennium-worn peaks masked from early ground view the low-level hit-and-run attacks of the Luftwaffe, made in pairs or by daring lone wolves. The chattering of 20mm wing cannon or the whistle of a 500-pound bomb hurtling toward us would be our first warning that the Germans had arrived. Our response, once we spotted the intruder, shattered the air with smoke, noise and colorful tracers chasing the bandit. A cheering section immediately formed after the aircraft passed beyond them to cheer on the gunners. If the plane trailed smoke or gave a violent shudder, the roar from the cheering section drowned out the gunfire.

We now held Mount Rotundo and were attacking Mount Lungo. K Company of the 30th Infantry Regiment led the assault. Upon reaching the summit of Lungo, they dug in on the terraces of the southern spur while awaiting reinforcements. The Luftwaffe soon registered their objections. We heard the whistle of a bomb, the blast and the drone of an engine, and then our AAs were on him. The German pilot gave it the gun and started to climb out of the valley. But the 40mm pompoms had him surrounded with their black bursts and flashing cotton balls. The cheer was deafening. Hot dog! He was blown to smithereens!

A ball of fire filled the sky as wings went one way, fuselage another. The flaming engine tore into the slope of Mount

Lungo. The bomb had been wide of its mark, so the downed plane was a clear victory for the good guys. The 441st AA Battalion's reputation was continuing to grow, and soon the enemy would learn to leave us alone. We were standing around congratulating ourselves on this spectacular display of warfare when Staff Sergeant John Petruska of K Company, a regular old Army type who looked more at home barking for a carnival than leading a mortar platoon that positioned itself by stealth, threw a damper on our celebration.

Through his binoculars Petruska had seen a medic rushing to the smoking crater where the engine hit the ground. The distance was too great to pick up details, but he could see that a stretcher had been carried away. A casualty ... not good. Our mood changed to the resignation that is so much a part of war. Did it always have to be one for one?

Scratch one ME-109, but the cost to our side was a courageous Infantry major who had just led his combat command to capture Mount Lungo.

It took the infantry nearly two weeks to slog their way through the rectangular-shaped quagmire of the valley ahead while removing thousands of deadly tank mines and nearly-undetectable shoebox mines from the mud, plus disarming the above-ground booby traps. We finally emerged from the valley between Mount Rotundo on the east and Mount Lungo to the west. Dead ahead sprawled the village of Cassino, which had crowned a hillside, nuzzling like a pup against the body of Mount Cassino. The village was now just a pile of rubble, and the Abbey of Cassino seemed to stare down at us with hate and defiance, like a mother enraged by the death of its child.

In bright sunlight, the Abbey's great white bulk with its long lines of windows and towers took on a pristine appearance, as if it were a monument to ancient gods. Sometimes it floated tantalizingly above the fog like the superstructure of a luxury liner on a sea of white. Like a giant albatross lurking above the flood plain of the rain-swollen Rapido River, the abbey seemed to watch our every move, staring down on us as we vainly attempted to follow Route #6 to Rome.

We ceded to the Germans superhuman and nearly-magical powers. Their powerful optical equipment could penetrate mist and darkness and see for tens of miles. They constantly manned their radios with operators fluent in English who could understand every nuance and cover all channels of our radio transmissions. They tapped our telephone lines. Italian spies directed German artillery fire and snooped around our campsites. The Germans lived luxuriously in the warm, dry abbey and ate the best of looted food and drank wine from the abbey's cellars.

Every time we looked toward that gorgeous white hotel, floating dry and secure above us as we lifted our muddy feet and shivered in our perpetually damp, dirty uniforms, our envy and hatred of the Germans increased. The monastery was an albatross around our necks. We couldn't do a damn thing. It was beyond our range until we sent another 2,000 or 3,000 Americans across the River Styx. It had to be destroyed just to deny the Germans the creature comforts we imagined they enjoyed.

Janey and I had flown about two dozen missions since entering the Mignano area. The valley floor seemed to hold the morning ground mist like a child clutching a blanket. Only the midday winds or temperatures forced the bashful countryside to shed her veil. While wallowing in the mud, we hoped but doubted that the engineers had thoroughly cleared the area of mines. The cold, incessant rain shortened tempers. The soggy soil increased the dangers of *Janey*'s takeoffs and landings, and once airborne, we were under the constant glare of the great white albatross. Was it hiding wily Germans with magic devices waiting to shoot us down if we flew too close?

14 • YELLOW FLAG

Locating our missing planes was becoming part of my standard duty at this stage of the war. It wasn't a pleasant task, especially if I had to separate salvageable airplane parts from human parts. On the other hand, I relished any opportunity to take a break from the daily patrol sorties and venture beyond the range of the whistling 88s and 170s of the enemy.

"Fly a one-hour dawn mission," Devol instructed. "Then before the sun creates ground fog, try to find Knutson's plane." Staff Sergeant Joe Knutson's plane was down somewhere in the area. He and his observer, Lieutenant Pete Sondrol, had gone out on an afternoon flight and ended up at an Evac Hospital in Naples. The casualty report didn't give details.

Staff Sergeant Sam Ream was my observer. Lucky for me, he had the excellent map-reading skills needed for a search. The only radio contact with the missing plane had occurred just before the plane left the ground. Minimal communication was normal procedure because radio signals, which are like flashlight beams shining through mist, can easily be traced to their source. Excessive radio chatter gives the enemy time to home in on a signal, so we used the radio sparingly.

The Germans were dug in on the north bank of the Volturno River. Army engineers were still under murderous artillery and mortar fire as they bent their backs to their unenviable task of maintaining a foothold on the enemy-held bank while attempting to secure a pontoon bridge over 300 yards of cold, raging water. The past week's relentlessly steady rain had swollen the muddy river to flood stage, and as the infantry sloshed its way across the wide, water-logged Volturno Valley, casualties rose to over 300 a day.

We fired constant barrages of smoke shells on the German-held north bank of the Volturno to screen the construction crews, but casualties continued. The previous night, by sheer guts and physical endurance, they'd completed a 10-ton jeep bridge. The supply link was forged and smoke generators now were effectively masking the Third's engineers' next task: building a 30-ton tank bridge.

My dawn patrol orders were simple—check on the smoke generator screen and fill in with smoke shells if needed while watching for muzzle blasts from the Germans' long-range 170s. I'd fly *Janey* into the narrow valley between Mount Tifata, which stood 1,800 feet on the east edge of our front, then back west where Mount Castellone rose to 1,200 feet. The seven-mile saddle between the mountains was filled with ancient, sparsely forested foothills, which gave me ample opportunity to fly an erratic pattern to confuse the German antiaircraft gun crews. I flew the roller-coaster evasive maneuver that Devol had taught all his pilots. It took a stable stomach to fly close to the tree tops over hills and down ravines.

Ground observers from the twin peaks were providing the infantry with good information, so our flights the last couple days were primarily to spot any distant enemy guns that dared to risk our spotting their muzzle flash. Below us, we could see the jeep bridge bending in the swift floodwaters of the Volturno, but our 105mm guns and ammunition trucks were gaining the far shore. We would soon be chasing the Germans back to their Fatherland.

The town of Caiazzo had been nearly leveled by the past weeks' fighting. It was now ours and served as the base from where I started a search pattern for Knutson's lost plane. The one-hour patrol ended, and I started flying a series of sunburst rays, fanning out in a southerly direction. I had an hour's gas left to complete the search mission and get home. I began to fly five minutes out and then five minutes back to the base point, flying in a fan-shaped pattern of approximately 30 square miles.

On the third pass, flying directly south of Caiazzo, we spotted what appeared to be an oval green lake in a prehistoric volcano crater. As we flew closer, we saw it was a lush pasture. Possibly underground thermal springs provided the heat to prolong the growing season into October. I circled and, sure enough, below us, highlighted by trampled grass and deep wheel ruts, was the broken but familiar outline of an L-4B.

Why had Knutson been seven miles behind the lines? No bent grass was evident to indicate landing tracks, so I assumed it must have been a near-vertical crash.

I flew *Janey* higher to look for the best truck route to the crash site to retrieve the plane. The area was remote and had been ignored by the war. Only narrow stone-lined lanes led to and from the pasture. On both the north and south edges of the crater's rim were clusters of homes and barns, and in one of the settlements, we saw twin towers of a Catholic church. Less than a mile to the west, a slow stream of ambulances wound to and from the front, taking their cargoes of shattered bodies to the life-saving comfort of Division and Army hospitals, then returning north to pick up more casualties. The crossing of the Volturno River was exacting a fearful price. Ream marked the spot on our map as we headed back to home base.

"Get to it," Devol ordered. "Salvage what you can, and write a casualty report." Ream volunteered to accompany Croal and me, even though this detail was likely to have some grisly moments. Croal and Ream unloaded all the supplies from the ¾-ton weapons carrier to make room for whatever we would salvage of the downed plane. We planned to be back long before dark, in time for chow. All we needed for this job were the tools and tackle locked under the seat.

Creeping traffic slowed our progress. We were careful to stay at least a quarter-mile away from the ambulance convoys. The Geneva Red Cross Convention required respecting ambulance traffic if military vehicles were not intermixed, and this was one of the few rules of war that both sides actually acknowledged and mostly observed. As the sounds of gunfire faded behind the hills and the October sun warmed our shoulders, we relaxed and enjoyed our midday tour of the Italian countryside. With plenty of daylight left, we arrived at the crash site just as someone in the distance fired what sounded like a shotgun, perhaps an Italian peasant shooting game for dinner.

Croal and I walked to the crashed plane and Ream stayed to guard the truck. As we approached the twisted wreckage, people seemed to grow out of the ground and the stone walls. They swarmed around the wreck. Croal and I searched the site for clues as to why the L-4B had crashed. Scavengers had already been at work. The airframe had been stripped of fabric, revealing a bent and twisted fuselage but no shell damage. The wings were broken and useless, and both wheels were gone. Nothing of value remained on the engine block, which was packed with hardened dirt from the force of the crash. The depth of the engine crater suggested the plane had spun in, and the absence of landing tracks reinforced that conclusion. "Evading enemy aircraft," I wrote in my report. "Low-altitude downwind turn… spun in, result of enemy action."

The Italians clamored around us, making friendly gestures, apparently wanting to give us information, but the language barrier separated us. After several tries I could only understand, "*Pielots, no morte, andato via*" to mean, "Pilots not dead, gone away." I responded, "*Buono.*" They smiled, repeating "*Buono, buono, buono.*" We all smiled.

Then I stood beside the stripped airframe and said, "*Fini,*" indicating with my hands a horizontal scissors motion, trying to signify we would abandon the wreckage to them. As we started toward our truck to leave, shouts came from the far side of the pasture. Several Italians were running toward us, waving wildly and yelling, "*Bambino, piccolo bambino.*" They were saying something about a small child.

Croal, Ream and I got into the truck to drive to the far side of the pasture to see what had happened, but our truck became inundated by the crowd. Scores of people jumped onto it and clung to the sides. The extra weight mired us down in the mud, so several of them jumped off to push. On the other side of the pasture a hysterical group of women, all dressed in black, was bending over something on the ground. They were screaming and sobbing and wringing their hands, pleading for help in a language we could not translate but could so easily understand from the anguish in their voices. On the ground lay a small boy, about five years old. A tiny yellow flag was clutched in his dirty, trembling hand. The black skull-and-crossbones printed on the face of the triangular flag was the key to the whole story. It was a warning to Nazi troops:

"DEATH-DEALING and MAIMING EXPLOSIVE MINES ARE BURIED BELOW."

That remote rural area was filled with German land mines.

The women pushed us toward the little boy, expecting us to do something. The crowd quieted and gave us room to examine the child as he lay quietly, crying softly in pain. His right leg was shattered and his foot was joined to the leg by only a few strips of flesh. Blood was spurting onto the dirt.

Ream already had his aid packet open and with the calm assurance that comes from years of training, began first-aid treatment. All we had with us were three aid packets and three vials of morphine. We'd left the rest of our supplies back at camp. To comfort the little boy while Ream worked, the mother cradled her son in her arms and sang a lullaby. Looking up at us with tear-swollen, pleading eyes, she murmured, "*Gracci, gracci.*"

Ream liberally sprinkled the shattered leg with all three packets of sulfa powder and then bound the wound with two bandages, using the last bandage to lash the damaged leg to the uninjured left leg. I couldn't understand how such a small boy could survive such a huge wound. Perhaps he was in shock, for there was not a whimper and he eagerly snatched the hard candy Croal offered him. Ream's calm, deliberate, reverent manner gave us all assurance that everything would be fine.

Croal had not been idly standing by. With the help of the Italians he had removed the wooden bench seat from the truck to be used as a litter. The canvas cargo cover had been taken down to provide warmth and padding to comfort our *bambino*.

A doctor and a hospital was our next stop. Combat hospital units were out of the question. There the little boy would have to wait his turn while combat-torn soldiers were treated first. The Italians indicated by pointing and vigorous sign language that we should take him to a nearby village. Croal skillfully avoided the pot holes and ruts in the road to give an easy ride to the little boy, who still clutched the yellow flag in his tiny hand.

The treatment center had been a school ten days before. Now a handmade Red Cross banner marked a door that emitted a stench like that of a rendering plant. The interior was filthy. My combat boots squished and slid as I walked through the brown slime contaminating the floor. Dozens of injured people sprawled in the muck or slumped against the gray walls.

Blood stained the smock of the nun who came forward to assist us. "Yes," she gestured, then, "*Entre.*" Expressing hope in her voice, she inquired, "*Dottore?*"

"No," I said sadly, knowing she would be disappointed. We left the injured boy's mother kneeling beside him, singing her prayers. On our way out, we waved and said *arrivederci*. The crowd responded in a chorus of *graccis*.

We left our water canteens at the hospital, then we rejoined the ambulance and supply convoy's crawl back to the front in complete blackout. We vowed to return with medical and food supplies and to persuade our medic to spend an afternoon in the village.

Within twelve hours the full Third Division crossed the Volturno and moved north. We never had an opportunity to go back to the village. Later, when I found a discarded yellow flag, I gingerly retrieved it and stuck it in my pack.

15 · *THE GRAVEDIGGERS*

From the air, the flash of any kind of light reflecting off metal or glass always called for a second look, and even if we couldn't confirm its source, we called for the fire missions to bang away. Knowing how we responded to the enemy's reflected light, we were very much aware of our own need to camouflage our equipment.

Protecting *Janey* was my main preoccupation. When she was parked on the ground, I blanketed her windshield and cockpit Plexiglas with tailored canvas covers. From 3-feet-wide green and beige burlap, I made weighted groundcloths and positioned them over her wings and fuselage to cover the large white Air Force recognition stars.

The burlap was a loosely-woven fabric with a coarse nubby texture, but it did the job. We had several bolts of the material in our supply truck when we landed in southern Italy, but we were using it up fast. Only one bolt was left. Where had it all gone and what would we do if we ran out? We'd been using the burlap for groundcloths, sometimes leaving wet or moldy ones behind, but we could no longer afford that luxury. When all the wing and body drops were counted, we had only a few to spare. We saved the uncut bolt for windshield covers.

We were in one of the dirt-poor sections of Italy, the Mignano Valley. The ground was so barren, we wondered how the people lived. Begging and theft intensified. Burlap, for some reason, was a prime target for theft. We had to guard it carefully.

Devol went back to Naples and left me in charge of the Air

Section. During the night we lost several cases of rations, four cans of gas, and most of our burlap wing covers. I had posted only one guard by the kitchen truck; but it just didn't seem possible that all this could have happened if the guard was awake. But it had happened, and we had to recover our lost property. If we didn't find the wing covers, our white stars might attract enemy bombs or artillery fire.

It's amazing how a group of men will pull together when their backs are to the wall. It wasn't long before the culprits were found, an older man and two skinny boys. I decided to administer some instant justice to discourage future thievery or our unit would soon be hungry, immobilized, and naked to the German gunners.

Through interpreter Stein, I demanded the return of all missing items. The older man spoke defiantly, "*No capice.*" I was furious, madder at myself than him. I made him lie down, and I marked four corners on the ground to indicate his length and width. The two young boys cringed, wide-eyed with fear as we tied their bony hands around a knobby olive tree and put the man to digging. My intention was to have him dig a hole for a sump pit to bury our wastes, but his lying on the ground gave rise to the idea of pretending it was a grave. Digging in the hard, rocky ground was too difficult for the man, so we pressed the two young boys, slender as they were, into service too. The digging still went slowly and, as the midday mist cleared, the late summer sun brought out sweat on our diggers. We gave them water to drink, but we ate our noon meal watching them dig. By early afternoon the pit was only about a foot deep.

At the perimeter of our camp, a few Italians clustered to watch the ritual, so I decided to put on a show. I made the older man lay down in the pit. We laid a shovel handle across the opening and playfully argued over the depth. It was unsatisfactory, so we indicated by sign language that at least another foot was required. The diggers went back to work.

We were enjoying our afternoon fun and the lull in fighting. Artillery fire had been slow all day and the air missions were only routine patrols. We kept our weapons very much in evidence, and in our play-acting, we even fixed bayonets on the guards' rifles. This was the first time the bayonets had been out of their scabbards since the last inspection to check for saltwater rusting. And they *were* rusty!

As the afternoon went on, we watched for Captain Devol's plane in the distance, but instead, the low dark clouds signaled that our valley was being isolated. The pit was now over 3 feet deep and our diggers were giving us hopeful looks.

No, it needed to be even deeper, for the *signor*, the older man. Prolonging the ruse, Stein went to the spectators and asked that the thief's family be summoned, for soon there would be a *morte,* or death. Shrieks and a cloud of dust from scurrying feet filled the air as our audience disappeared.

A *patron* soon approached our perimeter and asked to speak with our *commandante.* Stein brought him to me and his message was simply to wait *una hora.* We agreed, but kept our prisoners digging. Within the hour they returned most of the wing covers and two gas cans, empty, of course. The older man, who had actually lived in Cleveland, Ohio, at one time, explained in broken English that the food and gas were gone beyond recovery, but that another burlap cover was on its way.

Two wailing women were introduced as the wife and sister of the older thief, and much to my shame and embarrassment, his wife kissed my hand while he fell to his knees and started praying. The joke had gone too far, but we could not let our audience know that it was all a charade, or we would continue to lose gas, rations and wing covers. When the final missing wing cover appeared, we released our captives.

An extra guard was placed on duty that night, and our camp was secure.

Captain Devol was delayed by a coordination meeting with the 36th Division, which would relieve us within days. We'd been in continuous contact with the enemy for nearly two months and needed a respite from battle. We would leave the Mignano Gap and at last be free of the albatross's evil eyes.

16 · *THE SILVER STAR*

We were finally relieved from the horrors of Monte Cassino by the 36th, but a road junction posed a deadly problem. Both Divisions had to pass the spot and it was being interdicted by German artillery fire. The offending guns were holding up the whole relief operation and causing heavy casualties. Although static conditions had enabled us to register our guns on every suspected German gun position, the forward artillery observer could not locate this gun position; and firing on a known gun location didn't necessarily silence it.

The Cassino Valley had been socked in for several days with fog and drizzle, and the artillery planes had been grounded. The dogfaces couldn't be relieved without running the gauntlet of hot steel and high explosives at the road junction. Third Division HQ called Captain Devol to determine the feasibility of a fire-direction flight.

"No deal," Devol responded. There was no safe way to risk a Cub to find a fog-shrouded German gun position. A persuasive offer, however, came in from General John "Iron Mike" O'Daniel. "There's a medal in it for somebody," he said, "so try something. We've got to stop those guns."

Devol turned to me. "Schultz, what do you think?" I knew there was a valley about a half hour behind us that should be high enough to be clear of ground fog. The locale was fixed firmly in my mind, and although fog shrouded the valley, I felt that if I could get the mission fired in less than two hours, I would still have about an hour to head south, where *Janey* and I could break free of fog and land safely on the Naples Plain.

I mulled the flight path over and over in my mind. I would take off heading due west, climb to 3,500 feet within six minutes, hoping to clear the fog. Then I would turn 45 degrees to a southwesterly course and climb until I cleared the soup or saw water below me. If I read the map correctly I could fly *Janey* out of danger with an hour's gas to spare.

Sergeant Weber of the Ninth Field Artillery volunteered to go as my observer. I lifted off *Janey* in a fogged-in valley with hills and mountains on both sides. Once we were up, the mist defined the muzzle flashes and we located a couple of 170mm gun positions. Although the 88 seemed to be the Germans' favorite gun, their 170mm howitzer was a formidable weapon. It could be horse-drawn and moved manually into the narrowest of gullies to hide from our return fire.

Under cover of smoke, Weber and I were able to adjust our gunners' fire and they smothered the area with high explosives. I don't know if they blew up the 170s or just blew up the crews, but the guns stopped firing.

"Well done!" crackled over the radio, with an added, "Good luck." The mission had run over 90 minutes and now I started out of the valley, climbing in slow circles to avoid a 3,000-foot peak to the south. As soon as I reached 3,500 feet, which seemed forever, I headed *Janey* straight south by compass. Twenty minutes had been wasted gaining altitude. Now we had barely 30 minutes to break free of the wispy gray curtain that surrounded us. When we finally cleared the threatening peak and ridge line and headed south, the haze thinned. Then I spotted an old friend.

"Look! Vesuvius!" I shouted to Weber. With its plume of smoke curling from the crater, it was a landmark we couldn't mistake. Within minutes the Naples-Rome railroad tracks were visible below us, fading into the southern horizon. We tried the radio, but we were beyond range.

"Hold on!" I yelled. "We're going down to the deck to get out of this ME-109 altitude."

The railroad was straight and the map features indicated I could follow it without fear of mist-hidden obstacles. Pastureland began appearing, so I decided to land near the road. We still had about 15 minutes' fuel and plenty of daylight. Following the dictates of Fort Sill, I firmly believed it was always best to give a field at least two slow low-level passes before cutting the power to land. I made two passes and the field seemed good enough.

"We made it!" Weber shouted, as *Janey* rolled to a stop. "Damn, we made it!" He cheered and patted my back. It had not been a bad flight. And we were safe.

But the field was rough, too rough to take off from unless I had no other choice. The road would be our ticket out when the sky cleared and we were gassed. Sergeants are always the best promoters for any enterprise, so Weber took off down the road while I stayed to guard *Janey*. Three or four hours of daylight were left, and we were less than an hour from Naples. If we could get gas within a couple of hours, we could spend the night in Naples.

Hours went by and no Weber. Finally at about dusk, he pulled in with two MPs in a ¾-ton truck. Daylight was gone and a night in Naples not possible, so we gassed *Janey* and spent the night under her wings. We stretched a canvas cover between the wing and the ground as wind break, and with extra canvas and blankets, our nest was as comfortable as we could make it, considering we were camping out in the early-winter rainy season of sunny Italy.

With the first light of dawn we pushed *Janey* to the road and bade farewell to our benefactors. It was an easy takeoff and the sun was doing a great job of burning off the mist as *Janey* headed due south. Within an hour we were at the main Naples airport, taxiing toward some Cubs scattered on the field. They were part of an Air Force L squadron.

Elation soon turned to frustration. Contacting the Third Division by radio was impossible. We hitched a ride to Fifth Army HQ and were able to send a message to Captain Devol that we were safe in Naples at the 12th Air Force Supply Depot.

Weber and I spent a memorable night in Naples, enjoying Italy's creature comforts and diversions.

Our mission had been successful, and when we returned to our unit we learned that we'd been recommended for Silver Stars. At last I had a medal for valor, although within my heart I knew there had been little valor in the flight. But a medal is a medal, and I desperately wanted one.

Division's orders were to rest and regroup for a couple of weeks to integrate new replacements, so the fighting stopped and endless paperwork began. It was a welcome break from flying; but on the downside it meant someone else would fly *Janey,* possibly one of those hotshot new replacement pilots. I was nervous.

It was hard to conceal my eagerness for the Division Award Parade that followed every major action, but when the parade was called, my name was not among those to receive the Silver Star. Three division pilots received Air Medals and I received a cluster to add to my previously-awarded Air Medal. Devol assured me that since the recommendations for Weber's and my Silver Stars had gone in on the last day of the action, perhaps they hadn't had time to clear. That sounded unlikely, but I still held on to the dream of future parades. My hometown newspaper in Waterloo, Iowa, had already reported that I had received the Silver Star. Obviously, the newspaper had picked up news about recommended medals, not the medals actually awarded.

Days stretched into weeks. Weber was sent to the States for an OCS short course and received a battlefield promotion to Second Lieutenant. Devol was ordered back to the States as an instructor, and I was promoted to Third Division Air Officer.

General Anderson, our Division Artillery commander, took a group of us to Corps Headquarters and briefed us on the Anzio landing, only weeks away. We had plenty of training to do with the new pilots, and I was to work with the Navy on a new LST jeep carrier. The new baby flattop would have capacity for five planes, and they would give the beachhead up to eight hours of air observation.

The days surged by; and then one day, a letter arrived from the Medal Review Panel. It was addressed to Captain Devol, but as Division Air Officer, the paperwork was now my job. So I opened it and read:

> A.W. Schultz, G.M. Weber, Silver Star Denied, Section 2.
> Silver Star for individual valor, not group. If you disagree, resubmit.

If I had made the flight alone, there would have been no question. The Silver Star would have been mine. But there were two of us. What could I do? Weber and I had both received ample rewards, and truly there was no valor in our flight when it was compared to the daily duties of the Division's dogfaces.

17 · *THE BANDITS*

```
Shorty?-----------Click
Glenn!-----------------------------Click-Click
Edkins?-------------Click
Geist!-----------------Click-Click
```

The only way one could hear the conversation and its clicking inflections was through headphones tuned in on the infantry radio. Sergeant Glenn Geist and his assistant radio operator, John Edkins, alias Shorty, were trying out a new design for a Cub radio antenna. Geist and Jones were in one Cub, Shorty and Smith in another.

It was December of 1943. We were warming up and drying out, three valleys and 20 miles behind the battle line at Monte Cassino. After fifty-nine days of wet, cold, bloody fighting, the 36th Infantry had taken over our positions. We could at last enjoy time to sleep, bathe, change uniforms and eat normal food. New arms had been issued, battle damage was repaired and older equipment updated. We could only faintly hear the boom of our front-line artillery, and now with dry feet, life took on a rosy glow.

Wars can be won with good communication; the better our communication, the better we could control and coordinate all the components of the Army. Geist always worked to improve our radio equipment's range, reliability and clarity, and this respite from the toe-to-toe slugging match at Monte Cassino provided a perfect opportunity for him to test his new ideas.

Early in the Sicilian campaign, Major General Lucian Truscott, then commander of the Third Infantry Division, gave Geist a command car with a powerful base radio. The purpose was to organize a radio section within the Division Artillery Air Section to keep Truscott in touch around the clock.

Our idyll was shattered by the short rat-a-tat-tat from the wing guns of Messerschmitts and the POM-POM-POM-POM of our 40mm antiaircraft guns. Looking skyward, we saw our two Cubs diving for the ground as two ME-109s darted behind the low-lying hills.

"BANDITS! BANDITS! BEHIND YOU!" I wanted to scream into a microphone. But I wasn't wearing a radio headset, and my warning would have come too late anyway. We were in a rest area, far behind the battle lines, and the damned Germans had hit and run.

Belatedly, the heavy fire from our .50-caliber flak wagons split the air with their sharp barks, but the Germans had disappeared. The sound of firing reverberated in the distance, but we didn't see the telltale smoke that would indicate a hit on either of the ME-109s or where the two Cubs landed.

I had been in command of the Division Air Section for only a few days and was just beginning to feel the heavy responsibility. The men in those planes were my men and their planes were my planes. If anything happened to them, I'd have to explain why they were in the air. Shouts came from the distance as a truck raced toward me, blinking its lights. I jumped aboard.

"Shorty and Smith cracked up!" Sergeant John Koster reported. "The ambulance and aidmen are there. Geist and Jones plowed into a grove, but they're OK."

There was no fire, a good sign, as we approached the crash site. Edkins was walking around the overturned plane, another good sign. However, the body on the stretcher was still. The gathered faces told the story. Lieutenant Alvin Smith was dead. Six weeks overseas and to be killed on a training flight in a rest area didn't seem fair, but war is never fair.

A message came for me on the telephone switchboard to

report to Major Walter Kerwin at DIVARTY Headquarters.

"Schultz, why were two planes talking in single names and microphone clicks?" He wanted to know as soon as I entered the Command Post tent.

I explained that we were trying out a new, shorter antenna that ran from the leading edge of the wing above the cockpit to the tip of the rudder fin. I was still standing. Kerwin, a West Pointer, played by the rules. Lieutenants didn't sit in his presence unless invited to do so.

"Geist, I'll bet. One of his ideas. Always something new!" The major motioned me to a stool.

After sitting, I continued the explanation. "When the men push the Cubs into cover or off roads, the antennas strung between the wing tips and the tail fin often break, and they break when we camouflage the planes with branches. It's a repair we make constantly. Geist ordered some special wire he believed would work on shorter protected runs. I gave him permission to use the two planes to test the idea."

"It worked, too, sir," I continued. "The Cubs were two valleys apart and still receiving strong signals. They were returning to base when they were jumped."

Kerwin leaned forward on his table. "Don't let this upset you, Schultz," he said. He must have been reading my mind. "This is a bad start, but death is part of war. Be thankful you don't have to write the letter to his family. Smith's duty assignment is the 10th Field Artillery Battalion. His commanding officer will handle it."

While I was there, Kerwin explained some facts. "Always remember, battalion pilots belong to the battalions and are commanded by the battalion's COs. Your authority is to coordinate their flights with DIVARTY's daily plan. The battalion CO can yank his planes as he needs them. Infantry orders come through DIVARTY or battalion unless they come from Truscott himself."

"Anything else, sir?" I said.

"Yes, tell Geist good going, to keep it up and to stop by

sometime," Kerwin said as he stood, ending our conversation.

Geist was visibly shaken as he stood by his radio car; however, he did relish the words of greeting from Kerwin. "If we only had some way to tune into Air Force radar net, perhaps we could have spotted the bastards and Smith would still be alive." The premise for a new project was already taking place in Geist's fertile mind.

Miraculous was the only word we could use to account for Edkins' still being alive. The landing defied description, and the more we discussed the landing and Smith's wounds, the deeper our sense of wonder grew. There was no doubt about it. Shorty had survived because of Smith's flying skill and courage.

Smith had been hit by two slugs from the ME-109's .30-caliber wing guns. The engine was shattered and had seized. It could not have been running on impact. The spars and struts had been damaged yet had held together to bring the passenger back safely. I hated postmortems but this one wouldn't leave us; we wanted to talk it out. Edkins wanted to talk. He tried to shed light on Smith's condition or remember what kind of noise the engine made. He couldn't recall any words from Smith, just rushing ground, a braking spin and the cartwheeling plane.

"When the flying grass and dirt stopped, it was quiet," Edkins said, his eyes glazed. "I was hanging upside down from the seat belt and I couldn't get the damn buckle to release. Sticky blood was all over everything. Smith was hanging loose from his belt and I could smell gas. I yelled and prayed."

Smith's last actions were textbook correct. He had cut the ignition to minimize the chance of fire, and by tromping hard on one brake had caused his plane to ground loop, averting a deadly head-on crash into a stone wall. Undoubtedly, his last thoughts were centered on saving his comrade.

18 · *THE WAILING WALL*

Second Lieutenant Erwin Rosner, my newly-appointed executive officer, had done a commendable job in shepherding the Air Section back from the ten-day rest outside of Rome and relocating the unit on a field south of Pozzuoli, a coastal town on the Tyrrhenian Sea.

Although Rosner had picked us a good campsite, the field wasn't long enough. Inexperienced pilots and our new Stinson L-5 required a larger field. Rosner's field gave us seclusion from military traffic and excellent camouflage, but another 300 feet of runway would make takeoffs and landings a piece of cake. After considering all alternatives, including a move to another field, it was agreed that if we leveled a 50-foot-wide opening through the low stone wall, we would add another 500 to 600 feet to our runway. I set out to make a deal with Captain Ralph Holland of our Division engineers. We needed a bulldozer, and in exchange we'd give the engineers sightseeing flights over Mount Vesuvius. Six rides to six men got us a bulldozer to use from midmorning to midafternoon, but it had to be back in motorpool, cleaned up for 5 o'clock inspection.

On the appointed morning, the lowboy and bulldozer pulled onto our field, with the dozer ready to go. Holland and I immediately had *Janey* airborne to survey the airport construction. We circled slowly at about 500 feet, watching the bulldozer advance toward the offending wall. Suddenly a host of black-clad Italian women and men ran from all directions toward the wall.

From our vantage point in the air, it seemed they just wanted to watch the show.

"Schultz, we need you," Geist's voice stated over the radio.

"Wilco," I said, trying to put a note of exasperation into the word. "Holland, we're going down. Trouble," I shouted above the engine noise. Though I was irritated, I knew Rosner wouldn't cry wolf. I buzzed the field and the Italians cleared out of the way and I brought *Janey* in.

Stein, the jeep driver I had inherited from Devol, was holding court with the milling crowd and gesturing wildly in his loose-fitting field jacket. The women were shrieking and wailing. They didn't want us to touch the wall. The men grumbled and spat and paced in circles. Stein, only five-four and dwarfed by the throng, spoke in Yiddish, which some of the Italians seemed to understand. The spitting stopped, but the women continued to wail and cross themselves.

Had our bulldozer desecrated the grave of a beloved saint or an ancestor? Did the wall have sentimental or historic value? Did it cover the entrance to a sacred grotto? "What have we done?" I asked Stein.

"Well, it seems they hid last years' tomato paste from the Germans beside this wall." Stein explained.

Holland and I talked it over, and Stein translated the good news. "You can dig up the paste. We'll wait," he announced to the crowd, adding, "*To-te, to-te,*" which in American-Italian seemed to mean Fast! Fast! The women started removing the multitude of irregular-looking vessels that held their precious tomato paste. They moved with both haste and care as the odd-shaped jars were lovingly packed with straw and nestled into waiting donkey carts.

I approached Stein to offer my thanks for controlling the situation. He was talking to several Italian women and the man I assumed to be the *patron*. "Schultzie," Stein said, turning to me. "They like us. If we give them flour, shortening, sugar and coffee, they'll cook us a feast of tomato pie tonight. How about it?"

George Hasse, our head cook, had been watching this

three-ring circus, so I called him over. "Stein has a deal for us. You work it out," I said. "It might be a real break from our regular ration." With great pomp, even before Hasse and his assistant Gus Browsey caught their breath, Stein was again giving a speech in his Yiddish-Italian mix. The smiles on the Italian faces left no doubt he had told them yes.

Stein was in charge of the guest list. He invited the engineers, who made short work of the wall and finished the leveling with time to spare for the midafternoon return of the bulldozer. The party began at dusk. A deep-dish tomato pie with a thick crust was the main course. Wafers of vegetables and chunks of Spam were mixed into the sauce. We drank the local wine, which we referred to as Dago Red. It tasted a lot better than the powdered lemonade that came with our canned rations.

The *patron* had a special wine that he shared with Holland, Erickson (Holland's CO) and me. From a decorative bottle, which he handled with great care, he poured small glasses of a thick, honey-yellow liquid. We toasted our new airstrip, replacement pilot training center, and home for our expected new, more powerful L-5 with its Air Force radio. Regretfully, the L-5 didn't become a reality until we were beached on Anzio.

Left: **Executive officer Edwin "Irv" or "Roz" Rosner.** *Right:* **T-4s Glenn Geist and Vincent Romeo tend the base radio and aircraft alert system. This was an ideal radio car location, hidden from air observation by the tree, on open ground to increase radio range, and with a ditch nearby to flop in should the German 88's send us some incoming.** *—Edwin Rosner*

19 · *PAPER DOLL*

With the snappy stride and smart salute of a recent Officers Candidate School grad, Second Lieutenant Hubert A. Boone reported to the Piper Aircraft packing crate that served as Third Division Air Section Headquarters on the Naples airfield.

We were sitting on ration boxes around the sheet-metal tent stove, scorching bread and smearing it with real butter—the Army was fattening us up for the cold and fighting ahead. We were two pilots short and the invasion date was rushing upon us.

A week before, I had been allowed to move my Air Section to the Naples airport to take delivery of the replacement planes and facilitate the major maintenance work. Air Force Liaison Supply had saved the 6-foot-wide, 7-foot-high, 24-foot-long heavy wood cases used for sea transport of our Piper L-4Bs. The cases made ideal living quarters, a palace compared to our drafty, damp pyramid tents.

Boone could hardly wait to get into action. "Where do I bunk?" he wanted to know. "How soon can I get a pass to Naples?" He didn't waste time.

"We've got a bunk for you in this crate," I answered. "I'm First Lieutenant Schultz, but everybody calls me Schultzie."

"Call me Boone." he said. "I've had to fight my whole life over Hubert, and I don't like Daniel, so just make it Boone." And with that request he joined the circle of men who were sitting around the stove, feasting on scorched toast. We showed him how we scorched slices of bread on the cherry-red stove top, smeared it with the first real butter we'd had in months, and topped it off with some British marmalade for a tangy orange flavor. It was a real feast, thanks to our trades with the British. Our supply, however, was getting low. Lieutenant Bill Richards asked for the chance to restock the marmalade.

I suggested we try for some Scotch and corned beef as long as we were at it, then added, "We've got plenty of C-rations to trade. With the radio out and you two lightweights aboard, you could carry five or six cases. It would make a good orientation mission. Boone, you're hereby assigned to be Mess Supply Officer." With the satisfaction that I had made a shrewd tactical decision, I went back to scorching another hunk of bread sliced with a trench knife.

As Boone headed for the empty bunk to stow his gear, the perfectly-whistled notes of "Paper Doll," a popular song State-side, filtered through the GI blanket hanging as a privacy curtain in our packing-crate cabin.

Despite the nearby pleasures and temptations of Naples, not a single soldier in our Air Section spent more than a night in the Port of Naples MP Stockade. We could always bribe or trade. We had surefire trading stock that would tempt even the true martinets among our MPs—a flight over the smoking crater of Mount Vesuvius.

A flight over Vesuvius was in reality a flight around Vesuvius, for *Janey* and the other Cubs couldn't fly that high nor withstand the violent thermal currents generated by the smoking core of the mountain. A few bounces as we approached the smoking volcano gave credibility to the apprehensions we always expressed to our passengers. Then by flying around the beautiful Bay of Naples and circling their unit, we disembarked satisfied passengers.

20 · *THE COTTON BALLS*

Explosions of fire danced on the beach as dawn approached. As the big Navy guns shelled Anzio, the LST swung into the wind for *Janey*'s short takeoff run. By the end of the deck she had climbed more than 5 feet and was well clear and gaining altitude. Again I regretted refusing to fly off the deck of an LST for the Sicily invasion.

The second and third planes were to take off at ninety-minute intervals. The radio waves were crowded, so communication had to be held to a minimum. Barrage balloons were being set up on the landing beach. From a distance their cables looked like silk strands, but at close range they looked as thick as tree trunks.

A fine-weather day was dawning. The beach was illuminated with shells bursting but clouded with dust from the flying debris. Farther inland, an early-morning mist covered the marshes with a blanket of white. We were counting on the wind to dispel the mist, and right on time, land features began to emerge. Sleepy German veterans from the Russian front were our adversaries, and we had surprised them before they were alert. All was going well for our side. My prearranged radio contact acknowledged *Janey*'s presence with a curt, "Stand by."

I flew the length of the beachhead, inland from our barrage balloons, and then expanded my path toward the mountains, now rising clear and bright to the east. Except for small bomb craters, the airfield at Anzio was undamaged, and I saw that we could easily operate our Cubs from there. Then I spotted tanks moving toward the beachhead, their muzzles pointed seaward. Germans?

I glanced at the map strapped to my leg. I might need to call in coordinates to give the Navy guns a target point. But the tanks bore white stars; they were our tanks, and must have raced 3 or 4 miles inland before being called back because they were past their objectives, marked by red lines on our invasion maps. In the smoke, dust, and panic of combat, the white stars weren't always visible and could draw fire from Navy guns as well as the Army artillery that had made it ashore. With their muzzles pointing in our direction, the tanks could easily be regarded as enemy tanks. Once a shell has left the muzzle, there's no calling it back. Casualties from such friendly fire seem less tolerable than other war casualties.

Below *Janey*, other vehicles and troops were rapidly approaching their objectives, and in many cases, had overshot them. To fire the Navy guns now would not be safe. Only a few 105s were in place. I watched the beachhead develop. Shortly my radio control ordered, "Check bridge Mussolini Canal—coast highway."

I'd been in the air an hour and fifteen minutes, so *Janey* had plenty of gas to complete the mission in a safe, thorough manner. I flew toward the bridge, following the road, an unbroken ribbon of pavement on each side of the canal. By flying inland from the sea, I reached a point where I could clearly see that the bridge span was intact and that the abutments looked abandoned. I took *Janey* down for a low pass to check for telltale scars in the roadbed, a dead giveaway that the dreaded Teller antitank mines had been planted there.

"Roadbed intact, span intact, checking for mines, over-out," I radioed. I turned *Janey* to fly with the sun behind me to avoid a reflection from the mist-moistened roadbed. I'd be flying low over territory still held by Germans, where trees and scrub obscured the ground, but resistance had been light so far.

I came in about 50 feet above the road, and as I

approached the bridge, I could see the low circles of sandbags on each corner of the bridge. Men were inside each circle. The low morning sun had protected me until I crossed the bridge, but now what looked like cotton balls streaked past me. The Germans had opened fire, and tracers from their machine guns were trying to home in on *Janey*. Just feet above the ground, I kicked her into a steep diving slip. Thank God for the ditch on the seaward side of the road and all the hours they'd made us practice doing slips. I didn't hear any noise from the Krauts' machine guns as I kicked the rudder to fishtail away from danger and run for the beach.

But there was no sanctuary on the beach, and ahead stood a forest of barrage balloon cables. I banked *Janey* again and climbed over the road, heading landward, away from the balloons and the machine guns on the bridge. The cotton balls had stopped chasing me, but I was dripping with sweat. Control slowly came back to me. I was alive, and had accomplished the mission.

"Mines on both approaches. Machine guns both ends. Want Navy fire?" I radioed, feeling a lot like Joe Penner, the shy salesman of 1940 radio fame who would knock on a door and mutter, "Nobody's home, I hope, I hope."

"No," Ground Control answered. "Tanks are moving. Over-out!"

It wasn't long before the soft, dry stubble on the edge of the commercial field absorbed *Janey*'s wheels for a safe landing. Flight Number One on Anzio had been completed with *Janey* and pilot untouched. Our tanks and engineers would clear the bridge. Our battle-hardened Blue and White Devils would clear the beach, and we would cut the coastal highway. The Germans would be trapped at Cassino, and we could roll into Rome for a holiday.

I was glad to be on the ground at Anzio, but I needed to move *Janey* from this field. Its paved runways and taxiways made perfect immediate storage areas for all kinds of war materiel so that I was getting boxed in as supplies deluged the shore line. We would soon be unable to move out and take off. Only an order from Air Force brass could evict the Supply and Motor Pool troops from this field and restore its function as an airbase, but until the landing was completed, the Beach Officer and his Beach Party of MPs were in charge.

With the funnel and chamois, plenty of 5-gallon gas cans, and several helpful soldiers, I managed to get *Janey* gassed and ready for her next flight. Enough space remained clear for Rosner, the second plane off the LST, to land. Within an hour a ground crew arrived to keep the landing lane clear.

Smoke and confusion plus the spasmodic sound of small-arms fire reminded me that although we were safely ashore, we weren't secure. As I walked across the road to the MP post to inquire about the location of DIVARTY HQ, black puffs of ack-ack smoke and screaming sirens filled the sky overhead. Two Stuka dive bombers were welcoming us to Anzio, and our 441st antiaircraft crews were giving them a reply. Puffs of sand erupted along the beach as the Stukas' wing guns sought their prey. The bombs whistled down and the wing-mounted sirens continued to scream like demons even after the Stukas had pulled out of their dive. I jumped into a ditch for cover, fearing that the whistling bomb had my name on it.

One bomb fell wide of the cluster of landing craft and splashed harmlessly into the sea. The other landed a hundred yards away from me, and about fifty yards from *Janey*. Even though I was across the road and huddled behind the bank of a ditch, the earth trembled and heaved and I felt like I had been squeezed hard by a very big bear. It must have been the Germans' equivalent of our 500-pound bomb.

Dust, smoke and debris flew over us and as the cloud settled, I knew I had to get *Janey* off the beach as soon as possible. The high howl of the Stukas' wing sirens and the whistling of the bombs kept us hugging the ground for some time. The bomb had put a couple of rips in *Janey*'s fuselage fabric and had thrown up a thick coating of sand, but she was flyable. The bomb had hit in a grassy area and the force of the blast had gone skyward in a geyser of sand.

Lieutenant Rosner landed and reported the same conditions I had. "Can't shoot Navy guns," he said. "The lines are too vague, lots of troops way out in front. The enemy can be handled with mortars. Did you see the big oval field just east of us?"

I had. "I'll go try to land. We've got to get out of here," I said as I settled into the front seat of my wounded airplane. As *Janey* cleared the ground, I could see Chuck Croal with our ¾-ton truck and Geist in his radio command car coming into the area. I waggled *Janey*'s wings to acknowledge their presence, and turned away from the growing forest of balloons to find safety on an inland field.

What had been the Pontine Marshes of Roman times was now Mussolini's greatest public-works project, and the results of the reclamation effort shone clearly below as *Janey* rose to cruising altitude. At first it looked like a cobweb of ditch lines without a center, but it soon became apparent that the deep straight main ditches led to the big Mussolini Canal. The canal then formed a huge collecting arm that emptied into the sea just past the bridge where an hour before I had dodged the deadly cotton balls.

The large oval field I had seen two miles inland in the morning began to look like our best bet. We could land three or four times within its length and once very comfortably in its width. The north side of the field had several short steep-walled V-shaped valleys emptying into the large oval. The west and south limits were defined by ditches that carried a small stream running eastward into the main canal. The eastern landing obstacle must have been engineered, for it extended a thousand yards in a true north-south direction and lay like a baguette of French bread walling off the area.

I made several passes over the field and with each pass felt more comfortable. It might be a little far forward, but it provided easy telephone wire access to a good road network. I landed *Janey* into the wind between shallow waterways that divided the pasture into 40- or 50-foot strips running north and south. The soft stubble cushioned *Janey*'s landing and I'd used less than half the oval's width to set her down. I taxied to the far end, took off downwind and cleared the ditch by 8 or 10 feet. It was a perfect field.

I tried another strip defined by the shallow waterways and again the landing was soft and short. I stopped *Janey* and left her engine at idle while I started to explore the waterways.

In heavy spring rains, the waterways might run full because the field and the plateau above had a strong tilt to the south, but for now the waterways posed no problem. The grass in the bottoms had a hint of green, but the bottoms were solid, and they were shallow enough to taxi a plane through them. Takeoffs and landings might be risky, however. The valleys along the north bank were manmade and must have served as pens for sheep, goats, or donkeys. They would eventually be used for aircraft revetments, I thought, but we could immediately use them to shelter troops. I laid down landing panels on the strip west of the baguette and flew *Janey* back to the beachhead.

One plane had been unloaded from a truck and was being assembled; it would soon be ready to fly. I reported the location of the new field and ordered the other planes trucked forward. The order was received with enthusiasm because large-diameter shells were exploding in the sand.

Ed Hill came down from the 39th Battalion with orders to get his guns registered, so *Janey* and I took him up. Rosner would land on the new field and fly the first mission from there. Geist and his radio crew would wait for Sergeant Reis to land and direct him to the new strip. Then we would all move forward.

The bright mid-winter sun bathed the brown countryside in clear light, emphasizing its drabness. From a distance, the beige walls of the multistoried homes with terra cotta tiled roofs looked sharp and crisp, but as we flew closer to them, the ugly stains on the stucco and the trash-littered yards betrayed the broken promise of the grand government project. That landscape had been planned by Mussolini's Fascists as part of a visionary development.

"Give us a target," barked the radio, bringing Ed and me back to the real world. Ed picked a crossroads due east of a cluster of farm buildings at 8,000-yards' range and reported, "Suspected enemy tanks, E 4500, R 300, one round smoke."

"On the way," rang through the earphones. We were now in business on Anzio.

Now came the routine of overs and shorts, rights and lefts. Fictitious targets were reported to keep up the spirits of the gun crews and to confuse the Krauts. I've often wondered if the Germans became overconfident by the number of tanks my observers and I reported they had, but just to keep them humble, we would often report that those same tanks were withdrawing.

We needed to get Ed's guns properly registered on at least three distinct points, so we picked out several crossroads. The airwaves came alive as more artillery battalions dropped their gun trails and asked for registrations. The next to fire missions would be Rosner, who gave me a wing waggle as he took over.

The beachhead looked like a dust storm with barrage balloons partially hidden by the smoke. Ack-Ack bursts added to the confusion. I was glad to get *Janey* down and open a C-ration on the front line, where it was safe. Two more trucks arrived with their planes. Geist hid the radio car in a ravine and got a telephone line on order. All had gone well. We had enough planes to keep a patrol in the air plus one on the ready. I looked at my watch and discovered I'd now been awake for nearly twenty hours, so I crawled into *Janey*'s back seat and closed my eyes. The distant sounds of combat that surrounded us was my lullaby.

Landing the long way, east-west, was risky because the waterways were not of uniform construction. Some were 10 feet wide and had a depth of 6 to 8 inches and others were 6 feet wide and 10 inches deep. The tempo of the invasion indicated we would use the field for only one night, so why worry about the deluxe runway when we still had plenty of good north-south strips? The capricious winds caused by the gullies to the north would only affect the planes as they taxied, thereby causing no major problem.

The sun shone as a red ball through the haze of battle. One more mission before sunset would close the day, and the mission might as well be mine and *Janey*'s. Captain George Snow of the Ninth's B Battery wanted to check his camouflage and do some registration, so up we went. Three battalions of DIVARTY were in place and all had at least three registration points. Now was the time to shorten the range and register in order to be prepared for close-in support with the 105s.

As always, the last rays of the sun cast a beautiful aura over the land. The fields took on a golden glow, the houses looked brilliant white, and plumes of brown dust erupted along a wavy line that separated the armies. The 60mm and 81mm mortars were busy holding the outpost lines apart, and our 105s and 155s would tilt the balance when we were ready, come morning.

Our landing had been a success. The Germans had stiffened their resistance but hadn't launched any counterattacks. Tomorrow we would cut Highway #6 and Highway #7 and trap them at Cassino.

21 · *THE FLIGHT OVER ROME*

During the night two more trucks loaded with Piper Cubs arrived and we were beginning to look like a full air section. The firing had not let up; in fact the tempo had increased. *Janey* and I had made four flights yesterday, and with this morning's dawn mission I felt familiar with the American sector of the Anzio beachhead.

The veteran British First Division held the ground on our north flank, and we were pleased to have them as comrades in arms. Fighting alongside them, we drew inspiration and confidence from their brisk, efficient manner and their matter-of-fact attitude.

Major Kerwin, the DIVARTY operations officer, radioed for me to report to the CP located on a dairy farm ahead of our airstrip and several hundred yards ahead of our 155 guns, not an ideal location for a command post. As our infantry and tanks moved along the main road past the dairy farm, it felt good to walk in the bright winter sun with an Army that had the spring of victory in its step.

"Schultz, every morning, just as soon as your first flight is down, come to the CP," Kerwin ordered. "There's daily planning to do. We must always have at least a couple of batteries in each battalion tied to my main control grid," he said, as we stood beside his special stand-up desk. "What did you register on yesterday?"

"Only crossroads and a couple of clumps of trees. At the

range we were shooting, I couldn't see a target. As a matter of fact, I haven't had an enemy target yet."

"We'll hold this line for a few days. I'll give you some terrain features I want to use as registration points. Don't plot them on your map, just do them as I send them and have the observers be sure to get a good spread at each location."

After a lunch of doctored-up C-rations (it's amazing what a few onions can do), I trekked against the traffic flow back to the airstrip. Rosner and Boone were waiting, along with a reporter from the *New York Herald Tribune* requesting a flight to check the front.

"Whose flight is it?" I asked Rosner.

Boone spoke up. "Mine."

"I want to fly over Rome," the reporter requested.

"OK," Boone smiled, giving me a knowing look. "Schultz, you better have another plane take over patrol. We may not be able to cover the whole Division area and Rome."

I ordered Reis to take off a half hour after Boone and fly a regular patrol, without thinking of the precedent I was setting. Rosner now assumed we would skip patrol missions to fly the Press, a policy that led to disaster within a week.

Boone took his passenger over our lines and told him that the distant Castel Gandolfo on the western slope of Colli Laziali was the western gate of Rome. A couple of well-timed German antiaircraft bursts in the distance convinced the reporter that he'd seen enough of The Eternal City. "He shook my shoulder and said he'd gotten his story," Boone reported later. "So back we came. I'd seen enough Kraut AA smoke for one day too."

The race for Press coverage was on. For the next few days we ran a flying circus. The story must have grown during the night because when I returned from DIVARTY HQ the next morning, we had already flown three reporters and two more were waiting. They all wanted a flight over Rome like the one Boone had given the *Tribune* man. So we accommodated them, even though we never came close to

Rome or made the slightest effort to go past our lines. The Press wanted headlines, the reporters wanted bylines, and we wanted our names in our hometown newspapers. Sometimes they took our pictures, but they always took our names and the addresses of our local papers. We were all written up as heroes because of Boone's first "Impress the Press" flight.

The dull pop of mortar fire increased daily and the geysers of dust the mortar shells created became more visible from the air. The Infantry wanted to use its own forward observers to fire the 105s on enemy mortars. We pilots were left with the boredom of registrations, but the fear of flak from the 88s and attack from ME-109s and FW-190s kept us from becoming overly complacent.

Fighting dragged on. Interrogated prisoners revealed we were fighting our old enemies from Sicily, the Hermann Goering Panzer Division, an armored division of first-class troops, many of them fanatics who had cut their teeth in the Hitler Youth. Dark crescent-shaped scars in the fields indicated tanks had just made sharp turns on grass-covered areas behind the German lines, but we could not spot the tanks. We were certain they lurked behind farm houses, were hunkered down in gullies or hidden beneath haystacks, but because the Italians were now our allies, we didn't want to blow up every house or burn every haystack looking for a tank. Yet that's exactly what we did. It amazed us how many times a haystack started to wheel out across a field and how many black smoke fires we started. Black smoke fires were good news. They meant oil and rubber were burning, thus a vehicle of some sort was on fire. Once we saw black smoke, we'd use high explosive or white phosphorus shells to fan the flames. The Germans would then triangulate to locate the firing battery and send over a barrage of counter battery fire, giving us a chance to spot their guns from the air and direct another battery to fire on them. If our planes stayed near the suspected enemy gun position too long, the 88s might give us an air burst and then we'd have to dive for the deck, where we would be within range of their 20mm flak wagons. Then our infantry mortars would pop a few mortar shells on the flak wagons or the ground observer might call in the 105s. In any event, the noise and dust level would increase. From the air we could see that this went on with a minimum of casualties if every one had a fox hole or slit trench for protection.

As the tempo of daily fire fights increased and the sky held more black mini-clouds from German AA, the requests from reporters dwindled, especially after a bullet whizzed through the plywood floorboard of one plane and stung a reporter in the foot. But one incident especially diminished the enthusiasm of reporters who wanted to fly with us.

The newly-arrived but well-seasoned 45th Infantry Division had shared our airfield for a couple days. As they were leaving us, one of their L-4Bs, to the horror of all who looked up at the resounding bang, exploded in midair. Burning fabric and fiery chunks of metal and wood rained down. The plane had not been hit by antiaircraft; it had flown too close to the path of our own shells and either been hit by the projectile itself or had triggered one of our new proximity fuses. From that day on we had few requests to tour the front.

The proximity fuse had been touted as a great new advance. It would give the infantry the advantage of instant air bursts and thereby eliminate the time-consuming adjustments of three to five rounds of ranging fire, which alerted the enemy and gave him time to find better cover. But the proximity fuse would multiply the danger zones for our planes hundreds of times. Flying smart became an absolute necessity. The gun population on Anzio had been steadily increasing. In addition to the Third's guns, the 45th Division's artillery pieces and its support battalions were dug into the beachhead, and the 155 Long Toms of Corps Artillery were firing as well.

Flying smart meant debriefing each pilot as soon as he landed instead of allowing him to go to the latrine and enjoy a quiet cup of coffee. Flying smart also meant getting off our cots every time a mission ended and listening intently to the pilot who had flown the last mission. It was a chore to get a proper debriefing and to record on the situation map the new gun locations on our side, the locations of suspected enemy action, and the location from which we had drawn fire. New pilots griped that debriefing was useless because conditions could change in minutes; but the older pilots continued to fly smart.

Seven days later we were still on the same oval field. We'd accomplished lots of registration, but we often received the long German shells meant for the Ninth's Big Bangers.

Left: **Keith Rozen, the short and spunky Ranger officer, standing beside an unidentified Ranger trooper of the more typical height. Keith made up in attitude what he lacked in size.** —*Harry Rozen*

22 • *THE RANGER*

"Sam's boy reporting!" followed by a broad smile and a snappy open-handed British-style salute were Keith Rozen's first words to me. As he stood framed in the opening of my sandbagged dugout doorway, I had an instinctive feeling that he'd have an influence among us, but I was not sure if it would be good or bad. "I'm down here to help out. Where do I bunk?" he continued impatiently—he was friendly, but cocky.

"See the squad tent in the gully? Ask for Rosner," I instructed him. "Which battalion are you from?" I asked, trying to get my bearings on this second lieutenant, who was about my height, fifteen pounds lighter, and wore paratrooper boots.

"Rangers, man, Rangers," he answered with obvious pride. Most Rangers were at least 5-foot-10 or more, so he must have shown some special talent to get into that elite outfit. I picked up the field phone that connected the tents around the airstrip, gave three short rings, and when Rosner picked it up I said, "We have a Ranger guest. I didn't know he was coming, but we can use every spare hand. Make him welcome." Turning to Keith I asked, "What's your assignment?"

"I was told to report to you and be useful. We've been working with the 41st Battalion, but I understand down here I get to fire the Big Bangers and anything else that's not busy. Put me to work come morning, but for now I need some rest. I'll go check with Rosner."

The squad tent was a regulation 20-foot-square tent with 3-foot-high side walls and a 12-foot peak in the center. The floor had been dug down about two feet. Around the interior perimeter stood a wall of sand bags four or five high, to protect us from stray shrapnel. The regular evening briefing was held an hour after dusk in the basement of the dairy farm. Perhaps then we would discover why a Ranger officer had been assigned to us as an observer.

The dairy farm was a stone-walled cluster of farm buildings. The beige walls rose perhaps 20 feet above the surrounding fields and were topped with mottled red-orange tile roofs. It was a highly visible location for our DIVARTY headquarters and had been selected when the capture of Cisterna seemed certain within the hour, but the stiff German resistance changed all that. Now the dairy farm was close enough to the enemy that it could be used as an infantry strong point. DIVARTY, as a matter of principle, never liked to withdraw to the rear. We pilots wished they would. We hated to have our Cubs within mortar range of the enemy.

The afternoon flights went off on schedule, and it was time for a break. The chill moist wind carried the smoke from the cookfire into the officers' tent and the smell of brewing coffee was enough to tempt me from my dugout. I'd just made up my mind to chance it when the Germans started a slow ranging barrage against the guns ahead of us. As they raised their gun elevation, the shells cleared the hill masking our position and fell 100 to 200 hundred yards behind us. The hot, jagged shards of spent shrapnel kicked up dust geysers around us and clanged against the metal sides of our radio car and trailer.

Geist and I were both crouched against the back wall of our cave, hoping the Germans would start firing short rather than long. Then Geist got a call on the radio. The message said, "Try phone," and he did. The phone to Battalion didn't respond to repeated, single short rings, the Ninth Field Artillery Battalion code. We tried Rosner with three rings, and he responded, so evidently the break was out of our area.

By radio, we reported the dead phone. The wire crew would be sent to find the break, but they would not be happy. Fixing wire is a risky occupation because of the exposure to enemy shells and snipers, and it's a dirty job, too. The lines often run though ditches contaminated with sewage.

Later the wire crew barged into my dugout, red with rage and ready to kill. "Some stupid bastard cutting wood by your supply tent drove an ax into the ground and cut the wire," the sergeant reported, as he checked my phone.

I immediately called Rosner. "Ros, who cut wood this afternoon?"

"Rozen," Rosner answered.

Of course Keith Rozen would be cutting wood! The newest man always got the chicken details. Rozen's wire-cutting incident was to be only the first of the campfire stories that Sam's Boy generated.

January 28, 1944, had no sunset. A gray overcast ceiling hung low as darkness seeped from the ground. It was time to leave for the evening briefing. I stopped by the officer's tent for a quick gulp of coffee to fortify me for the lonely walk to the dairy farm. Keith Rozen was there, telling a story.

Five hundred yards of straight road led east from the Mussolini Canal bridge to the southwest corner of the dairy farm. The Ninth's 155s were dug into the western slope of the canal's west bank, and our airstrip's command post and crew shelters were burrowed into several small erosion gullies about 300 yards behind the guns. I had to walk through the area every evening just after sunset to attend the evening briefing, and two or three hours later I would retrace my route in full darkness.

As I approached the farm I was always challenged from somewhere in the dark, "Halt! Who goes there?" The password would be exchanged and then I could scurry on to enjoy safety and comradeship within the thick masonry walls and cavernous basement that served as our DIVARTY CP.

On this evening, General O'Daniel, Third Division's

executive officer, was in control of the meeting. Coffee, tea, and canned apple cobbler had been set out. The apple cobbler was a rare treat, and the presence of several infantry officers made it obvious that tonight's meeting had a special agenda. General O'Daniel lifted the canvas cover from the map board and began, "Tomorrow we take Cisterna and get out of the swamp."

Now I knew why a Ranger observer had been sent. I looked around the room and, sure enough, there sat two majors in paratrooper boots and the shoulder harnesses that only Rangers wore. Troop movement was to start at 1 a.m. the next day, January 29. I would need to have a plane and an observer above the advance route well before first light at 5 and a second plane ready for takeoff at dawn.

Major Davis of the Third Ranger Battalion sought me out as the meeting ended and said, "We sent you our best. If you can hold Keith down, you'll have a ball. He's good, but short. You two will get along." I understood. Serving with the pre-war Gentle Giants of the Regular Army's Third Division had made me wish for an additional six inches of height many times. Keith, with the Rugged Giants in the Rangers, must have shared the same longing.

After the briefing we filtered into the darkness and started walking our separate ways back to our units. The Germans were sending single greetings all over our area, without a time schedule or target pattern, just to make sleep fitful. We of course were doing the same thing to them, only we had more shells and were firing doubles and quadruples. The muzzle blasts and impact explosions gave the battle area a dull glow of light. As I started walking the straight stretch of road, the light seemed to increase and I began to fantasize that an 88 was trained on the road intersection by the farm. The gun crew, seeing a figure on the road, might decide to send a shell whistling toward me, and a large stray shrapnel fragment would rip my chest open and I'd lie on the road as the tanks in full blackout moved forward. Come dawn, all that would remain would be a helmet beside the road and brown-stained rags in the roadway.

I started to walk faster with each explosion, and soon the tempo of my walk increased to a fast trot. Then I broke into a dead run until I fell exhausted into the ditch just short of the canal. With sweat and tears streaming down, I trembled in the ditch and tried to lie flatter, cursing my buttons because they were in the way.

I don't know how long it took me to regain composure, but at last the trembling stopped and the shells seemed far away. I crawled back to the roadway, gingerly rose to my feet and started to walk toward the bridge.

"Halt! Who goes there?" a voice barked in the darkness.

"Hash," I answered, hoping the password for January 28 hadn't changed. A soldier's silhouette appeared in the gloom. "Schultzie, Captain Shaunessey has been back half an hour. What kept you?" I didn't answer.

I carefully opened the flap of the officers' tent to maintain the blackout and found the precaution unnecessary. Only a small candle gave off a faint glow. I shook Rozen and said, "Four hours to your first mission. It's 11 now, we'll call at 3. Tie optional."

"You bastard, sir," Keith muttered.

"Twenty-four hour delay. What does that mean?" Geist asked as I entered the dugout. "Just came in from DIVARTY."

"Ring them to confirm," I said.

"They confirmed. What's it all about?" Geist asked as he set the phone down. I knew that as much as I wanted to sack out right then and there I'd better give him the whole picture now, rather than in the morning. Geist could delay the wake-up call to Rozen until 5 a.m.

If war can have a ho-hum day, then January 29 fit the bill. By the time Keith and *Janey* and I had landed from the dawn flight, everyone knew the impending attack was to be the next day.

23 · *THE RANGERS'*
SACRIFICE

The twenty-four-hour delay was good news. The attack on Cisterna, Italy, would begin January 30, at 1 a.m. We were given no explanation for the delay, but we continued to fly regular front-line patrol missions. Once the attack began, we'd be flying the risky scouting flights needed by our combat teams.

Janey now sported a new coat of paint and patches to cover the multitude of shrapnel and bullet holes picked up since our invasion on January 22. The twenty-four-hour delay in risking her skin met with my approval.

Cisterna is an ancient city of white stone-walled buildings with orange tile roofs, 30 miles south of Rome, seven miles inland from the Tyrrhenian Sea. Nestled in the foothills of Mount Arestino, it sat astride Coastal Highway #7, which was the German Army's western supply route to the battle at Monte Cassino. Capturing Cisterna and controlling Highway #7 was our mission.

The Third Division had halted two miles southwest of Cisterna following our successful landing at the seaport of Anzio on January 22 and 23. Positions along the east branch of the Mussolini Canal were occupied by the First and Third Ranger Battalions. The Third Division immediately established solid, in-depth defense lines and supply depots to support the major encircling attack on Cisterna. Now the day was at hand. The Big Bangers had been sending death and destruction into German positions at an increasing tempo since midnight. The infantry moved forward at 1 a.m.

Before the first sliver of light broke the eastern horizon, Ed Hill, observer for our 155 howitzer battalion, and I were airborne. *Janey* climbed to 800 feet, the optimum observation altitude, as we flew through the smooth air toward the Cisterna battleground. Muzzle flashes visible to the east of our map's red line indicated German gun positions. Hill radioed, "Flashes, E-15—10-3, request smoke."

"Cease fire!" a strange voice on the radio barked. "We have contact." Our coordinates must have been wrong! Had we called for fire on our own troops? That should have been an enemy position. Ed and I exchanged bewildered looks. Had our troops advanced that far that fast? Had the Germans abandoned Cisterna?

I took *Janey* to 1,000 feet to be safely above small-arms range and flew directly over Cisterna. The white puffballs of enemy tracers immediately arched toward us, and we had gone far enough. Cisterna was still enemy territory.

Brief bursts of light flickered on the horizon several miles east of Cisterna, beyond the range of our guns. Shells were bursting just south and west in positions marked as German. Might they be shelling their own troops? Mortar flashes erupted from the impact area that the Germans were targeting, and mortar shells were exploding further west along the canal. The firing pattern indicated our Rangers were trapped. Their rapid advance must have led them into a German trap. Stone houses on the outskirts of Cisterna were serving as pill boxes, blocking any advance. Enemy 170mm guns in the foothills churned the earth and sprayed blankets of hot metal fragments to block withdrawal or reinforcement. Our Seventh Infantry Regiment was fighting valiantly from the western edge of Cisterna to forge a connection with the Rangers. Resistance had intensified and soon it became fierce pocket-to-pocket, hand-to-hand combat. As Hill and I circled higher into the brightening dawn, spectators to the horrible carnage below us, we felt frustrated. The troops were so intermixed that we could do nothing. Any assistance with heavy artillery might kill more of our own troops than theirs.

The commander of the First Ranger Battalion was dead. A Regular Army sergeant major had taken command and was maintaining radio contact with the Artillery. Shortly before noon, his radio fell silent. *Janey* had just gained observation altitude for our second mission when the Ranger's radio contact broke off in mid-sentence. Although they were trapped, the Rangers were putting up one hell of a fight.

The muzzle flashes of mortars, followed by the daisy-face pattern of ground bursts, became fewer and fewer. Soon, scattered white rags and erect figures started to appear. Tears fogged our eyes. Hill's voice became barely audible as he reported the sight below. In the face of overwhelming manpower and firepower, our Rangers were surrendering. The link-up could not be made, and our objective would not be taken.

A stillness fell over the shell-scarred ground below. Firing stopped as the green-uniformed Rangers and the few gray German figures formed clusters and started moving north and east toward Cisterna. To the west, the battle raged. Heavy artillery, both German and American, continued to raise clouds of debris and dust and send deadly shrapnel scything across the ground ahead of our slowly-advancing dogfaces.

The Third Division fought on for two more days. The big German 170mm guns sent a protective ring of flying steel splinters around Cisterna, while our barrages into Cisterna did nothing to dislodge the elite Herman Goering Division from the centuries-old caverns that spread below the city. Air Force strikes were spectacular—towering clouds of dust were followed by leveled blocks of buildings. But the Germans only burrowed deeper and emerged ready to fight as soon as the planes disappeared. The Third advanced to the northern outskirts of Cisterna, but was too spent to maintain the position. We sustained 3,000 casualties in the twelve days after the January 22 landing. On February 3 and 4, we broke contact and settled for a stalemate. We hadn't cut Highway #7; however, the Germans hadn't thrown us back into the sea either.

The staff briefing the morning of February 5 grimly reviewed our situation and made it plain that we must brace ourselves for a vigorous enemy counterattack. The combined attack on Cisterna had upset the German timetable. We didn't then know the full extent of the morale and battle damage the Rangers had inflicted on the new German troops. The Germans had to move fast to beat the miserable wet weather ahead. Spring and reliable dry ground would not come to Anzio until May, and mud would dominate the battlefield until then. We were outnumbered, and the Germans held the high ground surrounding our beachhead. Our fast-firing well-supplied artillery had blunted the Germans' advance when they tried to attack over open ground. Our artillery, however, couldn't overpower the Germans entrenched on the rocky hillsides and in the fortified buildings of Cisterna. We needed tanks and air strikes to dig them out.

"Axis Sally," the sultry-voiced announcer who nightly played American music on Radio Rome, repeatedly interrupted popular Big Band songs to report on the big parade in Rome. The 750 captured American Rangers were marched through the streets of Rome so the Italian populace could witness the great German victory. American voices, sounding as though under duress, recited a litany of rehearsed statements on how well they were being treated by the Germans. Naming individual names, they would encourage comrades to desert and escape the certain destruction that lay ahead. The program saddened us, and we wondered where Axis Sally had gotten her information. We feared that those 750 men were going through both a physical and psychological hell.

In the DIVARTY Headquarters tent, the swagger and confidence of the previous week were absent. As our briefing ended, Major Walter T. (also known as Dutch) Kerwin, ordered me to the operations tent to work out some missions. I followed Kerwin to his domain, slipping between the light-proof overlapping canvas flaps into the stuffy, dimly-lit tent.

The operations tent always had a two-man guard posted around the clock. The battle maps of our sector, Division Supply Dumps, and General Situation maps were on display when one lifted the light canvas drapes. Interior lighting from dim electric bulbs gave it an intimate and congenial glow. We called it the War Room.

"We were lucky and unlucky, Schultz," Kerwin began. "The twenty-four-hour delay at Cisterna drastically changed the balance of action. The Krauts moved a complete 14,000-man division into the line facing the Rangers January 29. They're planning to "Lance the Carbuncle" of Anzio as Hitler demanded. We set back his timetable, but it cost us those 750 Rangers taken prisoner."

"The attack won't be long in coming," he continued. "The German prisoners we've taken along the front tell us that seven new divisions are now surrounding the beachhead. We don't know the timetable, but the Rangers chopped the hell out of one of their best assault units and forced them to spend a lot of scarce ammunition. We owe the Rangers a great debt for the time we've gained. We have to take advantage of the gift … fast.

"Their 170s outrange us by 2,000 to 3,000 yards. That's a given. Our strategic bombing is denying Germany the freedom to produce and move military products. We must rely on the Air Force to stop the supply of ammo to the 170s and then the Tactical boys can blow them sky high," Kerwin said confidentially. "We'll use all the ammunition we've got and the big guns from Corps artillery to fire concentrations on each and every enemy staging ground and supply route. We must be prepared to fire even if the wire's out and the radio's jammed. We'll fire a pre-set rotation."

Kerwin walked to the beachhead map and pointed to the location of the 155 guns and the 8-inch howitzers. "These guns are registered as of today and will be controlled by Corps artillery, so forget them for now. Our Division's guns must be registered on thirty or more potential staging and supply routes.

Some of these targets can be picked up by ground observation, but some of them will be better served from the air. I also want your air observers to rate how close ground observers are coming to the distant targets."

Kerwin wanted to be able to interdict every sheltered point the Germans might use to organize attack formations. We had to hit them early and hard before they approached our outposts. He felt that by hitting their rear assembly areas, we could harass and demoralize their reinforcements.

I asked when he wanted us to start.

"That's the key," he said. "Only a few must know of this plan. Don't give your pilots or observers any details. Above all, the firing points must not be combined on any single map. Your CP is too open to view by wandering civilians. We need to ship them out of here soon. Two of your plane crews have been captured and we don't want pilots or observers to know the extent of our preparations. I'll send you the missions to observe and missions to fire, three or four a day. Blend them into regular patrol flights. Use many different pilots. Report the results directly to me in this tent ... daily! Understand?"

I understood. The depressing morning briefing now became a springboard for a new chapter in air artillery observation. *Janey* and I would be in the vanguard. Pre-set rotations would be much faster to fire than two of our favorite tricks, the French Square and Time on Target, and possibly more devastating—we'd find out soon enough.

An old soldier's tale says that the first shell that breaks over the soldiers' heads is the one that counts. Once the first shell has landed and the soldier is flat on the ground hiding in a tire track, his chances of survival are greatly improved. To take advantage of this fact, the French in World War I taught us their deadly trick called the French Square, which they had developed to catch the maximum number of enemies above ground and without shelter.

To set up a French Square, we selected a target by ground observation from a mountain peak or a church steeple or by air observation in an L-4B. Then we fired our ranging shells, purposely missing the target. To fool the enemy, we wanted the shells to fall 300 to 500 yards from the real target. In its simplest form, we shot at the four corners of a square that surrounded our victim. By correcting the shots that were over to the left and to the right and short to the left and right, the points where the lines intersected was our impact point. All ranging shots had been timed from on-the-way to impact. That factor enhanced the possibility that all shells from a single battery, where its four guns are within a 100-yard circle, or from three batteries, where the guns are within a 500-yard circle, would simultaneously rain death and destruction on the unsuspecting enemy.

To fire a French Square took time and patience, but the effort was well worth the trouble. We wouldn't hear from that enemy position for a long time. However, we had to move our position because we'd given the enemy ample time to determine the source of the French Square, and the only variables on our side during any counter-battery fire would be the terrain features, air density, the damage we'd inflicted on him and how skillful our deception was during ranging.

It took half a day to locate a worthy target and establish the registrations for a good French Square. Once we had set up a French Square, we could then use our initial registration points to tie in other support artillery and plow the countryside with a massive Time on Target. This enhanced version of the French Square used dozens of guns and heavier weapons all timed to land at a common point at the same instant, coming from all directions. From my vantage point in the air, it looked like a giant brownish-gray flower bursting into bloom with shafts of yellow flame and white smoke billowing from the center as the light dust rolled from the center like waves from a pebble thrown into a pond.

Casualties were horrendous if the deception was complete but very light if the troops were dug in. Grim as it sounds, the statistics for shells shot by size and weight and the number of men killed is not a direct ratio. Preparation, surprise and chance roll those dice.

With pre-set rotations, we were prepared in advance. When the Germans tried to follow Hitler's order to "Lance the Carbuncle," we would blow them sky high. It was a fitting tribute to the 750 Rangers who had bought us the time to prepare such a reception. The excellent physical condition and training of the American Rangers intimidated their Nazi captors. They were not the dispirited troops the Nazi propaganda usually described.

On February 16, the Germans launched six major attacks against the Third Division, but each was shattered before it penetrated our outpost line. We captured 200 of their men. And Major Kerwin's interdictory fire plan had proven its worth. Hitler gave up the beachhead and his army crawled back to their defensive holes.

24 · *THE TIGERS*

I wanted to ask Kerwin about moving our airstrip and radio car from behind the Ninth's guns. Fortunately, we hadn't lost a man, but we'd lost three planes. One was totaled by ground fire and two had been shot down in enemy territory. The constant rat-a-tat of small-arms fire made us realize just how much we depended on the dogfaces, who were holding the line a thousand yards ahead of our field.

By now Keith Rozen had returned to our good graces. His snappy conversation and cheerful willingness to take on any mission made him a sought-after observer. We spent the next few days firing more registrations and more secret concentrations. Then on the 5th and 6th of February, the Germans launched their multi-division assault against the British. Perhaps they were trying to even the score for having been driven from North Africa, and the full fury of the Wehrmacht fell on the British First Division. The narrow finger-like projections the English had made toward Rome were rolled back yard by yard and had now become indentations in our lines. To exploit a lack of coordination between the Allies, the Germans had also launched a major probe at the junction between the newly-arrived American 45th Division and the British. Coordination had been substandard, and before a correction could be made, some enemy penetration had occurred. But the enemy now had to reckon with the determination of the Allied forces. We counterattacked each German thrust and regained the small amounts of ground we'd lost.

The main event, however, was just ahead. On February 16, the blow fell. The Germans unleashed ten divisions against the Allied force, which was composed of the 45th, the Third, the Rangers and the British First. Early that morning Kerwin's secret concentrations started to rain in on the Germans' sheltered assembly points. Counter-battery missions exploded on suspected gun sites. On some guns that day, we fired a thousand rounds. If the Krauts had expected to rest before the attack began, they were disappointed. The Blue and White Devils kept them awake.

My February 16 dawn mission with Keith, who had become my regular morning companion, was frustrating and unproductive. The sky was overcast with leaden clouds, and the shards of dawn breaking over the hills gave us too feeble a light to observe complete actions. Gun flashes and shell bursts created a low cloud of smoke and dust below *Janey* that mixed with morning mist as it rolled across the landscape. The ground observers were in control, calling upon us only when needed, but we lacked a clear view of the Germans from the air.

With the multitude of guns firing that morning, we had two options. We could either fly low over the front, exposing *Janey* to small-arms fire and the flak wagons, or we could fly a mile behind the front and be safe from our own passing artillery projectiles but be a sitting duck for hungry ME-109s or FW-190s. Keith and I chose to fly low over the front, taking the chance that the 20mm guns were being held back to support a counterattack or to join the tanks for a thrust.

We made it back to the airstrip with no holes in *Janey* or us, and as I landed, I wondered where all the planes had gone. Only one was left, and it wasn't flyable. As Croal appeared, lugging two 5-gallon cans of gas, Boone ran up and shouted, "Schultz, every regiment wanted a plane, plus the Rangers and the 45th. I've got to gas up *Janey* and take a mission for the Ninth. Rosner will be down next."

"OK, go ahead," I agreed. "Who's your observer? Want Keith Rozen?"

"Rozen has to report to Colonel Darby," Boone replied. "I'll go alone."

Stein roared up in the jeep. "Hey Rozen, Darby wants you!" Stein yelled. "He's been calling every ten minutes!"

Keith jumped in the jeep and away they went. Stein didn't even slow down for the waterways that crossed our field every 50 feet, so Keith got one hell of a ride. The tempo and crescendo of the battle noise gave everything a sense of urgency. I walked toward Geist in his radio car and asked. "Glenn, what's going on? Why did Rosner send out all the planes?"

"Jeeps kept coming in with big brass wanting to take a look. Division sent down a colonel from the 45th, and then we had a couple of urgent fire missions. On top of all that, Boone took a call from the Ninth about some tanks and he had to wait for you. We could've used a couple extra radio channels too."

Two planes returned within minutes. Now we could restore order to our flight line. "Good going, Ros! You kept it going," were the first words Rosner heard from me as he parked his plane. I was glad I'd had time to sort things out before he landed. His passenger, an infantry commander, jumped out and headed for one of the jeeps hiding behind the long low French-bread-shaped hill on the east side of our field.

"What could you see?" I asked. "Were you high or low?"

"A little bit of both," he answered. "The mist is burning off, but the Krauts are using every trick in the book. Smoke, shriekers and, believe it or not, I saw a couple of flares. The smoke's giving the infantry observers fits, and it's the first time the Jerries have used shriekers in a long time," he chuckled. "They must think we're a bunch of raw recruits."

"How are the dogfaces holding up?"

"I couldn't see any breakthrough, especially in front of us," Rosner said with obvious relief in his voice.

"Hey you guys, over here!" Geist shouted. "Boone's calling fire on some tanks! A battery of the Ninth with radio direct—no, now it's two batteries! No, it's Battalion, half smoke." Smoke shells combined with high-explosive shells meant only one thing. The tanks had somehow been stalled and the Big Bangers were trying to set them on fire.

"Hey, he either hit a tread or one turned ... man, some Long Toms are in on the fun. Hold it! They're waiting for the smoke to clear," Geist reported like he was doing a live broadcast of the Kentucky Derby. "Four tanks, Tigers, first one crossways in the road! HE on the way, he's getting a battery of 105s firing as rifles from the side, all going through one radio." We could depend on Glenn to be more interested in the radio aspects of the battle than the artillery.

"He's got another battery of Long Toms to seal off the last tank!" Geist continued. "Man, are they keeping Boone busy!"

"Glenn, how long has Boone been up?" I asked, fearing the answer.

"One hour, forty minutes," Geist answered. "He should have another thirty, forty minutes if he hasn't been gunning it, if he had a full tank when he left."

Glenn then realized that *Janey* wasn't full when Boone took off. We never tried to chamois the last gallon out of a 5-gallon can. Croal and Boone had put in only two cans, and it normally took three cans to fill a plane. Boone would soon find out how much gas he had left. If the floating stick on the gas tank wasn't bobbing, he was flying on fumes.

"Rosner, get up there and replace Boone. Now!" I shouted. Rosner didn't quite make it to the observation point when Boone reported, "Engine dead, trying for Road E-6, our side." Boone had to glide out of trouble and land *Janey* on one pass, and even if he landed safely on Road E-6, *Janey* would be exposed to German fire of all sorts. It wouldn't take them long to destroy a Cub that was a sitting duck.

"Richards got the contact." Geist was at it again. "No, now Rooster's firing, Richards is coming in. We've got it covered," Glenn yelled with a mixture of relief and elation.

Before Geist's report had completely registered with us, Richards had turned in to land. I waited, anxious for news of Boone and *Janey.* "Did you see Boone go down?"

"Yeah." Richards replied. "He landed just north of the dairy farm and the dogfaces pushed his plane in the ditch. Mortar shells are falling, but they're in a sizable ditch."

Geist handed me the field phone. "It's for you."

"Schultz, this is Colonel Davis of the Fifteenth. Put that pilot down for a medal. I'll sign. He saved our skins. We'll paste those Tigers for a little while longer with HE and then I'm going to send out some bazooka teams to finish them off. You fellows do good work!"

Boone had survived the dead-stick landing and we were happy about that. We liked Boone. He provided great evening entertainment with his fine tenor voice and his renditions of "Buffalo Gals" and "Paper Doll." And his cheerful attitude helped keep our spirits high.

"Boone's on the horn!" Geist shouted, with a smile a yard wide.

"Schultzie, *Janey*'s OK, if the Krauts leave her alone," Boone assured me. "We shoved her in a ditch, and she's around a bend in the road. We can get her out tonight." Boone knew how concerned I was whenever anybody flew my plane, so he wanted to assuage my fears right away.

"You did a great job," I complimented him, with obvious relief in my voice. "Colonel Davis has put you down for a medal. You deserve it, IF you didn't hurt *Janey*," I joked.

Our conversation was cut short by the whistle of incoming shells. We dived for cover as the Germans gunned away at our Big Bangers with a barrage of long shells surpassing anything we had heard to date. It was a staccato outburst of snare drums combined with the throb of kettle and bass drums—360-degree surround-sound. Booms, crashes, cracks and krumphs accelerated the pace of everything that moved, everything except what I was waiting for—Rozen's return.

At last they rolled in from the extreme west, the beach

side, at the end of our strip. The pace was far from leisurely, but this time, Stein was slowing down for the water-filled ditches.

"Schultz, Darby's given me one hell of an assignment," Keith began. "First of all, I may have to fire the Navy along the canal. You and I can handle that, OK?"

"Sure we can," I answered.

"Now the secret stuff." Keith loved drama, and this batch of orders from the respected Col. John K. Darby, leader of the Rangers, held dramatic potential. "The Limeys are in trouble and us Rangers might just swing a Battalion over behind them to pull their chestnuts out of the fire. I'm to explore a march route that can be used even single file," he explained. To locate a good hiking route, we'd have to fly at 1,000 feet and expose ourselves to the Luftwaffe again, but we had no choice. Five hundred Rangers eager to avenge the loss of their 750 comrades could make the difference in a close-quarter battle with the Germans.

"The situation's tough," Keith continued. "It might come to hand-to-hand combat and that's where the Rangers shine." He paused.

"One more thing. The Queen's Own are disembarking without their heavy shooters, so we might assist them. We'll do it by flare if we can't get radio. All radio may be involved with the Navy. We shoot concentration B-9 by R-6 if they fire a yellow flare. They'll fire red if too close and green if too long. If we land short and shoot up the Limeys, it might lead to a lot of bar fights."

I understood the situation, but *Janey,* my good-luck talisman, was gone. I'd take Bill Richards's plane. It had already been gassed, and all I needed were extra flares. A shout from Feldman interrupted our preparations. "Hey Schultz, shall we paint BA on the side of Richards's plane so your Kraut cousins will know it's you?" BA was *Janey*'s Division designation.

Koster propped the plane, and it started on the first pull—a good omen—then off we went. Two massed waves of

FW-190s had already attacked the beachhead area that day, so it was with little relish that we started back toward the docks, the target of the German big guns. A haze of smoke from scattered fires partially hid them, and barrage balloons swayed on their tethers above the wispy clouds, giving a festive air to the grim, deadly scene.

The Rangers still held the south flank of the beachhead, defined by the north dikes of the Mussolini Canal. We made a quick radio check and everything checked out. The Navy would fire the prearranged salvos if called upon. I wanted to fire just one broadside to see the Navy 8-inchers impact.

The camouflage of the Ranger reserve camp couldn't have been better. If we hadn't known where to look, we would never have spotted it. We flew high above the woods where the ME-109s and FW-190s could easily spot us, but we had no choice. We had to fly high enough to locate and examine a good hiking route. From about 1,000 feet, the road was clearly visible, and if the Rangers were moving with small arms only, single file or squads, the north sector of the Anzio beachhead could be reinforced in less than two hours with a Ranger battalion.

No bandits yet. Two missions down and one to go. Keith shook my shoulder and pointed to the piney woods near the evac hospital. We'd heard that showers were being installed, and he wanted to check it out. Perhaps we'd luck out and the nurses might be giving them a trial run. We spotted the showers, but no nurses. Once past the dock area, I started toward the British sector, my eyes peeled for a yellow flare. As we flew closer to the front lines I saw no yellow smoke, just khaki-clad troops marching four abreast in parade formation, toward a crucial road overpass. I couldn't believe my eyes. Those soldiers were within easy rifle and mortar range of the Germans, yet they were marching forward in style, bagpipes inflated and drummers drumming, led by an officer with his Webley revolver drawn.

We needed a closer look, so I spiraled down in broad

sweeps, worried that the German bandits might be watching but mesmerized by the incongruous composure of these Scotsmen, and as I flew over the band, I relaxed the throttle. Now we could clearly hear the piercing cry of the pipes and the rattle of drums. The Queen's Own, in typical British fashion, were heralding their arrival with élan and an unabashed show of esprit de corps as they marched forward without any protection of support weapons.

Would their pipes and drums scare the Huns? During World War I, the Germans had dreaded the wailing of pipes and the rattle of drums because it meant the Ladies from Hell would soon be coming for them with bayonets, broadswords and dirks. But bitter fighting lay ahead for all Allied comrades in arms. Hitler had a score to settle. If the Wehrmacht couldn't win this battle when the Germans had numerical superiority and short supply lines, what would the invasion of France bring? A white panel triangle appeared, designating the British HQ. We were in the right place. I gave the wings a waggle and the panel disappeared.

"Good show," crackled over channel two. We had radio, but I saw no yellow smoke. I gave another waggle and sailed back inland over the piney woods. I didn't want to stay near the German bulge because they might have a couple of flak wagons ready for us. We'd completed Keith's mission. Now we'd recheck the march route, give the Third's front a couple of low sweeps and get down.

25 • *THE STALEMATE*

The report of an artillery piece followed shortly by a scream indicated a package was en route to the Germans. A report, followed by a delayed hiss, like a whistle between dry lips, indicated a reply from the Germans. The Germans wanted to silence the Ninth's Big Bangers, the 155mm Howitzers, and our batteries replied in kind. Most of the trajectories, inbound or outbound, seemed to arc right over the Third Division's Air Section, and this field had to be abandoned if we were to keep our sanity. Luckily we hadn't suffered any casualties, but we had lost two planes on the field from stray shrapnel.

Stein had taken Keith to Ranger HQ to report on his mission. Now forward observers were doing close-in firing, and our planes were maintaining patrol. A new record would be set today. One of our battalions, twelve guns in all, shot more than 10,000 shells. I recalled the day on Sicily when we first fired 100 rounds. Major Walter L. "Dutch" Kerwin's firing kept the enemy off balance. Every sheltered assembly area behind the German lines received some plowing several times a day. The gullies and draws, or wadis, as the British called them, would be first. They were marked on the Italian maps as fossi, and Jimmy Roosevelt's P-38 photo recon group had made several passes over the area at different altitudes and sun conditions so that the shadows could be read to determine the depth and width of these potential enemy staging areas and gun hideouts.

On the Third Division front, our outpost line had never been seriously breached. Even the tanks had been stopped before they were within bazooka range. We'd started lots of fires, and although some might be piles of burning tires ignited by the Germans to confuse us, many had been pay dirt. We were proud of our defensive ability and didn't relish the idea of stalemate. We were assault troops. If the enemy didn't attack with force tomorrow, we would know we had taken his worst without breaking, and we'd be capable of capturing Cisterna.

Brilliant white parachute star flares, shriekers, and 170mm heavy artillery from the Germans denied us restful sleep, turning the front into a surreal moonscape illuminated by brilliant flashes and accompanied by the thunder of war. Our guns were not silent. We blasted the distant concentration points with 155s and pasted the enemy's forward positions with 105s. We had plenty of shells and liked to shoot them as long as we were up. The barrel, or tube, of a 155mm Long Tom had a service life of 2,000 shells if fired with regular charge and 2,500 shells at maximum charge. We had fired many maximum-charge missions in Sicily when we were trying to support the north coast bridgehead that extended past our maximum standard charge range, but most of our projectiles were now powered with a regular charge. It was a heavy job, but barrels were changed under field conditions. Saving lives outweighed the wear and tear on the equipment.

By mid-February an unspoken understanding had filtered through Allied and German ranks. We wouldn't move unless the Germans moved. The slaughter would be on hold until the ground firmed. For a few months, General "Mud" made the decisions on Anzio. The Luftwaffe, however, didn't have to follow General Mud's orders. Late on the afternoon of February 18, a lone ME-109 strafed the beachhead at low level, and as we were shouting radio warnings, it rose over the Padiglione Woods, passed though a blazing sunset, then fired at one of our Cubs. As the Messerschmitt disappeared behind Mount Lapini to the east, the momentum of the Cub's flight path carried Lieutenants Smith and Jones behind enemy lines. The plane crashed and burned on the outskirts of Cisterna, beyond the range of any possible assistance.

Plenty of raw Italian winter weather lay ahead, and for the next sixty days the stalemate continued until the sun greened the grass and dried the ground enough to support the heavy vehicles of war. Every corner of our beachhead could be hit by Anzio Annie, the big German long-range railroad gun, the 340mm. We couldn't hit their guns. They out ranged us and our only help came from the Air Force. The one-gun-per-installation tactic the Boche used made the spotting of their artillery by aircraft nearly impossible. We lived with the worry of that lone shell fired by an incompetent gunner that fell long, short or wide of its mark and mistakenly maimed or killed one of us good guys.

Sometimes the Germans would fire big batches of old ammunition. Some were duds, and we marked those with white tape fences and walked a hundred yards around the mound the impact had created. After a couple of rains, the fences fell down and soon we were walking over them. Some of the stray evening shells, fired when the gunner could no longer read his sights, killed sheep, donkeys and goats. If the Germans shelled the same area the following days and the weather turned warm, the Italians wouldn't risk burying or cutting up the carcasses. We had to bury them.

Keith Rozen and I had spotted no nurses taking showers, but now that imminent danger had passed, a showering schedule circulated throughout the command. I could send five men a day on the first go-round. We drew lots, and the enlisted men were overjoyed with the shower rules, for only field-grade officers, majors and above, bathed alone. This procedure gave the medics a chance to conduct "short arm" inspections on the captains and lieutenants as a group. The enlisted man's indignity of group "short arm" inspections was now shared by the company officers.

Spring air, fresh and crisp, filled the colorful sunset of February 19 as I walked to DIVARTY HQ, trying to keep time with the low, distant rumbles.

"Schultz, we want you to move," Captain George L. Snow, DIVARTY Headquarters Battery CO, reported as soon as I arrived at the dairy farm. I didn't mind that we were moving or care where we moved. As long as it was away from the Ninth's Big Bangers and the errant German shells, the men would all be happy.

"We're moving to the large wadi," he continued. "The one on the west end of your pasture, about a half mile north. If you move due west to the ditch bank, we'll have a short telephone line and you'll only have to post one guard. We'll be guarding the east and west sides and the road leading in from the north. What say?" asked Snow, trying to sound like a Brit.

We would start the next day. Maybe this news would ease the gloom that had hung over the Section since the loss of Smith and Jones. Snow promised an earth mover to help us settle in.

True to his word, Captain Snow sent a bulldozer down our gully and we scratched out an area for our kitchen, radio car, and aid station. Just before night settled in, we started scraping up an Air-Force style revetment on the southwest side of our pasture, away from our main activities. It would be our gas dump and airframe repair shelter. We were beginning to feel safe now that we were over a half mile from the Big Bangers. Our only worry now would be random shelling and the new antipersonnel cluster bombs introduced last night. The Germans were always coming up with something new and fiendish.

By nightfall all ranks slept below ground. My personal shelter, dug deep into the bank of the ditch, featured a sandbagged entrance verandah that gave me a protected view of the evening fireworks display. It would accommodate me and the morning observer, plus a field radio, three phones, and a map board. My dugout was a duplicate of the radio car command post minus the large base radio and Geist's special equipment. When viewed from a short distance, the top of my shelter blended perfectly into the surface of the field.

Brass called it line straightening, but for the combat patrols during the next weeks, it seemed to be a deadly game played to keep the dogfaces busy. Even though the lines were being straightened, both sides were ready for a rest. General O'Daniel created a rest camp in a sheltering woods close to the beach. Company-sized units would move back for showers, the best food the beachhead could offer, and even movies in dug-down hospital tents. Returning troops raved about the treatment they'd received, and they looked great. They were clean shaven and wore clean clothes, especially dry socks. An overnight LST ride to Naples with a three-day rest at Sorrento was available to officers. Five days away from even the sound of artillery was a real rest. Sorrento was refreshing and I returned to the beachhead relaxed.

In late March, the Iowa 34th Red Bull Division landed on the beachhead and gradually relieved the Third's front-line units. The arrival of their Air Section was an excuse to have a multitude of revetments shoved up by the bulldozer and a broad lane of waterway depressions filled, enabling us to use the long east-west length of the field for landing away from incoming shells.

For the benefit of the new arrivals, Keith Rozen enhanced the myth of my good luck with my "German cousins." When a shell boomed in the distance, Keith would run over and stand by me, figuring he'd be safe from my Teutonic kin. We were both the shortest men in the air section, but his dark hair and complexion contrasted to my fair skin and blue eyes, so Keith would shake his fist and shout, "Shoot if you must this Jewish boy, but save your German cousin!" The comic-relief routine always worked and Keith gave our unit spirit.

The Zionist Brigade stories came from Izador Feldman when he joined us and discovered that there were three other Jewish fellows in the Air Section. This game served to break the tension of the fitful shellings we received and the ever-present knowledge that the one that gets you is the one you never hear.

In early April, Lieutenant Boucher landed unannounced on our strip with his own plane. He was a replacement for Smith, the pilot we lost on February 17. Boucher had over six months of Stateside flying time after graduation from Fort Sill, and just couldn't wait to be assigned a mission. I took him up in *Janey* for a general view of the whole front. I felt daring because I suspected the Germans had an 88 primed to fire on a crossroads near the factory building. The area had frequently changed hands, and was still contested. If a pilot made a quick pass over the intersection, did a 180-degree turn and dived to 300 to 500 feet behind the intersection, the Germans might send a ranging air burst that would scare the hell out of any passenger.

I buzzed the road intersection, then swung low, 300 to 500 feet behind it. "WHAP!" The rending, teeth-jarring air burst came right on schedule. *Janey* bucked and tossed. Black smoke billowed around us as I kicked the rudder and spun down to the deck, giving both Boucher and the Germans an exhibition of aerobatic stupidity. Back at the field, Boucher was overwhelmed. He'd been fired on during his first flight and was feeling like a seasoned veteran until Rozen said, "Hell, Schultz was just showing off. His cousins won't hit him. Stick close to the short German and you'll be safe."

That night it was Boucher's turn to hold court. Everyone burned for Stateside tales and the latest news from Naples. Boucher told us that there were other pilots in the Army replacement depot, just loafing and flying nurses around Mount Vesuvius, and he said there were plenty of planes parked at the Naples airport. Perhaps my request for planes would be fulfilled soon. I'd requisitioned four Piper L-4Bs from Fifth Army Supply in order to bring our Air Section back to its authorized strength of ten planes. Since the invasion of Anzio, on January 22, 1944, our airstrip had been constantly within range of enemy artillery. Four of our Cubs had been damaged beyond repair. One had been lost by pilot error, two had their airframes and wing spars shattered by shellfire, and one Cub had caught fire and burned from antipersonnel bomb fragments. Our skilled ground crews had been able to repair ground loop damage, to spread landing gear, and fix broken props, thus keeping the balance of our planes in the air.

I sent four volunteers to Naples. Ferrying planes from Naples to Anzio was a volunteer mission because the 80-mile flight over water was fraught with danger. The Germans held 70 miles of coastline between Anzio and our supply depot north of Naples. Once a pilot started back to Anzio, he had to fly a mile or more seaward to avoid enemy 20mm groundfire. Should he be jumped over the sea by the Luftwaffe, his chances for survival were slim unless he could reach the Navy's protective curtain of antiaircraft fire in time. The incentive for making those flights was a layover in Naples to wait for decent weather and to coordinate with the Navy a flight route that offered some AA protection. Waiting for decent weather and arranging for covering Navy fire usually took a couple of days, which included a short rest in Naples.

Glad as I was to see all our pilots back safe and sound, I was concerned to see only two Piper L-4Bs land, followed shortly by a Stinson L-5. Why only three planes, and why the L-5? To me, the L-5 wouldn't count as a full-service plane. I was fearful that the Press and VIPs would again be finding urgent reasons for top-priority trips from the beachhead to Naples.

Fortunately, within days the Army Corps Artillery arrived on the beachhead with their new L-5s. I pointed out to prospective passengers the advantages of flying in their L-5s. In the L-5, with average winds, Naples was less than an hour away, but in an L-4B, is was nearly two hours. But now we had an L-5. Although some of our recent replacement pilots had flown the Stinson, we didn't have even one pilot with a full hour of L-5 time in his log book.

Previously, during December of 1943, our Third Division had been in Naples refitting after 59 days of continuous action in southern Italy and Cassino. L-5s were at the Naples airport, and as the newly-appointed Third Division Air Officer, I contacted the 12th Air Force Supply to see if we could get one along with our replacement L-4Bs. At that time, my request was turned down. L-5s were for Army and Corps issue, not Divisional level. Though disappointed, we satisfied ourselves with a few flights and bull sessions with Corps L-5 pilots regarding the plane's performance.

Chuck Croal, my ground crew chief, was not so easily discouraged. He somehow managed to get his hands on a set of L-5 airframe and engine manuals.

Luckily, now that we had an L-5, we were on a perfect airstrip for checking out ten eager pilots in this new plane, despite our lack of an L-5-trained check pilot. Our east-west runway was over 3,000 feet long and our north-south strips were 50 feet wide and 800 feet long. I asked DIVARTY Headquarters to let me keep the new plane off regular patrol flights for at least a week to familiarize the pilots with its landing and takeoff capabilities. Our field's length and width gave us the opportunity to make several touch-and-go landings per flight and to get the feel of crosswinds. The L-5 couldn't compare with the L-4B for short landings and takeoffs, but it had many other benefits. Air Force-Infantry close-support missions were being planned for the future. They had worked well for the Third Division in southern Italy as long as air-to-ground contact was maintained. If the small-unit infantry commanders could contact P-47 Thunderbolts by L-5 radio relay for bombing missions, the infantry support potential was outstanding. The L-5 was equipped with an Air Force radio and had additional weight-carrying capacity to easily handle the 70-pound infantry radio system.

Air cover over the beachhead in clear weather was effectively discouraging the daylight hit-and-run raids of the ME-109s and FW-190s. The new Air Force P-47 Thunderbolts were able to carry substantial bomb and fuel loads. They were replacing the older prewar P-40 Warhawks, flown by the African-American fighter squadron that had provided cover for our early beachhead invasion.

My request to delay placing the L-5 in service rotation had caused concern for General "Iron Mike" O'Daniel. I was ordered to report to his headquarters. O'Daniel greeted me with the question: "What's the problem with the new plane?"

This was not the time to be shy. I told him I was concerned because we hadn't received the fourth requested plane, and now that we had an L-5, I didn't want it to get sidetracked into Brass, Press and courier flights. If that happened, we would then be two planes short of full strength, a severe handicap when Allied Forces started the Breakout. And I also wanted to caution General O'Daniel that, because of its size and sound, the L-5 would attract special attention from the Germans if it were used by infantry commanders for only preparatory reconnaissance flights. I wanted authority to keep the L-5 in regular daily patrol flights after we had completed our "home schooling" instructional period.

General O'Daniel agreed with my concerns and invited me to look at the air photos that had been covered with canvas when I'd entered the war room.

"This is our Breakout plan," he told me, tracing the valley we would follow on our drive to cut Highway #6 and close the jaws of the trap soon to be sprung by the Fifth Army's advance north from the Cassino front. Our D-day was May 23, and if all went according to plan, we would destroy the entire German Tenth Army. As I signed out of the war room tent on the secrecy roster, the supply officer gave me the bad news: No more planes until we reached Rome.

26 • *THE BREAKOUT*

There were just a couple of days left before the upcoming attack and breakout attempt. We had taken part in special plans, including the sweeping hail of .50-caliber machine -gun bullets we would unleash on congested troops, the modern-day equivalent of a volley of arrows sent over a castle wall. But the enemy had a treat in store for us, the *nebelwerfer*, a multi-barrel rocket launcher. It had been used on the Russian Front and a couple of times on Anzio.

Cannon to the right of us, cannon to the left of us, and into the Valley of Death charged the Blue and White Devils of the Third Infantry Division. May 23, 1944, was a memorable day as the Allies began the Breakout from the stalemate of Anzio. We tried to punch our way through German mine fields with flailing chains mounted on the fronts of our tanks. The engineers, under a hail of German fire, pushed linked sections of explosive-filled steel tubes, known as bangalore torpedoes, under the concertina wire to sever its strands by detonating the whole string of pipes at once. Battle sleds, fashioned from the casings of Italian torpedoes, were towed behind tanks, ferrying prone soldiers over the tangled mess of barbed wire. We thought we had set a record on February 16 when one battalion fired 10,000 shells, but new records were being set on May 23.

The Germans held their ground and the *nebelwerfer* proved to be an elusive target after it had unleashed its rain of death and disappeared to spew forth death again 400 yards away. It could be pulled by two stout men, so it was easy to relocate and conceal. Despite *nebelwerfers,* barbed wire, mines, and cannon, we good guys inched ahead. In Cisterna, the long-coveted objective, the soft masonry buildings seemed to absorb our shells and became rubble heaps.

Night fell and we had moved ahead, but at a dreadful cost. The guns rumbled all night and into another day. The Air Force strafed and bombed the German rear to deny them fresh replacements and supply, but the German soldiers had to be dug from their positions like olives from a jar—one at a time. Day two ended with the Anzio crescent shrouded by a smoky haze that turned the setting sun into a blood-red ball. We held new ground but Cisterna still sheltered Germans in caverns beneath the crumbling walls. A lonely statue in the city square still stood among buildings that had become piles of rubble.

The machines of war were used again that night, including the *nebelwerfer.* The naked light of parachute flares bathed the battlefield. Silhouettes of medics moved to retrieve the wounded, seeking the source of moans and cries through the rain of fire still exploding on the ground. Night had been good to the troopers on our northern flank. They had cut Highway #7 and were heading across the open ground. On the southern flank, Cisterna was encircled, but still held by the Germans. The Quarry, north of Cisterna, would be ours by midday, and that was where the dreaded 88s and the 170mm howitzers were hidden. We had tried to obliterate those guns with 500-pound bombs, white phosphorous shells, and high-explosive artillery shells dropped like mortar rounds, but the guns kept reappearing on aerial recon photos and continued to fire on the Big Bangers. I wanted to see the Quarry, and just for the hell of it, I wanted to spend the night there.

By late afternoon it was ours, and the road network carried a constant stream of vehicles. I sent Croal forward with a ground crew, and with Rozen flying as my observer in *Janey,* we headed for the Quarry. The map elevations there looked good, and as I flew low over the shell-pocked pasture, I could see that we had been shooting at flat rocky plates. What we had assumed were shell craters were actually just powder burns. The area surrounding the Quarry now swarmed with people; there could no longer be much danger from mines. As I landed, cheering natives surged forward to mob us. I cut the power to stop the revolving propeller before some over-eager Italian child was decapitated.

I called Geist and he came in free and clear due to our line-of-sight radio link. We could see the beachhead shining brilliant white. The haze of battle now swirled away from the beachhead and eastward, toward us.

"Bring up the sections," I told Geist. "We have a field." Other Third Division units were already using the Quarry area. At last we were free of Anzio and out from under direct German observation.

Cisterna was still a house-to-house battle. Reserve elements of the Third would help mop it up while the advance elements continued to Cori-Artena, and our goal, Valmontone, which sat astride Highway #6, the supply artery through which supplies were pumped to Cassino. The trap would then close on any Germans who might want to escape from Cassino.

During the night Cori fell and the Third Division was racing eastward to Highway #6, our original objective of the January invasion. We didn't have time to think of a telephone connection because the fields that had looked promising on aerial recon photos seemed tilted at nearly impossible angles for takeoff and landing. A fairly large clearing near the hillside village of Artena, although still held by the enemy, could possibly be our field for the coming day.

A blanket of snow covered the flat lands of Anzio as Rozen and I started the morning mission of May 27, the fourth day of our drive on Rome. The mountains to the east still sheltered the shadows of night, but the first slivers of sunlight illuminated the higher peaks and sent shafts of light darting toward the sea. Rozen kept tapping my shoulder and pointing toward Anzio. The enemy's view from the Pass was unusually clear. With a good pair of binoculars, he could have read the label on our ration cans. If they had used their Storches as we had used our L-4Bs, they could have blasted us not only off the beach, but off the map.

We pondered the damage the Germans might have done to us if they had fired as many shells at us as we had fired at them. We owed our Bomber Boys a great debt for their courage and sacrifice in the skies over Germany. The decisions and priorities of German war production had been affected by the results of early British Wellington raids; and our bomber raids of 1944 had not only altered the Germans' plans, but had seriously disrupted their production and logistics. The downward spiral in the quality, quantity, and variety of the German war production saved hundreds of lives for those of us in the infantry divisions.

The terrain as we approached the Valmontone Valley offered only one possibility for an airfield. Again we would be almost directly behind the Big Bangers, and would probably catch some long shells intended for them. We soon registered the Ninth's 155s on three points, and because the infantry didn't have active targets, we used crossroads to register their guns. Our registrations must be fired carefully. A Tabor, or battalion, of French Moroccan Goumiers, the fierce mountain tribesmen who dearly loved hand-to-hand fighting, was sneaking through the valley, terrorizing retreating Germans who might stray off the established paths along the eastern side of Highway #6. I had tried to drop food and ration to these fearless marauders while we were fighting at Cassino, and knew how perfectly their tan Gallabeyahs blended into the hillsides. They would now be operating without radio contact, and we didn't want to drop any shells on an ally that had an eight-to-one kill rate. They carried firearms but used them only when they could not use their knives to cut throats and lop off ears or other body parts as souvenirs. Their stealthy attacks turned the sheltering darkness into hours of dread for an outpost guard or straggler, who knew that if he dozed, he might never wake up, or wake to find his comrades lying silently by, minus an ear.

The scenery below us was lovely. Italy was now dressed in spring green, with flowers garlanding her hillsides; but I could spot only one area suitable for landing—and it was not a pretty site. I gave it three passes and turned to Keith to indicate I would try. "Hold on tight, it looks rough," I shouted, and he folded his hands in prayer. As soon as I cut the power to land, I aborted, and gave *Janey* enough power to sail past. There were too many rocks to dodge.

Keith looked relieved as I started for the Quarry. I reasoned that rather than crack up *Janey* by hitting a 6-inch rock on the field with a passenger, I'd try it alone. By flying alone from the back seat, with minimum gas, I could trim the plane to be tail-heavy and somewhat resistant to a nose-over if I hit a rock. Once down, I could get some help from the Ninth or a passing Third Division outfit for a stone clearing crew. My captain's bars would come in handy, for they gave me instant authority to recruit a work detail. With a little work, the strip would be satisfactory although far from desirable. The other advantage to this plan would be that I could establish an immediate forward base with wire and radio connections.

If the Luftwaffe had been active, they would have had a field day. Motor column control didn't exist. On the few narrow twisting roads, vehicles were bumper-to-bumper and troops were congregated in the clear spaces. Patton, Truscott and O'Daniel would have had heads rolling if they had seen the congestion. The roads would have been death traps if a couple of bold ME-109s or FW-190s happened to swing by for a visit.

The second mission was up, and when we landed I explained my plan to Rosner and Richards while Croal filtered about 4 gallons of gas into *Janey*. Four gallons would give me enough for an average mission, but not add excessive front-end weight. A 5-gallon water can, always a great front-line trade item, was strapped into *Janey*'s front seat as far behind the center of gravity as possible, in an attempt to make her tail-heavy.

Geist would stay put till I had telephone and another plane on the field with spare batteries and good radio signal.

Then he would move his command car forward. Croal and crew were to start as soon as I landed but were not to give the MPs any lip. Gas and ammo were the big items, so our progress along the road depended on the MPs' good graces. My parting orders were to fly patrols on one-and-one-half-hour rotation and start landing with me as soon as I had telephone and gas. I hoped we'd be in the valley tomorrow and would only have to use this field for a day.

I was just too short to comfortably fly *Janey* from the back seat. To taxi her, I had to crane my neck and shift from side to side in the seat as I did the snake crawl down the field after landing, and the horizon disappeared as soon as the tail went down. I wasn't a happy pilot in the back seat, but my only solution to today's problem required that I fly from the rear.

All went well on takeoff, but as I approached the front the sight of the road congestion made me cringe. I hoped the Luftwaffe was asleep or chasing our bombers somewhere else. The Ninth's guns were already dug in, and the gun crews were just sitting around. My stone-clearing crew would be easy to round up as soon as I landed.

My plan called for a stall landing, with minimum roll. As I touched down, a couple of small field stones popped out from under *Janey*'s fat doughnut-shaped tires, but we had made it, and I had perfect radio contact with Geist.

I didn't have to use my captain's bars to round up a stone-clearing crew. The fellows from B Battery of the Ninth came over and volunteered to help. Compared to the ciggy-butt and match-stick routine of policing barracks yards back in the States, this job was easy. The crew made short work of clearing the field by turning the detail into a baseball game. Most rocks were of throwable size and soon a throwing contest developed. Eager hands helped me gas *Janey,* for I had water to share, and with water, acquiring additional gas and C-rations was never a problem.

Wire chief Sergeant Joe Green provided me with a field

phone, which I set behind a small stone ledge. Now I was in business in a sheltered CP. Soon Richards and Hill would be landing and we'd be in great shape to handle any mission. I called up DIVARTY and reported my new field in operation, and called for Geist to move out. We'd keep two ground crews to care for the three L-4Bs and the L-5 at the Quarry. The new narrow strip couldn't hide more than five or six planes and the L-5 wouldn't be able to use it at all. At last a breathing spell. I opened a can of beans and franks, leaned back against my warm rock ledge and looked down on our former Anzio home.

Janey, flying over the destruction at Mignano after completing a fire mission against the Germans on Mount Cassino. The historic monastery was believed to serve as an enemy observation post and is barely visible in the upper right hand corner of the photo. Homeward bound, I flew *Janey* above ground fire range.
—1944 *Field Artillery Journal*

27 • THE PURPLE HEARTS

The new field was difficult to use. It was narrow, curved, and canted in every direction, but it was the only field we had. We had no choice, for we had to stay within two city blocks to have telephone contact with DIVARTY. In addition to its undulating surfaces and demanding shape, the field had the additional hazard of being located behind a battery of the Ninth 155mm big guns. Low stone ledges provided shelter for personnel when enemy shells came from the south and southeast, but our planes would be exposed to long enemy shells intended for those Big Bangers. I hoped to find a safer field the next morning.

We now held the village of Artena, nestled at the apex of a 7-mile-wide valley between Mount Laziala to the north and Mount Arestino to the south. From this vantage point we overlooked the city of Valmontone, which straddled Highway #6 and which had been our objective when we landed January 22, four months ago. If we could cut this highway, the Germans would lose their escape route as they retreated north from the Cassino front. But the Germans rained shrieking shrapnel on us and we couldn't cut through Highway #6. We didn't move out the next day or the day after. Neither did the Allied troops coming up from Cassino. The fighting produced gains measured in yards, not miles. Thousands of casualties had been sustained since May 23. The Germans were seriously diminishing the vigor of the American troops. When the Germans increased their range or their trajectory, figuring they had somehow missed the Ninth's position, those long shells hit the airstrip and exploded among our planes. As the first shell whistled by, we dived behind rock ledges and waited out the shelling.

The first day we had lost one plane to enemy shelling. The second day was a day of prolonged shelling and terror. By noon we knew the attack wouldn't capture enough ground for us to move. The Ninth kept firing in support of the Infantry attack, and the Germans kept responding with return barrages, converting our landing strip into a howling dust bowl. What saved us was that 10 to 15 percent of the shells were duds, thanks to the Air Force's strategic bombing that had crippled German industrial production.

We dug our foxholes deeper and dug a larger pit to shelter our base radio. The pit, 4-feet-wide, 3-feet-deep, and 10-feet-long, was a major undertaking through rocky soil crisscrossed with the roots of centuries-old olive trees. All officers and enlisted men alike took turns with picks and shovels. Captains Fain and Roundtree of the British Eighth Army and their crew moved their stripped-down tank closer to our excavation. If the German shelling swung our way, the tank would be driven over the pit to provide cover. We crowded into our foxholes. Too many of us were packed into this confined space full of planes and men.

Midafternoon a second plane went up in flames; and, just as we would have done, the Germans sent over six or eight additional shells just to keep the fire going. "Schultzie, what are we going to do?" Koster asked, as he crawled to our pit to report on the lost plane and equipment. "The truck's leaking gas," he continued. "She has three flat tires and we can't move her! She may blow too!"

"We can't move. This is the only field within wire distance of DIVARTY," I reminded him. "But you're right. This is a mess," I said. "I'll go talk to the Brass." DIVARTY was a quarter mile behind us and I walked the way there instead of driving. A dust trail from a jeep could result in more bombing. Major Connors took me into the CP tent to explain the situation map.

"Army changed our Corps' thrust," he began. "We'll hold our position and fortify for a counterattack. You'll have to use the present field. The British, French and American Fifth Army will be joining us any hour, so control assistance from your planes will be critical. I can't lose touch."

"Only five planes are flyable," I reported. "We're catching the wild shots at the battery of 155s in front of us. Could I keep some planes back at Cisterna and call them up by radio?"

"Radio's too crowded," he reminded me. "We can't rely on it, but you're right. We can't afford to lose more planes. Can't let you get beyond wire contact either," he emphasized. "I need at least one plane and pilot I can talk to. Our choke point on the Germans could explode, and the situation could swing from victory to disaster within minutes. Any ideas?"

"You only need one plane on the strip at a time?" I asked.

"Yes, you keep one plane that I can contact by phone or runner and you can move the rest off that strip. But keep looking for a strip you can use safely that's still within wire range."

Connors had given me an opportunity to modify our operation. I ran back to report the good news. No wonder Connors was so well liked. He was easy to talk to and left us feeling that we had provided the solutions to our own problems.

Rosner saw me coming between the trees and by now several pilots were helping deepen our new pit. "All but one crew can move out," I announced. "Crews will rotate. One plane with pilot sitting on the field. When the mission is over, that pilot and plane can go to Cisterna." The announcement produced smiles of relief.

"Planes will come forward by the clock to be on the ground while patrol is being flown. If the plane's not on the ground, then the plane flying the mission must land before going back. We have to maintain a constant wire link."

"What about the radio crew?" Geist asked.

"Send back all the guys you don't need. You and I will sleep in the pit under the tank with the morning observer."

Word spread fast and preparations for the move began. Koster, Schumacher and Croal came to the pit to outline their plans, and without a word from me, Croal took night duty so that he would be on hand for the dawn mission with his beloved *Janey*.

The new arrangements produced an obvious upswing in morale. The schedule allowed the sections to trickle out so the withdrawal would cause a minimum of activity and attract a minimum of attention from the Germans. Captains Fane and Roundtree and their crew stayed to roll their tank over the radio pit if shells started to land close. And they continued to brew tea for us.

The planes and their crews disappeared. Only *Janey* was left. I secured her near the tank for the night, hoping she was a safe distance from the Germans' normal shelling pattern. As dusk closed in and the air took on a chill, a pair of untended Italian donkeys tried to make love. The few of us who remained sat along the edge of our pit enjoying the evening's entertainment and drinking tea prepared by our British guests. The donkeys didn't disappoint us. We were soon enthralled by the neck-biting and braying of their mating ritual. As the tempo of the dance and the intensity of their passions increased, so did our encouragement and support. Soon the erection of the male and the obvious willingness of the female indicated that a perfect union was about to commence. Yet the connection wasn't being made. Although the female was standing perfectly still, the male's ardor was affecting his aim, and his mighty thrusts were missing their intended target. Corporal Willie Lang, our Wisconsin farm boy, had encountered the same problem back home and knew exactly what to do. He left his ringside seat, and with a deft and steady hand, guided the male's outsized body part to its rightful place.

"Good show!" our British guests shouted, then led the rest of our crew in cheers. The union was complete, and the donkeys were locked in a rapturous embrace, thrashing, stumbling, braying as the male passionately nipped the female's neck.

So absorbed were we in the consummation of this union that we sensed no special danger until we heard the impact of a shell a hundred yards from our position. The damn Krauts were hitting us with an artillery salvo! Without hesitation, we dived for the pit. The donkeys didn't interrupt their lovemaking but instinctively moved to a safer location. Without bothering to uncouple, they stumbled into the pit with us. Three radios, six men, and two donkeys in the throes of passion were all taking refuge in a foxhole while deadly shrapnel whistled overhead. The donkeys brayed, thrashed and kicked as men yelled, grunted and swore in pain. Canteen cups full of tea flew through the air as a cloud of dust enveloped everything in the pit.

I don't know which happened first—the climax of the donkeys or the end of the artillery salvo, but at last the ordeal was over and we pushed the donkeys out of our pit. Radio wires had to be reconnected and canteen cups retrieved, but there was no need to call for a medic. We were safe, but we all limped a little from kicks in the shins and shoulders and chest as we tried to restore the dignity lost while sharing our pit with two passionate donkeys.

Due to Geist's radio tinkering we didn't miss our favorite evening programs. Lord Haw Haw, the turncoat British aristocrat with pro-German sympathies, told us how we were losing the war. And American pop music accompanied the insulting commentary of Axis Sally and her sidekick, George.

Willie Lang recounted other animal matings in which he had offered technical assistance at a critical moment. Darkening skies to the west, east and south roared and flashed as though heat lighting were heralding a summer storm, but we could see the secondary light and hear the muffled *kruuummp* that indicated Kraut artillery was landing somewhere. Death still stalked the night. But a familiar voice called, "Hey Schultz, tell your cousins not to shoot, I'm coming over to spend the night with you!" It was Keith Rozen.

"Adolph! Fritz! Hold your fire!" I shouted back. This banter helped us keep our sanity while the shells sought us out. We scrunched closer together in our pit to make room. Geist unplugged the radio speaker, checked the phone line, and put his earphones on for the serenade of static and combat talk that would keep him awake all night. We were packed like dry figs in a box.

Colonel Darby of the Rangers wanted a special dawn mission. And of course Keith, being a Ranger, would be the observer. Three Allied Armies—the American Fifth Army from the south, the American Seventh from the north, the British Eighth from the east—plus the knife-happy Moroccan tribesmen filtering through the mountain canyons, were about ready to join forces and annihilate the enemy. When we had started using this field a day or so ago, Keith had located his section as far away from the Ninth's guns as possible. When he had made and reported his first observations, he retired to his cot, but moments later we were all diving for the ground as the alarming whistle of an 88 passed overhead and was followed by the THUD of a dud.

"Damn you, Schultz, you'll do anything to get my para-trooper boots," cursed Rozen. "I'm sticking by you for the rest of the war! Your cousins knocked me off my cot." True to his word, Rozen settled in beside me, using the English tank as an anchor for his lean-to.

Salvo after salvo of heavy artillery was called down on Highway #6, the road to Rome. American industrial might had provided us with abundant ammunition and the lowly Italian pack mules had shuttled it to our forward gun positions. The Italian mule skinners courageously hauled the supplies of war forward, returning to base with dead and wounded soldiers.

At dawn on the third day, Keith and *Janey* and I took off downhill, away from enemy lines, hoping to confuse them. We flew about a mile away from the front line, then rose above the horizon from a different point of the compass. The rugged peaks of Monte Greco held back the early rays of the rising sun and allowed the valley that contained Highway #6 to remain covered in a wispy haze. Plumes of smoke, white, brown and black, curled skyward in the morning air, indicating that the previous evening's interdictory shelling had hit pay dirt somewhere. Our steady barrages straddled the road and swept clouds of fire, debris and dust in huge rolling coils. Anything on or near the road was dead or immobilized. Ground observers were controlling the fire missions, and as soon as the relief plane waggled its wings, Keith and I returned to enjoy our morning British tea. During our flight, Rozen's air section had arrived and reestablished his lean-to next to the British tank. His cot stood ready; and Keith, being a man of style, donned his blue silk pajamas and settled in for a midmorning nap.

The stench of cordite and the shriek of shrapnel filled the air. In that instant, each of us sent up a prayer as we moved our bodies to make sure that we had avoided this latest greeting. As waves of concussion seemed to burst our eardrums, Keith yelled, "I'm hit!"

Captain Fane sprang into action and by the time our small party had crawled from cover, Keith's concern was centered on his pajamas rather than the severity of the wound.

"Take it easy with the silk," he barked. "They're the only pair I have. Pull them off, don't cut them," he ordered. Keith had been hit on the cheek of his right buttock, a long shallow cut, the kind that bleeds buckets of blood. We had no medic, but we did have sulfa powder and bandages. Bandaging a butt, however, had not been covered in our first-aid classes, thus presenting many opportunities for hilarity, once we knew that the bleeding was not in direct proportion to the severity of the wound.

"Keith, have a drink of my special on-death's-doorstep

scotch," I offered. "You deserve it." I wanted to be of some assistance until an aidman came.

"Not on your life, Schultz! You did this on purpose!" he accused me. "You had your German cousins shoot me so you could take my boots. Fellows, promise me, if I pass out, you won't let this Kraut steal my boots."

Geist used the phone to call for a medic and a stretcher, as we watched Fane wash and treat the wound. With great mock concern, we held learned discourses on how to bandage a butt. Most certainly the wound qualified for a Purple Heart, but how should it be phrased in dispatches describing Keith's service to his country?

"Cry your hearts out! I've got a million-dollar wound," Keith snickered. "Think how much fun it'll be to have this wound dressed by pretty nurses, not a bunch of dirty dogfaces. I'll be in the States by the Fourth of July, selling war bonds," he boasted. "Wait till people see my wound! Hey, I'll let them bet on the number of stitches in my ass and then charge them to see me drop my drawers to count." The ambulance finally arrived and the stretcher bearers hauled Keith away.

Keith's shell was the last shell to land on our field. The four Allied forces were linking up to trap the Krauts. Rome would soon be ours.

The battle to break out of Anzio had started May 23, 1944, at 6:30 a.m. The fighting was the deadliest and the most difficult of the European war. Two American Armies, a French Division, and a British Corps converged to annihilate the German Tenth Army. To perform this feat without killing our own with friendly fire required careful planning and observation. Air observation and radio relay was mine and *Janey*'s contribution to that Big Show.

The Third's first objective, to cut Route #6, was soon taken and we rushed forward to complete the link with the advancing Fifth Army from the south. Planes and pilots were performing efficiently and losses were light until the Germans were compressed into a small corridor and flak darkened the sky like a baby thundercloud. On May 27, 1944, the fifth day of the Anzio beachhead breakout, such a shamrock-shaped cloud enveloped and exploded around the plane of pilot Bill James and observer Lyle Jenkins. The plane fell from the sky into disputed territory.

The field phone rang. A change of objective had been ordered. Major Roberts of the First Battalion of the 15th Infantry Regiment had to go forward to contact his recon units. *Janey* and I were next up so we took off with our passenger. Once up, we discovered the radio channels were jammed so Roberts ordered me to land. I objected because the terrain below appeared to me to be unfit for takeoff, but he was in a hurry, so I put *Janey* down in a small strip of pasture beside Highway #6, the road to Rome. As the sounds of battle faded in the distance, Roberts commandeered a jeep and was off to turn his troops to meet their new objective. I attempted to fly out of the pasture but couldn't take off in the afternoon's light, warm air. I had to wait till morning for the heavy, cool dawn air to get the lift *Janey* needed to clear the trees.

Division vehicles were on the roads, and I was able to commandeer a weapons carrier to search for our downed plane. I found it lying on its back, stretched over a rock-covered, dry gully. It was a complete loss. Bloodstains spotted the passenger compartment, but no bodies were inside. I learned that one man had been killed and one badly cut, and they had been taken south toward Naples, not west to Anzio. There was no easy way to check on their condition, for they were now out of our unit's jurisdiction. The plane was hopeless. Its tail section had been shattered and stripped of fabric by the antiaircraft blast, its fuselage was bent beyond repair, and the 70-pound radio had ripped from its rear mounting. The radio must have flown through the cabin like a huge boulder. If anyone had lived, it was a miracle.

On June 4, 1944, Rome was ours. On June 5, Stein chauffeured me through Rome in the jeep. I was in an overcoat, my teeth chattering with the chills of malaria. I didn't feel at all like a conquering hero. That night I went to the evac hospital and on June 12 was discharged from the Naples convalescent sanitarium.

Three of my pilots were dead and two wounded. Two observers had been killed and two wounded. Kelly was still in Rome, but Jenkins might be on his way home. I decided to take a chance and visit the hospital where First Lieutenant Lyle Jenkins had been sent. He was still awaiting orders for the trip home when I walked in. Jenkins rocked back in his hospital chair and told me about the day the lights went out for him. Grinding pain had coursed through his body until heavy coarse hands had lowered him to the ground. Loud shouts and the rattle of friendly and enemy fire had filled his throbbing head until, sharp as a bee sting, the medic's vial of morphine had delivered its merciful oblivion.

"Schultz, what are you doing here?" he asked in the slurred voice of a man on strong pain killers.

"Came to see you," was my halting answer. I was unprepared to see this man in such broken condition. The administrative desk told me Jenkins was scheduled to be shipped back to the States within the week. This was good news, but when I saw the entire upper portion of his body in a wooden framework, surrounded by a plaster cast with only his left arm free from tethering, I nearly let out an audible gasp. Our eyes met with a compassion that's hard to explain, and as I shook his left hand farewell, our eyes moistened. There is no way to convey and explain the bonds that form among comrades in arms unless one has been to hell and back.

28 · *DRAGOON*

For the third time in fourteen months I paced the darkened stern of an LST, sweating the moment of invasion: 8 a.m., August 15, 1944. I would fly *Janey,* my L-4B spotter plane, above the invasion as our assault troops hit the beach at Cavalaire, France, for Operation Dragoon. We'd land in daylight, without the protection of dawn's misty shadows. My grasshopper would take off from our homemade mini-aircraft carrier, created from an LST by the Navy's resourceful Seabees.

The invasion fleet headed directly from Naples to Southern France. Three U.S. Infantry divisions—the Texas 36th, Oklahoma's 45th and ours, the Blue and White Devils of the Third —were spoiling for a fight. General "Iron Mike" O'Daniel had given me a direct order at the final briefing. "Schultz, you're the old man of this air section," he said. "Get in the air and keep a careful watch for yellow smoke. Let's get it right this time—no friendly-fire casualties!"

I knew what O'Daniel meant. This was the Third Division's fourth invasion. After-battle casualty reports had three times listed friendly fire as contributing to the gruesome toll. Exploding yellow smoke grenades were now the universally-understood signal on D-day: Cease-fire instantly.

French Resistance bands, French Commandos, U.S. paratroopers, Allied glider forces, and our own invasion troops would be landing on a crescent-shaped strip of land 13 miles wide and 3 miles deep. Our allies would have an abundant supply of yellow smoke grenades. The spotter planes would play a vital part in this mission. There were ten of them on board LST 906, and I directed the launch of those planes.

On our last afternoon in Naples Harbor we were saluted by a bulldog-faced man standing in the bow of a British Navy launch. He was smoking a big cigar and flashing a V-for-Victory sign as his vessel toured Naples Harbor. Having Churchill himself bless our attack fleet bolstered our confidence. We cheered him at the top of our lungs, and I raised my swagger stick in salute. But seared in my memory were the flaming vehicles suddenly abandoned on the beach and the torn bodies tumbled by the surf onto the sands of Anzio. I could never forget the price we had given in the blood of comrades to win that narrow strip of land.

The Third Division had suffered nearly a thousand casualties in one day, May 23, 1944, in its desperate effort to break the German grip on Cisterna and tear free of the Anzio marsh. That captivity had left us bitter. We reached Rome on June 4, greatly reduced in numbers, but still walking proud and eager to avenge Anzio. Now it was time to settle the score.

The Navy crew of LST 906 didn't welcome its new ten-plane cargo. There had been only three planes to launch at Anzio the previous January, and after completing that mission in three hours, LST 906 had sailed for home base by dusk. This new mission would require spending 12 hours or more as a highly-visible target off the fortified coast of southern France.

Although LST 906 remained offshore, beyond the range of shore batteries during the daylight hours of D-day, it held a steady course into the wind while we launched the planes. As a solo ship on the outer edge of the armada, the Navy crew feared their exposed position would attract special Nazi attention. They would be sitting ducks for German U-boats and E-boats. And because LST 906 would be cruising outside the protection of barrage balloons, beyond the beachhead's concentrated umbrella of antiaircraft fire and on the outer fringe of Allied fighter cover, some German ace might want to paint the symbol of a ship on the tail rudder of his ME-109. But the bitterest pill of all for the

Navy crew was that, during launch, the ship was directed by me, an Army officer.

During my hospital stay I'd appointed Lieutenant Fred Boucher to guide the loading of our ten planes on the LST. His diplomacy and experience in the military system made him the ideal man to be liaison with the Navy. An experienced Stateside pilot, Boucher had joined us as a replacement during the Anzio breakout, and he had been fired on during his first ride in *Janey*.

For Anzio, our three planes had been hauled to the docks by truck, assembled and loaded in a single afternoon. But for this invasion we became a circus act for the Italians living around the Naples harbor. We had to land our ten planes twice on the crowded pier—once for the practice and then for real. And it was hardly a secret operation.

Our practice launch had rated 90 percent. One plane was lost when an over-eager sailor inadvertently raised the barrels of the forward 40mm anti-aircraft guns just as the plane passed over the ship's bow. The pilot escaped injury, but got a saltwater bath and a chance to test his life vest. The plane sank.

Arranging the cooperation of the dock master, Navy Seabees, Navy hoisting engineers, Army Quartermaster troops, Italian civilian dock workers and the officers and crew of LST 906 was a monumental task for me. The dockside activity in full view of thousands of civilians made any thought of secrecy absurd. The only surprise would be whether we would land east or west of Marseilles.

LST 906 had been forced to spend ten nights moored to the pier. The Germans still frequently bombed Naples Harbor and extra nights at the pier were a trial for the crew, who were confined to the ship. Fear of dockside sabotage and shipboard theft required reinforced guard duty every night.

Our throbbing engines and churning wakes left little doubt that we were forming into battle order. As our ships gained way, darkness dimmed our view of Mount Vesuvius, whose smoke plumes had been a navigational guide for many flights. Sleep didn't come easily on deck, and below decks poker and crap games blossomed. We formed and reformed in clusters of twos, threes and fours, then dissolved into singles as each sought his own private space. The LST's fantail was my favorite spot. I could watch the effervescence of plankton bloom and fade in the trailing wake.

Self-doubts didn't dominate my thoughts as they had before other landings. But images of black smoke from an exploding munitions ship at Licata, the scream of a diving Stuka at Anzio and faces of missing comrades sabotaged my attempts to compose myself. I went below. When conversation lagged in the stale air and dim blue light, I made my way through the blackout protection to the clear night air, where I could review my last briefing instructions:

> 1. DIRECT THE NAVY 8-inch guns to fire on Cape Negre. Use smoke and demolition shells to knock out the German guns that covered our assigned invasion beach.

> 2. Immediately REPORT YELLOW SMOKE —the warning that we were firing on our own troops or French Resistance.

> 3. WARN THE NAVY'S SMALL-CRAFT CONTROL of underwater obstacles and offshore sandbars. Navy Air would be circling above to provide fighter protection and would have primary responsibility. I was to act only if asked, otherwise keep radio channels clear.

> 4. TARGETS OF OPPORTUNITY—I hoped some clearly-defined targets would show up or some of the ground observers would call for help. I wanted to direct the fire of the Navy 8-inch guns and give the Germans a bath of smoke, fire and shrapnel.

    5. RESPECT FRENCH PROPERTY—Identify all targets. Don't shoot first and ask questions later, as we did in Italy. We had assumed a house was hiding a machine-gun nest or a tank. We had directed fire on it, hoping to see a plume of black smoke. Now we had to be sure before we fired.

I vividly recalled flying above the canals and gullies south of Cisterna as several hundred of our Rangers surrendered at Anzio. Watching our guys march away under guard, while I was unable to fire a shot in their support was a feeling I didn't want to experience again. Soon the hum of aircraft engines overrode the sounds of the splashing waves as flight after flight of bombers roared in to scatter bombs on the Germans, who were waiting for us on the beach.

    Clouds of flaming debris rolled above the open water from the shore: American air power was performing at its best. Whooshes and booms shattered the morning calm as Navy rocket launchers and guns hurled their projectiles shoreward, leaving behind clouds of foul-smelling sulfide smoke and shock waves from the muzzle blasts. The noise was ours; the enemy was not responding. Our barrages were being fired to cleanse the landing beaches of mines, and the bombs were intended to destroy shore fortifications and to demoralize the enemy.

    LST 906 separated from the formation of huge gray ships and headed into the offshore breeze which dissipated the gossamer wisps of vapor from the face of the early-morning sea. From the ship's bridge, the captain shouted, "24 knots over the deck"—plenty of wind for a Cub to get airborne.

    Janey's engine started on the first spin of her propeller. Tech Sergeant Ted Royston's face broke into a broad smile. His plane had performed to perfection with the entire ship watching. I let the engine warm up as eager sailors held the struts. I revved *Janey* up to 1,800 rpm and checked both magnetos. Perfect. I depressed the mike button and said, "7:35 a.m."

    "Roger!" came the reply. The code sign had been exchanged with Division control.

Slowly I eased the throttle past 1,800 rpm. The sailors released their grip and off we went, racing down the deck. *Janey*'s wheels left the plywood with 20 feet of runway to spare.

A beautiful sight unfolded below as *Janey* climbed into the azure sky and headed toward the thunderclouds on the beach. Our armada was arranged in mathematical precision across the sparkling Mediterranean. Some ships were shrouded in smoke from their guns and rocket blasts. Others were surrounded by tiny gray dots that left streaming white wakes. Their small landing craft were scurrying into assault formation.

At midnight, eight hours before our H-hour, French Commandos had landed at the rocky base of Cape Negre and clawed their way up the narrow ledges of the 350-foot cliff. The heavy German gun batteries on Cape Negre were sighted to dominate the landing beaches and sea approaches to Cavalaire Beach, our objective. If the French raiders succeeded, it would give the infantry a shrapnel-free landing beach and the engineers would be free to clear the mines that our barrages and bombs hadn't exploded. My prime mission of the invasion was to assist the Navy in silencing the guns of Cape Negre if the French Commandos should fail. Watchful, I flew *Janey* toward the towering dark cliff of Cape Negre, growing bolder when I saw no muzzle flashes or exploding shells. I stayed out of 20mm antiaircraft range as I circled, and when I was over the crest, I encountered the friendly waves of celebrating French troops and the welcome sight of drooping gun barrels in blackened fortifications.

Viva la France! They'd done it! The French Commandos had wiped out the guns and crews! I radioed a message to the cruisers standing by, "Mission accomplished."

Looking seaward, white bow sprays defined the fast assault vessels as they sped toward the beaches in orderly waves. Geysers of water shot skyward when some of the lead boats triggered mines. A few boats became impaled on jagged underwater barriers. Line upon line of frail-looking landing craft rushed for the sand to discharge their loads. Crouching figures darted out as the boat ramps opened, a few fell in twisted positions at the water's edge. Plumes of sand rose up as land mines exploded, littering the battle site with dead and injured bodies. The Germans' mortar bunkers that had survived our preparatory bombardments began firing.

My radio contact checked in. "No bandits. Stand by." I had a grandstand seat to harrowing sights as I flew above the landing zones, witnessing scenes of triumph and carnage. We held the shore but were paying a price. Soon I saw the flash of our own mortars as we advanced to destroy the enemy's strong points.

The second plane off the LST was flown by Lieutenant Boucher. As I completed my first loop of the invasion beaches, I saw his plane clear the flight deck. Everything was on schedule. I would respond to the demands of the infantry divisions and Boucher would handle the Corps and Navy. The eight remaining planes on our mini-carrier would launch at intervals of one hour and 45 minutes.

The big German guns seemed to be on vacation. I'd been flying a routine evasive pattern, losing altitude by slipping turns, then regaining observation altitude by climbing as I flew away from the enemy. I watched warily for the tracer trails that had chased me above the beach at Anzio. None came after me. The Seventh Regimental Combat Team's beachhead swarmed with landing craft, disgorging supplies, vehicles and troops. The combined efforts of the French Resistance and Allied Airborne troops had cut communications. The Air Force's success in destroying transportation had disrupted the Germans' ability to respond to our attack.

A purple smoke grenade exploded to the west, signaling that Cavalaire, a small seaside resort, had been taken. Slowly I banked *Janey* into a turn and began gaining altitude to see over the land mass of Cape Lardier. As the 15th Regiment Combat Team's beach at Escalet came into view, a second purple grenade sent its column of smoke skyward. At H-hour plus one, both ends of the 13-mile beachhead were secure.

I pressed the radio mike button. "Smoke east and west at 9

o'clock," I reported.

"Roger. No bandits. Stand by," Base responded.

First Lieutenant Rosner, my executive officer, was the next pilot off the LST. Once he was airborne, my observation mission ended and with about 45 minutes of gas left, I needed to find a suitable landing site for six of my ten planes. The other four planes were assigned to the Seventh and 15th Regimental Combat Teams. I needed a field close to communication lines and capable of nesting six planes. Landing space along the Third Division's beach was nonexistent because the sand was swarming with men and vehicles. Level land between the beach and the seaside hills scarcely provided room for roadways, which were narrow and crooked, loaded with traffic and lined with steel latticework utility poles. *Janey*'s gas-tank float indicator was bouncing close to the bottom. I had to get down! The distant countryside beyond the shoreline seemed asleep beneath the tall umbrella pines. Barrage balloons along the beach steadily multiplied. If they had been multicolored instead of metallic gray, the beachhead would have resembled a carnival. Above the purr of *Janey*'s engine I could hear the scattered pops of our mortar rounds. Our dogfaces were firing their mortars to flush out the German machine-gun nests and snipers. Bodies were sprawled in grotesque postures of death along the roadways, behind walls and in flower gardens, indicating that much of the fighting had been bitter and hand-to-hand. Surrendering Germans were being marched to safety. For them, the war was over.

One last swing over the beach failed to reveal a good landing strip. I circled wider, passing over the seaside town of St. Tropez in the 45th's sector. I wanted a strip close to the beach with enough length to land and large enough for my six planes. Trees for hiding the planes would be a plus. A pink stucco three-story manor house was nestled at the apex of a broad, horseshoe-shaped stream delta about 300 yards from the coastal road. On either side of the entry lane, the level ground was newly-planted in a young vineyard. It would be a short, rough landing, but I could see no alternative. If I landed parallel to the rows, the straddled vines might rip the bottom of *Janey*'s fuselage. If I landed across the ridges, it might be bumpy and stand *Janey* on her nose. On either side of the field, however, we could hide three or more planes in the surrounding trees.

As I flew over the vineyard for a final check, the gas tank float stopped bouncing, indicating empty, and my full bladder demanded release of the Navy coffee. I had to land here. I cut the power and came in parallel to the furrows, my kidneys ready to burst.

The young grape vines bent easily and the berms were shallow. No sound of ripping came from underneath, but as I coasted to a stop, GIs ran along the roadside waving their arms wildly and shouting at me. I lifted my earphones to hear, "Mines! Mines!" I cut *Janey*'s engine and slumped in the seat, wiping my sweaty hands on my trembling legs.

"Don't move!" one shouted from the lane, enunciating very clearly. "You are in a minefield!" It wasn't the first time I'd wet my pants. "BA-1 in minefield," I broadcast to HQ.

I sat there in *Janey*, my butt protected by a pee-soaked parachute, two feet above a field of deadly booby traps. Sweat drenched my upper body but at last my kidneys were relaxed. Southern France is warm in August, and I was trapped in the middle of a hot sunny minefield that might explode any moment if some watching German flipped a detonator switch, or if an eager GI tried to help me, or if a curious dog came wandering by and tripped a wire! If a mine exploded within 10 feet, my chances were none; within 20 feet, slim to none; within 30 feet, slim at best. I was protected only by painted linen on three sides, an engine and gas tank in front, and a wet nylon parachute underneath.

Captains don't cry, but I wanted to. Twenty-three was too young to die, and I had bought a gift for my two little sisters back in Waterloo, which I hadn't mailed yet. Would those German cousins my Jewish buddy Keith Rozen always claimed I had do this to me? Had I come this far, survived so much, just to be blown to bits because a stray dog or cat's tail brushed a tripwire?

Or perhaps because a blowing piece of trash happened to lodge against a grapevine?

The hands on my watch advanced only thirty minutes in what seemed like an hour. Help was not coming. The 45th Division area I'd landed in was being crowded by the westward shift of the 36th Division. Heavy mining of the San Raphael beaches and underwater obstacles had forced a change in strategy. The engineers of the 45th were being used to clear the mined beaches. The clearing of the mines around a potential headquarters would have to wait. So I waited. On the subject of minefields, our manual stated: When in a minefield, stay quiet and wait for the mine-clearing crew. I wondered if the author of the manual had ever perched in a fragile shell of fabric and wood two feet above a gruesome death?

"Roz, I'm in a minefield," I radioed Rosner. "You're it."

"Roger, Wilco, good luck," Rosner's New York accent crackled over the radio. There was nothing more for him to say either. I was 75 feet from the line of palms along the entrance road, and I'd stopped 50 feet short of the low garden wall. Ten lines of young vines separated me from the entrance lane. I reached around to the map pocket behind my seat. Yes! my liberated Zeiss binoculars were there. I'd check each line of vines. I didn't know what to look for, but maybe I could spot something to help me escape this trap.

And there was something. With typical German uniformity, every other row had a wire running on the ground between the vines, made visible possibly by wind erosion. I had luckily straddled an unmined row, but the mine's trip wires were within a few feet of *Janey*'s wheels. As I scanned the vines again, I saw black blocks, each about the size of a half-pound of butter, lying on the ground about 10 feet apart, nestled close to the young vines. Thank God they weren't heavy-duty Teller mines, capable of blowing a tank or armored car to bits and sending shrapnel screaming in a 30-yard circle. Exposed TNT blocks were bad, but only if you were right on or next to them.

As I looked out the other side of my plane, I could see

another twenty rows of vines where the same configuration existed. The clear space between the vine rows seemed to be about 7 feet and *Janey's* wheels had rolled safely almost 300 feet in a straight line. The Krauts must have been depending on trip wires, or had they possibly sweetened the deadly mix with wooden shoebox mines? I yelled to a GI on the road and asked, "Seen any mines explode?"

"No," came the reply. "We only saw the trip wires and wanted to warn you," shouted the busy GIs. "The engineers should be back soon." My alternatives were to stay in the plane, lie down between the rows or crawl the 50 feet to the stone wall. I pondered the options and my responsibilities, but it was my responsibilities that forced me to a decision. I cocked my earphones so one ear was covered and I could get some idea of the invasion progress. Then I heard a faint "Mayday." It was Boucher. He had to ditch because of engine failure. I had to get back into action, wet pants and all.

I yelled to my roadside comrades that I'd try to crawl to the wall. They said the area behind the wall had been swept for mines and flashed me a Churchill V. I crept gingerly out onto one of *Janey's* wheels and threw the 2-foot by 10-foot white landing panel across the fuselage to form a cross, a warning to other planes. Now the moment of truth. I would have to place a foot on the ground.

The bare ground between the wired row and the clear row looked undisturbed. With my helmet, binoculars, pistol, aid kit, and canteen, I lowered myself to the ground and crawled on my belly in a frog's swimming stroke. It was slow, dirty and hot. Prayer came with each breath and thanks for each explosive block I passed. At last I could see the low wall ahead. What had been in the German's mind when he set the trap? Would he have planted a shoe-box mine at the end of each row, or at the end of the trip wires, or was the entire mine field controlled from some distant hidden dugout?

The moment of decision couldn't be delayed. I scrutinized the texture of the dirt, searching for any irregularity. The dry alligator-skin soil indicated that water had stood at the row's end until the combined effect of sun and wind had turned it into vapor. That could have taken days—a positive sign. Should I get to my hands and knees and move forward three more feet, stand erect, make one leap and pray? I'd clear the wall. If I did, I'd present a large target for an exploding mine.

Crawling the last three feet seemed to take forever. But, with one more prayer, I stood, made a long leap and landed face-down on the grassy terrace behind the wall. Cheers from the dogfaces on the road interrupted my prayers of thanksgiving.

The manual said: Stay put. I'd broken the rule but now I walked in the sunshine, ready to get back into action. My problem now boiled down to getting transportation to the Third Division beach and arranging some way to keep track of *Janey*. The Wire Sergeant of the 45th's 180th Regiment told me the manor house was scheduled to become headquarters as soon as wire connections could be made. "I'll watch your plane if you'll give me a ride," he promised. "I had six hours of dual-engine training before the draft caught me."

I agreed, and he agreed to drag *Janey* to the walled end of the field as a sign whenever the mines were cleared. Then I'd come and fly her out. I walked to the road to hitch a ride.

Our two combat teams were rapidly moving inland to secure the first day's objectives. Headquarters hadn't established its base for the evening but had relayed contact with Rosner. He'd selected a strip about 2 miles inland, beyond the seashore ridge line. Since he liked long fields, I felt confident he wouldn't put us in a box. The roads were busy, so I held out my thumb, and at last a bunch of footpounders stopped to give me a ride right to the edge of Rosner's field. Now that I was with my own unit, I found a radio-equipped jeep and made a beeline for the map coordinates Rosner had given me. He was right on the button and indeed the field had good potential. At H-hour plus four all was going well: one plane totaled, two on the ground and two in the air, and the Luftwaffe hadn't paid the beachhead a visit.

29 · *SIGHTSEEING SORTIE*

The surrendering soldiers coming out of the trees and ravines were an unusual lot for German soldiers, short, young, fat, skinny, or old. As they approached we could see they were not Germans, but Poles, Russians and Balkans who perhaps joined up as an alternative to a forced labor camp. There were very few German noncoms, and no officers. The enemy resistance had been scattered and listless, and these prisoners were glad to be in our hands. They could expect no mercy if they fell into the hands of the French Resistance.

With Rosner's radio we reached other planes in the air to assign targets. With relish I reported "Mission accomplished" to the Battalions and Divisions. The beachhead air cover wove a protective net overhead and the steady flow of traffic moving past our airstrip gave us a feeling of strength and security.

Our L-shaped pasture airstrip paralleled the west side of a hard-packed gravel road for approximately 600 yards. The short leg extended west along a low stone wall for about 400 yards, gradually rising as the pasture blended into a vineyard with 4-foot-high mature vines loaded with pea-sized green grapes. The legs of the L were 200 feet wide, giving us ample side clearance to land even in heavy crosswinds. Proximity to the road and the cork trees along the stems of the L made this field a perfect place to land and hide our planes

But when would the Germans counterattack? We needed Geist's radio car to give us the power to reach past the pine-crowned ridges that surrounded our valley. The first ground crews were to follow the regimental combat teams. Our only contact would be by radio. I started getting a little anxious and felt a lack of control. One battalion of artillery with its two planes had been assigned to each combat team to provide close-fire support, hoping for some rapid pursuit of a retreating enemy.

Our sixth plane radioed, "Number five down."

"Number two OK," Rosner responded.

Rosner knew we couldn't wait for the ground crews to gas a plane, so he went to the road to bum some gas from a passing truck. We'd chamois it ourselves. But our safety cushion was gone! The plane was lost. Later that night we learned the pilot was safe, but we were now down to three operational aircraft. We'd been prepared to lose two planes, but now with 60 percent of daylight still remaining, some planes would need to fly two or three missions this first day.

Planes seven, eight, nine and ten left the LST 906 without mishap. The lack of enemy resistance made us wonder what the Germans had up their sleeves. The prisoners were talkative, but we hadn't captured an officer high enough in rank to have information regarding the sector's defensive or offensive plans. I took the 16:00 mission. It was my turn anyway, and I wanted to fly over the mined vineyard and check out *Janey*.

The highway below us was clogged. Men were marching in the ditches and along the edges while two lines of vehicles tried to move on a one-lane road. The infantry battalions had added armored, self-propelled guns, which were fired by their own ground observers, lightening the burden of support formerly required of the artillery. My mission, therefore, became merely radio relay and checking on a few bridges for ambushes and buried mines. If a German flak wagon had appeared, it could certainly have clipped my tail feathers, but either nothing was around or it was letting me pass. Most bridges on the narrow roads were still intact or only slightly damaged. We kept rolling on. Where were the Big Guys we had fought from North Africa to Anzio? Were they on the run, or were they preparing an even bigger surprise for us?

The valleys were broad, with vast stretches of deep-red soil that resembled the red hills of Oklahoma. Some fields were a fertile brown where they had been freshly turned, and every valley sported green and beige patches of crops. The lower slopes of the palisades were brown and green with trees and scrub growth, accentuated by the straight lines of the well-tended vineyards. The surrounding cliffs ranged from charcoal-gray to caulk-white. One could easily imagine the prehistoric sea covering these mountains and the wave action that carved the caves and grotesque shapes into the hillside. Wind, rain and sun had worked their wonders to create a fantastic vista.

Farm houses outside the villages wore terra cotta roofs modulated in color patterns resembling decorative Indian corn. I could imagine the progress of the family that had started with a small square house, then added a larger rectangular barn, then another house and then another shed or barn forming an L or a U or a square farmstead that had become rooted in the floor of the fertile valley.

My wristwatch showed that it was time for a radio check. I had hoped for a certain answer and got it in Geist's reply: "Stand by, no bandits." Since the day the Messerschmitts hit us behind the lines at Cassino, Geist had figured out a way to listen in on Air Force warning systems. Being able to monitor their channel gave us an added margin of safety.

The enchantment of the clear blue sky and the slanting rays of the late afternoon sun made me glad I still had an hour's worth of gas and could extend my mission to enjoy my first unhurried flight over La Belle France. To placate my guilt for goofing off, I looked for hidden antitank guns or machine-gun nests, thereby justifying the need to fly low and around each building. Many were covered with a pale beige stucco that had been troweled to a smooth surface that reflected the sun and seemed to light the surrounding valley floor.

Gray buildings were the most common, and from an altitude of 800 to 1,000 feet they appeared uniform in color, but as

I flew lower I detected three distinct surfaces. From only a couple hundred feet I saw sharp shadow lines on sides of the buildings where the mortar had been eroded by the forces of nature while the building withstood the passing of centuries. The gray stones used in the construction were the size of home-baked loaves of bread and were laid as nature created them. At some point in the early history of Provence, skilled masons began trimming stones. The trimmed stones, in addition to the mortar joints tooled flush with the stones' surface, resulted in a uniform light-gray finish.

Other buildings appeared constructed of huge slabs of dull, white marble with black veins, but upon closer inspection, flying by at 50 to 60 miles per hour, I saw they were light-gray plastered surfaces with streaks of black or mildew-stained cracks around the windows, under the eaves, and over the doors.

I flew on to check on *Janey* before the golden-red rays of sunset yielded to the purple shadows of dusk. When I flew over the ridges to St. Tropez and circled the 180th Regiment HQ manor, I saw that *Janey* had been pushed back against the garden wall and the young vineyard was now serving as a ration dump and truck park. The mines had been cleared out, and I planned to come back for *Janey* in the morning. One last radio check announced my coming in, and again I heard Geist's report: "No bandits. Roger, out."

Rosner had selected a good field. Though it had a slight tilt, it would serve our purpose for the coming night. There had been no fire missions but plenty of bridge checks and radio relays. My brief sightseeing sortie had passed unnoticed. I gave a debriefing report and marked our map with a couple of potential fields for the coming day. We'd close the day with three planes on the DIVARTY field ready to fly at dawn, on August 16, 1944. *Janey* would be back in flying rotation as soon as I'd completed the dawn flight and retrieved her from the 45th's sector. Four planes were on special duty with regimental combat teams. We had lost two planes but no pilots on our D-day, August 15, 1944.

30 · *CHEERLEADERS' SKIRTS*

The gentle bleatings of farm animals, a slight chill in the air, and a mist rising from the ground greeted the dawn of our first day in France. During the night, Ed Hill had arrived to fly as my observer, and today we would use Rosner's plane. Schumacher's careful attention to Rosner's plane made it pleasant to fly, and it started on the first turn of the prop. Roz, like me, didn't want anyone else flying his plane, but we were all used to sharing when necessary. As I climbed into the plane, I reassured Roz, "I'll baby her for you; she'll never know she was up!"

The sun was just beginning to clear the ridges to the east, and plumes of smoke rose, momentarily spreading out as they lost the power of heat to drive them skyward. As far west as we could see, the smoke pattern stretched like beacons, telling us how far our advance had taken the Division's forward elements during the night.

The Division's first mission after securing the beachhead was to cut the enemy supply routes north of Toulon and Marseille. The trail of fires gave us clear evidence that we were well on our way to accomplishing that mission. Hill and I analyzed the smoke to determine which were cook fires, identified by white smoke, and which were burning military vehicles, identified by belching black smoke. We hoped the black smoke was all German. As we flew a couple of hundred feet above and beside the road, it became evident our dogfaces were riding on anything that moved, and they were moving fast.

If German bandits showed their faces today, they would be

blasted into confetti. Our 40mm pompom AA guns were hidden in groves along the roads, and the .50-caliber flak wagons manned by black American gunners were parked on side roads. Vehicles were spread out at specified intervals and the ring-mounted .50-caliber machine guns on all trucks were uncovered and manned by alert, trigger-happy troops.

Sideward glances told us the French Resistance must be doing its job. Fires smoked in the small settlements along the main route and several cars were burned out, indicating the enemy was on the run. We were flying over the Seventh Regimental Combat Team's march route and their pace was brisk. They were the men of Truscott Trot fame. Since I had no direct mission and our radio contact checked out, we decided to fly the entire length of the column until we reached the Recon Troop tanks. Once on the ground I'd report the map coordinates to the Division command post. The next decision centered on either staying low and risking flying over a pocket of German troops with machine guns or flying above the surrounding hillsides for an expanded view and becoming a potential target for 88s or marauding bandits. Day in and day out, low is safest, so I flew low until Ed and I spotted the lead tanks.

I climbed to 1,500 feet in a gigantic circle so we could see far beyond the dust clouds of the probing tanks. No burning vehicles. That meant we weren't running into roadblocks protected by antitank guns—a well-concealed antitank gun always seemed to get one or two victims before we could destroy it or bypass it.

As we started home, the upcoming report started to form in our minds. At the rate our troops were moving, any airstrip picked now would be useless by noon and our moving would only slow down the vehicles that really needed to use the narrow hard-surfaced roads. I'd recommend that as long as we had good radio links, we should stay put until early afternoon. Ed made notes on gun and supply stations we flew over, plus the farms and villages where the FFI (Forces Francaise D'Interieure) had displayed crudely-painted sheets to identify their CPs. We had seen paratrooper groups and they all seemed to be moving with a purpose and merely gave us friendly waves. All stops were open; we were marching to victory. When I approached the strip to land, the Ninth's Big Bangers were still limbered to the prime movers. It was obvious that the point of our Division ranged more than 10 miles beyond our present position.

I'd flown over to the 45th sector and seen activity around the pink manor house, so my first order of business after briefing Rosner was to have Stein pick me up in the jeep. We headed for St. Tropez to retrieve *Janey*. The jeep trip along the beaches and over the seaside mountain roads proved slow and nerve-racking. Supplies were rushing westward, and we had to go east against the grain. At last we passed through the 45th's checkpoint, on our way to *Janey*.

The wire sergeant of the 180th, the one who had promised to keep an eye on *Janey*, was relieved to see me. His unit was moving out at noon and he didn't want to leave *Janey* alone. I renewed my pledge to take him for a spin in the air someday.

Stein filtered only four gallons of gas into *Janey*. I'd be taking off short into still air, and I didn't want any unnecessary weight. Stein and the extra gallon of gas had to stay behind. The wire sergeant rounded up a crew to clear my takeoff path, and after an exchange of V signs, *Janey* started bumping across the vineyard. Truck traffic of the past twenty-four hours had mashed the earth like a well-packed parking lot. As soon as I cleared the road, I banked *Janey* sharply, kept her nose down and her engine at full rpms, committing one of the cardinal sins of flying—a low downwind turn—but I couldn't risk flying through that forest of barrage balloon cables.

Barrage balloons were an early feature in the grand show of any invasion and a regular feature around our supply bases and ports. The balloons were sent aloft as soon as possible to discourage visits from the Luftwaffe, and were set at staggered heights. Any minuscule mistake while flying near the balloons could mean death for a pilot. Even the cables tethering barrage balloons were equipped with explosive charges so that, in a collision, whatever didn't get sheared off or entangled would be blown to smithereens.

I nursed *Janey*'s airspeed at 60 mph while completing my 180-degree turn and was soon able to gain altitude as I flew inland into the wind. Everything below me seemed to be moving north and west: tanks, men, and heavily-loaded supply trucks with the added cargo of dogfaces hanging from the sides like spaghetti ready to fall out of a bowl. Someone must have really chewed ass, because convoy discipline was now very evident. Vehicles were the regulation 50 feet apart, evenly spaced. General Patton would have been proud.

I needed to get back to our landing strip near Collobrieres but couldn't resist the temptation to watch the show below me. Not carrying a full load of gas limited my gawking, however. When I finally landed *Janey*, I appreciated Rosner's choice for a field. The texture of the hay stubble cushioned *Janey*'s wheels, retarded bounce and made my mediocre landing appear perfect.

The latest news greeted me. We'd lost a plane, saved the pilot, killed some enemy—and the plane might be repairable. Second Lieutenant James R. Smith of the 77th Armored Field Artillery Battalion did it all. The 77th had been attached to the 15th Regimental Combat Team for the invasion. Smith was number seven off the LST and had completed his mission of observation and radio relay. The sun's rays streamed through the top of his wind screen as he approached the landing strip that his ground crew had staked out on a broad stretch of cleared beach. Something, perhaps the sun's rays, had distracted him, and the inshore breeze blew him into a barrage balloon cable. Like magic he was spun 180 degrees around the cable and flew off like a wounded duck. Sergeant Howard B. Nickelson of the Third Signal Company witnessed that "Believe It Or Not" encounter between the Cub and the booby-trapped steel cable:

> I was the photographer sent to take photos during the landing at Cavalaire. I wasn't on the first wave, but after the infantry landed and secured the

beaches I landed. After taking several photos, I noticed a Cub headed toward the beach from the sea. He was, I estimate, 1,000 feet above ground and I believe he was making a pass over the landing strip for a look-see. Prior to that the 36th Engineers had dozed out a short strip several hundred feet above the beach. I didn't see the strip because I was busy along the beach. The Navy had anchored a barrage balloon in line with the strip. The Cub's right wing hit the cable about half way up, and the plane slid along the cable until the force broke the balloon from the cable. The plane made a tight part circle around the cable, flopping and tipping and miraculously freeing itself. The pilot miraculously got it all put together, got on even keel, circled and landed on the strip. A neat bit of flying. The story amazingly had another rather unfortunate ending. Barrage balloons have a charge tied to the cable that detonates on contact. When the cable came flying out of the sky, it landed close to a tree where some German prisoners were sitting. The charge detonated, killing or wounding several of them.

By noon of the second day, we were still racing through the valley and Artillery had not fired a shot in anger. Stein, always eager for a trip to the rear to enlarge his trading network, had been standing by, anxious to get going. I left Rosner in charge and headed for Division Headquarters. I might have to go all the way back to Division to get Top Brass guidance on how to respond should the 15th ask for a replacement plane.

Narrow roads were easier to navigate than those ruled by General Mud, but only slightly, especially after the surface had been pulverized into a mire of face-powder-fine dust. Everybody on the road looked like an outlaw from the Old West with a handkerchief over his face to filter out the churning dust.

DIVARTY deferred my question to Division and told me there had been a call for me to go to Division anyway, so I'd get my guidance there. Another mile in the dust bowl suited Stein just fine because we weren't far enough back to find decent trading goods. Division Headquarters was Spartan, merely tents among the low branches of gnarled cork trees in various stages of being stripped of their bark.

Lieutenant Colonel Grover Wilson met with me as soon as I arrived and wasted no time expressing his dominant concern. He wanted to know when and if we could fly far beyond the road network and search every terrain feature that might possibly hide a large body of troops as well as light and heavy tanks. It just seemed impossible that the Germans were giving us so much ground. We needed insurance that the pockets of troops we were bypassing were not the teeth of a trap. Memories of our first days on Anzio had not faded.

Wilson wanted a flight later in the afternoon. I was instructed to channel any request for the transfer of a plane from my unit to the 15th through him. He didn't like the fact that we'd lost three planes so far. He got a hearty laugh from Smith's airborne circus performance and was pleased that Smith had escaped injury. I assured the colonel we were trying to repair our barrage balloon wound. The mood and timing seemed right, so I asked if I could have all Press flights cleared through him too. He agreed, relieving me of another burden that I'd let get out of hand on Anzio. I walked down to the supply area and, sure enough, Stein had a trade going. Much to his regret, we had to head back to our strip, which was now so far behind the lines we couldn't hear small-arms fire.

A familiar figure was standing by the command post tent as we drove into camp. "When are the replacement planes coming?" Fred Boucher asked, without hesitation or embarrassment. "My *Sad Sack* is totaled for the time being and I want to get flying."

"I don't know," I responded. "Can we salvage *Sad Sack*? I heard she looked like a wet noodle when they pulled her out of the sea." Fred was taking a lot of ribbing for dumping his plane. A common joke was: "*Sad Sack* gets the Purple Heart and all Boucher got was a bath."

I had Sergeant Reis round up the pilots for a briefing. "Fellows," I reported, "Division is darn leery of the speed we're moving and think this may be a trap like the one the Germans pulled on the Rangers when we advanced toward Cisterna at Anzio. The foothills leading to the valley floor have dozens of ravines, and they want us to give each one a good look. Be especially watchful for roads of any type. It'll be risky. I don't know if we can do it from 800 feet, above rifle range, or down at 300 where we'll be easy targets. I'll fly Wilson up a few of the valleys myself and see what he thinks, but this is his request and he'll be on top of these missions.

"To make this work we'll have to pay careful attention to our maps and let Geist know which ravines or trails we're following. We'll get a master map and number the draws so we know if there are roads leading into them. Any questions?"

"Can we get air photos?" asked Second Lieutenant Robert Peterson, our newest replacement pilot.

"How about large-scale maps?" Lieutenant Virgil Dahms asked, remembering the maps we had on Anzio.

"I say we make two passes," volunteered Bill Boyer, the observer from the Ninth Field Artillery Battalion. "The first pass high to separate the girls from the boys and the second one low enough to look up the girls' skirts."

"After I've gone up with Wilson and know what he's expecting, I'll let you know." I responded with a chuckle. "Until then, Boyer, you're in charge of the low passes."

Just then the colonel pulled up in a jeep, and after brief introductions, he and I climbed aboard *Janey*. I pressed the mike button and asked, "Any bandits?"

"Negative," responded Geist.

That brief exchange wasn't lost on Wilson. He knew that the higher we flew, the greater the danger we faced from any ME-109s and FW-190s that might sneak in below our fighter cover. The first part of our flight path was due west, and the sun would favor the enemy if they dared challenge our Air Force and come in high from the sun.

Colonel Wilson wanted to see what could be seen from high and low, and it was my job to fulfill his wishes. As we flew over the finger-like low ridges that fanned onto the valley floor like the pleats of a cheerleader's skirt, it became evident that many could be discounted, for they were too narrow or steep for vehicles and void of foliage. Some had ample foliage to hide troops but were isolated from the valley floor by deep waterways and didn't even have goat trails for access. We spotted several valleys with features a lurking enemy would appreciate: trees, narrow roads, low stone walls, and brush-covered berms that could hide a large number of troops and equipment. Wilson marked those locations on his map. We'd check them out, he said, as we flew east, back to base. Fear of radio interception presented a problem. We shouldn't identify the coordinates of suspected locations over the air; but if we were downed, the information would be lost with us. I suggested that for today we assign odd numbers to the valleys west of our base and even numbers to the valleys east of it. The colonel agreed. We marked forty "skirt pleats" when we descended to 1,000 feet for the trip home. The colonel checked other low-level spots before the light began to fade. At 200 feet we saw sheep, goats, cattle and horses that had been tied out to escape the plundering Germans. In one major valley the rural road, lined with stone walls, seemed a perfect hideout. I was afraid to follow it, but it ended harmlessly in a small animal enclosure. We drew a blank as to where the Germans were hiding.

It was a lucky day. I landed *Janey* without a bounce and as the colonel left the plane he thanked me for the ride and said, "You'll be hearing from me, Schultz." As Wilson's jeep drove away, Stein grinned from ear to ear. "I hope we see more of him," he remarked. "His driver's from Philly and has some good connections." Two days in France and Stein already had his trading network organized!

My briefing to the pilots outlined what we had seen and how we could add a factor of safety. If we made the low-level passes at the end of missions with one plane high and one low, it might bluff marauding bandits into believing that if they shot at one plane, the other plane would spot them and bring retaliation.

The battalions were operating as separate units in support of the Regimental Combat Team. One of the four battalions, the Ninth FA Battalion, was shooting the Big Bangers, 155 howitzers. Having the 75mm Tank Destroyer and Armored self-propelled 105mm howitzers directly attached to infantry regiments and battalions changed the role of the spotter plane.

A Tank Destroyer and a Self-Propelled 105mm looked the same from a distance, so both were called TDs, for Tank Destroyers. A TD could stop on firm ground, fire a smoke shell in the direction requested and within two to three minutes follow the ranging shots with a dozen deadly air bursts. The thick steel sides of the gun carrier vehicle offered good counter battery protection to the gunners. In contrast, our regular artillery pieces required 10 to 15 minutes to fire the first shot and provided very little protection to the cannoneers. In a rapidly-moving situation where seconds counted, the TD became the weapon of choice. The infantry loved TDs because they stayed alongside them and could parry the thrust until the four-gun batteries or twelve-gun battalions could join the battle; thus TDs reduced the demand for the spotter plane.

Fred Boucher's *Sad Sack II* was pulled from the sea and deposited on a jetty. Some parts were salvageable.
—*US Navy*

31 · *MASSACRE*

In the first two days in southern France we had covered 20 miles, and that pace continued on August 17 and 18 until we ran into company-sized resistance at Brignoles. Until that fight, the Ninth hadn't fired a shot. We overcame the roadblocks and by August 20, we controlled the road hubs surrounding Aix-en-Provence. For three days our Division command post occupied Aix while we regrouped and consolidated our positions. By August 23, Allied forces had cut the German supply routes to Toulon and Marseille and crossed to the North bank of the Durance River. Now the East bank of the Rhone opened before us. Why had the Germans let us come this far?

The French Resistance fighters, motivated by four years of Nazi domination, brutality and atrocities, fought with every weapon at their disposal. The Germans lived in fear of being captured by the Resistance and refused to surrender to those vengeful French fighters. Many small German outposts, therefore, were wiped out to the last man. Even battle-toughened SS noncoms feared the FFI, and small parties of German soldiers readily surrendered to the first American who fired on them.

Even the infusion of experienced Wehrmacht noncom and junior officers didn't halt the retreat of the 19th German Army. Twice our footpounders were loaded onto trucks and, in two motorized marches, they covered over 150 miles, bypassing countless defensive positions the enemy could have manned with a minimum of disciplined troops and extracted a fearsome toll before they withdrew or surrendered. Daily we gave thanks for the combined effectiveness of the Air Force, who denied the Germans daylight mobility, and the French, who turned their nights into hell.

Tank Destroyers proved their worth in battle; however, we weren't fighting the Tiger and Panther tanks of the Goering Division. Perhaps because Patton was rampaging through northern France, the Germans had to dispatch top-quality war materiel there in an effort to stop him. Very little forward recon was required from the Air Section. Our daily patrol flights kept us ready for the German counterattack, if it came.

Our replacement planes hadn't arrived yet, and to the older pilots' chagrin, we had to allow our personal craft to be in the daily rotation. If everyone felt as possessive of their planes as I felt of *Janey*, there were some smoldering fires of resentment, but we had to do it. Lieutenant Fred Boucher had lost *Sad Sack II* and could hardly wait to get *Sad Sack* painted on number three, but I didn't mind when he flew *Janey*. He had more experience than most and had a nice light touch, as evidenced by his smooth landings.

Late in August, Boucher took *Janey* to fly the dusk registration missions with his favorite observer, Sergeant Joe Jones of the 41st FA Battalion. The low voices coming from Geist's daytime speaker always kept us informed as to how the missions were going if we cared to pay attention. That August afternoon, all seemed well until, after the last registration, I heard the code name for Lieutenant Colonel Davis of Seventh RCT requesting a bridge check. I ran to the radio to reject the order because of the lateness and the low light level, but I was too late. Boucher answered, "Roger. Wilco. Out." I looked at the sky. Maybe, just maybe, enough light reflected from the gray stone and chalk-white bluffs surrounding our valley, and besides, I didn't want to make an ass of myself by aborting the mission a lieutenant colonel had ordered.

A few days before, the main valley floor had terminated

into smaller valleys like the space between spread fingers, today the ridges leading from the valley floor looked like pleats in cheerleaders' skirts. The darkness seeping up from the valley floor gave the hollows between the pleated ridges a shadowy sameness. Boucher should have more than 30 minutes' gas, enough to complete the mission and do a little searching for our home gully. Fifteen minutes later, Geist shouted above the murmur of the loudspeaker, "Boucher wants a flare."

"Send *negative*," I shouted back. I didn't know what to do. I wanted to buy time.

"I see him," yelled Bill Richards from across the field where he had been idly listening. "Tell him to swing 90 degrees port."

"Ninety degrees port, two minutes," Geist broadcasted, adding his own mileage estimate.

"Get lights ready," I ordered. Now the entire section was listening anxiously. Boucher dipped *Janey*'s wings, indicating he'd heard and would follow the directions. I could see the bright Coleman gas lantern in the kitchen tent being lit, a couple of warm glowing kerosene lanterns were going, and out of tents came some forbidden unmasked headlights fastened to radio batteries. Even Geist brought out his elaborate truck light, which was powered by a truck battery.

In the dimming light of early dusk, the Coleman lantern seemed as bright as the sun. We felt certain it had alerted every German within cannon range. It was immediately shrouded with canvas.

"Another minute," coached Geist. *Janey*'s wings dipped again. Seconds stretched into hours until at last Glenn shouted at the top of his voice, "Lights!"

All of the lights came on at once and we heard Boucher sing out, "Gotcha!" Immediately, the lights went out again and back to their hiding places, but we started to sweat. Had the Germans been watching and listening? Would they send over a barrage of 88s as a thank-you for the impromptu sound-and-light show? We heard *Janey*'s throttle cut back and she rolled to a stop near the command post tent. Boucher bounded out of the plane, threw his arms around me, nearly squeezing my breath away. "You saved our lives, you saved our lives, Schultzie, you saved our lives!"

I stood speechless, proud of the way the men had responded to the emergency, but knowing that I had only been a bystander. "It took the whole Air Section, Boucher," I said, "especially Geist! We were with you all the way, and we're happy to have you back—and *Janey*, too!" I hoped the Germans were asleep. The noise of celebration for having the lost sheep back inspired the cooks to make extra coffee before dousing the stoves, for they knew this would be another night of story telling when we had finished listening to the music of Axis Sally and the enlightened commentary of Lord Haw Haw. The enemy must have been busy retreating because their 88s didn't reply.

Second Lieutenant Paul J. Matthews had joined us at Brignoles as an observer on August 18. Robert Peterson, who flew for the Tenth FA Battalion, picked him up. They flew into our field about an hour before our excitement and concern over the lost plane. Matthews's first ride started with a scary takeoff between slanted pointed poles in a valley floor, a greeting, called "Rommel asparagus," prepared by the Germans to gore glider troops. Now he had seen the lighter side of Air Observation. Today the Tenth Battalion, as part of the Seventh and 30th RCTs, would be starting a wide motorized swing to help spring a trap on the German 19th Army that was squeezed on the east side of the Rhone River and could not be supported by the main body on the West.

Montelimar was to be the choke point. Air Force strafing and bombing had isolated the German 19th Army in a long corridor. Now it was the ground soldiers' duty to pull the trigger. If the plan worked, it would pave the way for a junction with Patton's Army and visions of being home for Christmas.

Dawn sent its first slivers of light along the eastern horizon and soon layers of orange, pink and yellow defined the distant ridge lines and outlined the tall, umbrella-topped trees. To the west, flashes of mortar bursts followed Route #7 north of Montelimar. The infantry had immobilized the Germans while waiting for the Third's Big Bangers to join the destruction. The Ninth's 155 howitzers, directed by a ground Forward Observer, had started a rolling barrage with a mix of white phosphorus and high explosive. The 105mm howitzers were moving closer, for it now appeared certain that a Panzer attack couldn't be launched from the trapped forces.

Tricks have always been part of German fighting. Veterans of the Third knew that a destroyed tank might be manned and serving as an above-ground pillbox. A flak wagon in a ditch at a crazy angle and blackened with soot could come to life and swing into action, and 88s with burned tires might suddenly send projectiles of shrieking death down a road. The enemy had to be stomped to death, and even then you'd better give the corpse a wide berth.

As Paul Matthews and I flew above our bursting mortar and artillery shells, we kept a sharp lookout for armored vehicles or pockets of troops that might have fled the main roadway. They could be lurking in ditches and behind stone walls, screened by brush and trees. I relished directing a pounding onto a trapped enemy column, for I not only feared the potential of the German soldier, but it gave us all a chance to avenge Anzio. Let the Germans suffer a thousand casualties in one day. It was their turn; we were just evening the score. The hills surrounding Route #7 provided the ground FOs a good elevated view, and the Air Force had isolated a 15-mile stretch of road by destroying bridges. Now a combined Army-Air operation was destroying the bulk of the German 19th Army.

Rosner had relieved me, with Matthews as his observer. The merging of our Division's units on a broad front promised to be a sight to see. Task Force Butler, unleashed at St. Tropez fifteen days ago, had cut a wide path on our right flank. Butler had reversed the old route Napoleon had taken to invade Italy, and Butler's rapid advance helped create in the Germans a series of panic-driven decisions that helped spring that trap. Good news abounded. The 45th Division started toward Grenoble and resistance evaporated. Now that the Third had re-formed on a consolidated front, our next move would be to load the infantry into trucks and move in giant leaps.

I flew a midday mission with Pete Smith, preparing a new registration on the north end of the stalled German column. The autumn heat and the bright sun shining through the smoke of battle emitted a sickly-sweet stench of death mixed with the obnoxious odors of burning rubber and oil. Shells continued to rake the roadway until fires had burned out and white flags were flying from every building and gully. We still watched for Nazi tricks. Some might surrender, while others prepared an ambush. Fanatical SS troopers might have their own plans for us. But when I saw the horses, I knew the Germans weren't trying to pull any scams. Only twenty-seven months before, I'd been in seventh heaven riding Prince, my favorite mount, in the 1942 Christian College Spring Horse Show. I spent many happy hours in the saddle at the University of Missouri, too, and now I was directing fire on these helpless, innocent creatures.

Our barrages into the tree-lined gullies and fence lines flushed wounded horses out into the open spaces. As they ran through the patchy shrouds of smoke, trying to flee the fire and hot steel shards, they dragged what I at first thought were leather reins but on closer inspection proved to be uncoiling intestines. The injured horses staggered and fell to the ground, writhing in panic and pain, whinnying and squealing piteously. I wanted to yell Cease-fire! This wasn't fair! But we had forced the Germans to move with horse power; now if we were to stop them we must either capture their horses or kill them. And if we could see the horses dying, we knew that in the cover of gullies and trees, Germans were dying too.

The French peasants would make short work of the horses. The carcasses would be stripped to bare bones as soon as the shelling stopped. In Italy the horses would have been butchered before the smoke cleared. Red meat was a precious commodity. The people had been hungry for years and were opportunists by default.

Even at 800 feet the sweet stench of burning flesh and smoldering hair from animal and human bodies caused my skin to crawl. It conjured up bitter memories of our road from Anzio to Rome. Our patrols were mopping up as prisoners emerged from hiding. Fires still smoldered and an occasional grenade or artillery shell burst, sending a fountain of shrapnel skyward.

My final flight of the day followed Route #7 northward into the 36th Division's sector. In the dimming light, the route became a line of flaming colored gems, modulating in size and brilliance, belching puffs of putrid smoke and the horrible stench of the battle into the air. I was flying the Division photographer, Captain Robert G. Reeves, above the carnage at near-stall speed as he tried to record the scenes on film. The sun dropped through the battlefront haze to a thumb's width above the horizon. Holding his nose, Reeves tapped me on the shoulder and shouted, "Too much stink, not enough light. Let's go home."

"Roger," I responded, giving him the thumb and fore-finger OK sign. All planes headed home when the sun was a thumb's width above the horizon. When the sun sank below the horizon, a pilot's depth perception was cut in half. *Janey* didn't need another Boucher-type landing.

Janey's side window and door panels had been removed to give us better observation, a nice way to fly as long as the weather cooperated. However, when I landed on wet grass or muddy fields, the rear-seat passenger got a bath. As the weather cooled I gladly sacrificed clarity of view and reinstalled the top window half of the door for its protection from the rushing cool wind. But on that day in August, I was glad the panels were missing because the rushing wind of the slip stream purged the stench of death from the cabin.

As *Janey* rolled to a stop and turned toward the tree line

surrounding our field, a brilliant green light momentarily blinded me and bathed the cabin in green. Geist was eloquently pointing out that he had our signal light working. Twenty-four hours ago, we had desperately needed a signal light we could aim like a gun. Fortunately, we had survived its absence, but now Glenn had it working and ready.

"Good going, Glenn," I yelled as *Janey*'s engine stopped. He and I had an unspoken secret: We both had failed in our duties the night Boucher had to land in near darkness. I should have read the code-of-the-day message that was delivered in the wee morning hours, at considerable risk to the messenger from infiltrators. If I'd read the message, I'd have known the color of flare I could have risked firing when Boucher asked for our location. Geist, as radio and signal chief, should have had the signal light ready. Luckily no one suffered, not even one of the planes, but we realized how our lack of preparation had nearly caused a disaster. Photographer Reeves thanked me for the flight and promised some pictures if they turned out. They would be great mementos of the day Anzio had been avenged, but I shuddered at the thought of seeing those innocent horses suffering forever in his photos.

The massacre was not yet over. That night we began a bold thrust as our footpounders were loaded onto trucks to begin two motorized marches that covered over 150 miles, by-passing countless ideal defensive positions. An organized enemy could have manned the terrain features with a minimum number of disciplined troops and extracted a fearsome toll.

More good news greeted us. A replacement L-4B was waiting at St. Tropez, and of course Fred Boucher knew it long before I landed and claimed it as his *Sad Sack III*. As long as he believed it to be an accomplished fact, and Rosner had volunteered to fly Fred to pick it up, why should I interfere? The Air Section somehow ran itself well without me.

Ninety miles in one night had to be a record. As I landed *Janey* from the dawn mission 60 miles north of base field, it seemed the Germans were completely demoralized.

32 · *DEJA VU*

Our 90-mile advance through enemy lines would have turned Rommel green with envy and left Jeb Stuart doubting his ears. Although the dawn mission filled me with apprehension, the smell of victory perfumed the air. Major Karl Connor of the Ninth FA Battalion had ordered First Lieutenant Joseph Bucholt to scout 60 miles north of our base to a point near Lyon. There Bucholt, who normally acted as executive officer of a firing battery, would establish a reorganization point for stragglers and a repair and gassing depot for the Ninth's vehicles. Joe liked flying and air observation. On Anzio he and I had fired many missions together. The dangers of this mission were understood. Realization that the Krauts had broken contact with us had not sunk in. The first day, we expected a fortified roadblock or a tank-supported hundred-man counterattack somewhere. But they hadn't counterattacked, and we were becoming both complacent and worried.

Dawn's first light crested the eastern hills and gave the earth a rosy glow. Flying on such a day was pure joy. Smooth, dense, misty morning air slowly released its grip as light emerged from the countryside, fulfilling the promise of another day. Our fears vanished as we soared above the sleeping ground. We were immortal. From our perch above the commotion, we watched the world come to life to begin another day of killing. I circled the still-smoldering carnage at Montelimar, once again to savor the revenge of Anzio, then we headed north above waving dogfaces. They were riding in trucks for a change, and I wished for a camera or that I had Old Blood and Guts as a passenger. Although we hadn't seen any ME-109s or FW-190s in days, convoy perfection were the only words that described the scene below. Our properly-spaced vehicles contrasted with the wreckage of a disorganized German convoy burning out of control. It exemplified the classroom lesson on convoy control: Proper vehicle spacing insures survival.

I had drawn the route we'd fly on a large-scale road map for Rosner. If we didn't find a suitable strip at the end of an hour, I'd take the next major road for 5 minutes toward Lyon and the 36th Division, which was on our left flank. We were moving past our detailed maps, and it might not be possible to radio map coordinates even by relays back to Division. The follow-up planes must be on the lookout for our white landing panels within the one-hour-and-five-minute terminus zone.

Below us on nearly every crest, a .50-caliber flak wagon had pulled off to give the march route protection. The side roads were alive with recon jeeps probing the farmsteads. FFI, painted in crude white letters on civilian vehicles of all descriptions, appeared as if by magic. Small clusters of farmers stood along the roadway waving up to us. Tanks made their crescent-shaped scars as they turned in the cultivated fields. Division wanted to be on the constant ready for the counterattack and confuse the German antitank guns, which we assumed were hiding just around the next bend. The K-7 self-propelled 105 howitzers were intermixed with the infantry trucks to give immediate heavy support should they meet resistance that required more punch than their mortars and bazookas could deliver. Our land forces were an awesome, seemingly invincible, sight as we moved forward.

Narrow scraggly hedges and low stone walls defined the roadways in the undulating fertile valleys. Trails engineered by animals and broadened by centuries of use made their way up the craggy yet gentle hills. Eons of Mother Nature's crafting had formed this countryside into a truly pastoral setting. *Vendange*, the French word for harvest, would soon begin, and the golden glow of the countryside foretold a harvest waiting for the local farmers, not Nazi occupiers.

The pockets of resistance and hidden 20mm flak wagons that we feared might catch us unaware had not materialized. Joe and I received several missions to explore bridges and villages for activity, but after we had hesitantly approached the areas, we left, feeling rather sheepish. All we could report were FFI cars and waving people. A motivated German or satellite soldier could make the Swiss border in a couple of days if he hid at night and wore civilian clothes.

We left Lyon behind us. I flew *Janey* cross-country 160 miles in two days toward Besancon, where the pace slowed and roadblocks appeared. Each bend in the road became an ambush site. Demand for air-directed missions increased, and radio relay dominated our flying time. ME-109s and FW-190s didn't appear, and the 20mm flak wagons must have returned to Germany or went up north to fight Old Blood and Guts.

The infantry circled Besancon. Another albatross, like the giant white monastery on top of Mount Cassino in Italy, stared down at us, and like the Italian monastery, the 200-year-old fortress of Besancon had a commanding view of everything that happened in the valley and everything that moved around the bend in the river. It had to be neutralized, its guns silenced, before traffic could move safely north and east to our next objective, Vesoul.

Four smaller fortresses ringed the main fortress, providing protection from ground assault. They were overcome by the guts and courage of dogfaces. As I flew through the picturesque valley above the chatter of small-arms fire, it looked a simple task to blow the fortress out of the way. But our flat-trajectory, high-velocity 105mm shells exploded against its sides and merely sent up a shower of chips that cut tree branches or raised dust. The air was crisp and clean, and luckily for us, the 20mm flak wagons had moved farther east, so at our leisure we were able to use the 155mm howitzers as mortars and drop the 6-inch shells into the fortress courtyard.

We shot a lot of shells, but only a few burst in the inner yard. A 155mm shell wouldn't explode consistently at extreme elevations. White flags didn't appear when the dust settled, so something else had to be tried. A close-in bombing mission could be the answer if it could be arranged in a timely manner. But an Infantry Division is a proud unit and likes to handle its own problems its own way. We quickly realized that this albatross had a vulnerable point. It had been constructed of heavy blocks of gray and brown local stone laid without mortar, and its entry port was closed with a heavy steel door. Because it was nestled into a hillside only a couple of hundred feet above the valley floor, its steel door provided an inviting target.

After careful consideration and maneuvering, a single new M-1 155mm howitzer we'd been using since Anzio was bore-sighted to shoot super-charged delayed-fuse projectiles at the steel door. Shell after shell slammed into the steel door. The stone arch doorway exploded with a *krumm* and a cloud of evil-smelling cordite smoke, but no visible damage resulted. As always, it was up to the infantry to start lobbing 81mm smoke and high-explosive shells inside the walls. After an afternoon of heavy 100-pound shells slamming against the door and a night of shrieking shrapnel and choking smoke within the walls, white flags appeared. The troops that surrendered were tough experienced soldiers, but the noise that reverberated within the fortress was more than they could stand.

We were soon passing through the gateway to the Vosges Mountains and on to the Rhine; we thought we'd be home for Christmas.

33 • *THREE STRIKES*

I was required to visit Headquarters and DIVARTY, but it was a mere formality. We were expected to support the 15th Regimental Combat team, but the replacement planes hadn't come. I'd wait one more day and then fly back to trade a couple of Lugers and get one by bypassing the system. I had no hesitations about bypassing the system and avoiding its attendant Brass, chicken routines and screwball ideas. And working with the system had nearly proven fatal.

Captain Mike J. Strok of Air Force supply had almost killed me in Italy. I had been sent to Strok to have bomb racks added to *Janey* to give our grasshoppers an expanded mission. His crazy modifications of *Janey,* which theoretically would enable us to drop food to the knife-happy French Moroccans and string wire to our pack mule artillery units, were best left to theory and not field experimentation. It was a happy day for me when a Secret Air Bulletin finally brought an official end to Strok's suicidal inventions. I hadn't received any medals for flying with his modifications, but I felt I deserved at least one.

As Stein drove toward the radio car, my sixth sense told me all was not well. Gloom spread across Bill Richards's normally cheerful face as he relayed the facts.

"We believe Boucher and Alpert are down," he reported. "None of the FOs saw it happen and there hasn't been any smoke. Fred has been out of gas for two hours, and no radio contact. I've checked with the 41st and they didn't give him a mission. We haven't heard from the infantry yet. When I get up I'll fly his sector to check the roads and pastures. We haven't alerted Boone yet."

Richards moved up another notch in my esteem. His report had been right to the point and his actions were proper. If something happened to Rosner, either Boucher with his varied flying experience, or Richards with his field experience would make an excellent replacement.

We had been on this strip for three days, and it was wise to avoid a consistent landing pattern. Our pasture was about two city blocks long by two hundred feet wide, surrounded by vineyards and scrub trees on three sides. Low palisades to the east of the Dours River formed the eastern boundary. Wind currents from the palisades were not affecting our flying because the early September weather in central France was balmy.

Boone dropped in over the tree line shortly after Richards and his observer cleared the ridge line to the west, then turned north toward Vesoul, our Division's next objective. Boone's landing brought nods of approval as he taxied past us to the sheltering tree line. This was a good soft field, but we were too far back and today we'd move again. I alerted Geist to have everyone ready to move by midafternoon.

Boone's report didn't shed any light on Boucher's location. In fact it added confusion because the 41st had asked Boone to relay a couple of radio messages that Boucher should have handled. Boone's flight pattern had been below 800 feet and he had followed common procedure by not flying past the lead tanks or recon vehicles. He hadn't been asked to look for *Sad Sack III*, and he hadn't.

Second Lieutenant Warren T. Reis, who three months before had received his battlefield promotion from staff sergeant, was on deck for the next flight. I pushed him up a half hour early and hoped we'd soon have Richards's report. But Richards's flight had been very routine. He flew all five routes north and observed the countryside in the bright midday light, but there was no sign of a plane in the trees or on the ground. Roadblocks of fallen trees were holding up the advances and

Bill's aside, "We aren't fighting the *Hitlerjugen*," made today's upcoming move sound dubious.

Fortified roadblocks on hillside roads are easy to defend, costly to remove, and the artillery cannot truly blast them away. It takes a dogface, walking or crawling through a minefield and avoiding trip wires, to fasten a chain to the obstacle to pull it clear. The muffled sounds we continued hearing were definitely the sharp cracks of the German 88s or 57mm anti-tank guns trying to hold us up.

"Glenn, get me the 41st on the phone if you can. Hold on the move order, just be prepared. Don't strike the canvas," I said with regret. I'd seen singles and pairs of ME-109s in the distance. With most of our AA protection with the infantry far ahead of us, three days in one location might invite disaster. I wanted to move out of there.

First Lieutenant Joseph L. Bucholt, a recent Stateside replacement with the Ninth FA Battalion, happened to be our newest observer. I decided to take him along on my search for a new strip as part of the next regular patrol flight. While waiting for me to get ready, he examined *Janey*'s patched skin.

Rather than narrate tales of blood and thunder, I passed the patches off by commenting, "You just can't be too careful when you use branches to hide the stars and glass." It seemed a satisfactory explanation to him.

"We'll be doing some low-level field dragging if I see a couple of long pastures in the 15th's area," I continued. "I want to find a strip that has vehicle tracks or animals grazing, so we don't set down in a minefield. You watch for gullies, rocks and wet spots. Tap me on the shoulder and point if you need to get my attention onto something. I'll watch the tree lines for clearance. We make two drags before we land, so even though I slow the engine, we won't land till the third pass."

"OK, I understand," he replied. "Let's go." Bucholt was eager to get airborne even though we were 15 minutes early. I had him click the mike button. He nodded when he got two clicks back, a signal that the radio was on and working. Corporal Vince Romeo, Geist's assistant, stepped from the radio car and threw up his hands in exasperation, indicating he hadn't made the phone connection to the 41st.

To show off, rather than call for Croal or Schumacher to prop *Janey*, I stood with my left shoulder lightly against the engine cowling, my right foot wedged under the right wheel, and, with my right hand, I pulled the prop around to the second compression spot. I reached in the cabin and turned on the magnetos, moved my left hand to grasp the cabin door frame, then with my right hand I spun the prop with a fast downward pull. *Janey* coughed into a steady purr. Joe's smile of admiration told me my showmanship hadn't been wasted; he hadn't seen that done before. My secret allies, Croal, Schumacher and Royston beamed with pride. They knew a little guy like me could do that trick only with an impeccably-tuned engine.

A waggle of the wing and Reis headed back a little early, reporting, "Dull, over, out."

Joe pressed the mike, "Roger, any mission."

"Standby, out," chimed in a third voice, and we were on patrol. If this mission proved fruitless and I found on my return that the 41st had not called in with information about Boucher and Alpert, I would have to report them Missing in Action.

Our advancing front moved against the geographic shape of a spread hand facing our northward push and into its crooked fingers. Two rocky, barren hills and two small ridges covered with dense growth joined a forested plateau, split by a broad river valley. The bright autumn sun made observation crisp and clear. Sunlight would flash off the windshield of a downed plane, and the brilliant colors of the landscape would contrast with the olive-drab canvas of a Piper Cub.

Roadblocks took their toll of lives as Germans stoutly fought from them in terrain that definitely favored the defenders. We flew between each widely separated finger as far as we could see our vehicles. *Janey*'s altitude bounced from 600 to 1,000 feet. I dived her to the deck as we approached each visible roadblock, fearing that armored flak wagons might be part of the Germans' deadly defense. The attack was stalled. The infantry Forward Observers were in control and I hadn't seen a single field that we could safely use.

Joe made a couple of radio relays and our time was about up. As Rosner approached and gave us a wing waggle and a radio check, he said nothing about SSIII (*Sad Sack III*), the code I'd given Geist.

I climbed to 1,500 feet, partly because as CO I felt I had to make an effort I wouldn't assign to others. I wanted to give the area a good search for our downed comrades, and I felt like giving Joe a special treat.

Janey always had the best of care, so without hesitation I made a second climbing full-throttle pass to 1,800 feet and then pulled *Janey*'s stick back into a reduced-power full stall. Next I let her fall off to the right into a three-revolution spin, losing about 1,400 feet. I felt guilty about showing off, but it was fun and I knew it would be confusing and possibly taunting as hell to the enemy. Some overeager Nazi might even report he'd got a Cub with his pistol if he had happened to shoot in our direction during a spin. This was Bucholt's first ride in a small aircraft. The smile on his face and his loud laugh expressed joy, but he didn't tap on my shoulder and yell, "Do it again!"

We headed home. I landed and went to the radio car, but the news was still the same. No report on Boucher and Alpert. Richards and Stein were gone now too. Apparently they went to 41st HQ to get direct contact and to report what Richards had seen. A likely story! I knew they were loose in Besancon. I was peeved that they hadn't asked my permission to go, but I was anxious to see what booty they'd bring back.

The sounds of battle remained the same. I called up DIVARTY to check for any special orders; we were to stay on schedule. I rang the Tenth FA Battalion and, after a long delay, left a message for Captain Tanner to call. There was still a faint hope that for some reason Boucher had landed at their field. Boone followed Rosner for the dusk flight. Sunset flights were in demand for they were dazzlingly beautiful to watch.

Ed Hill flew with me the next morning, September 9. As we flew north to the roadblocks that had stalled yesterday's progress, we had no doubt they would be cleared. Darkness timidly gave way to streaks of yellow and orange light along the ridge lines to the east and a rosy glow tinted the hems of the clouds that hovered over the ridges. Smoke from bursting shells obscured the main roadblock, and traffic wasn't moving north. All roads were void of traffic. We were stalled.

"Ready. Over," were Hill's only words, just to let them know we were in radio range.

"Standby, loud and clear. Over. Out," a ground station replied. Out indicated they didn't want additional conversation.

Piloting *Janey* in the smooth morning air was exhilarating, and as I climbed in a twisting pattern of figure eights from a low of 300 feet to a high of 800, I hummed the "Skater's Waltz." I still didn't want to risk flying between the valleys. The heavily-forested ridges might be hiding enemy stragglers or infiltrators.

"Bandits! Bandits! Bandits!" shattered my reverie. I immediately dived *Janey* to the deck and turned right. Trees whizzed by, level with the wind screen.

"There," shouted Ed, pointing over my shoulder to the black puffs of 40mm antiaircraft shells exploding about a mile south of us, just about over our air strip. "Not after us." I stayed low, however, and we watched the trucks below us swing their .50s around to follow our path. They were our allies if whatever it was came after us. Our mission time would soon be over, so I cautiously climbed out of hiding to get enough altitude for valley-to-valley radio range. I was ready to get back to base for hot coffee and to read Division's orders of the day and perhaps hear news of Boucher and Alpert.

Ed clicked his mike and we got back two clicks, a signal that we still weren't needed. The relief plane finally appeared in the distance. As it waggled its wings I could read BD, the 39th FA Battalion marking, not BB, the marking of Boone's plane. Something was wrong. As we came in low from the south and

I cut *Janey*'s power to land, trucks and the twisted wreckage of a plane were about 400 feet past the end of our runway. One vehicle had Red Cross emblems. I dreaded landing. I didn't dare stop *Janey* on the runway and run to the crash site. No pilot ever blocked a runway or left his plane in the open, so I taxied to the closest trees. Before I had time to cut *Janey*'s engine, Stein was already there with the jeep to take me to the crash site. "Boone and Boyer are dead," he shouted. "An ME just came out of nowhere and got them just as they lifted off."

The bumpy ride to the crash site was over in seconds, but a flood of memories scrolled before my eyes, documenting the nine fun-filled months Boone had been with us. In January, fresh from the States, he taught us the words to "Paper Doll" in the aircraft crate we called home in Naples; in March, on Anzio, he stopped four Tiger tanks and landed *Janey* in no man's land; in July in Naples he tried to teach what he called the Texas national anthem, "San Antonio Rose," to his new Italian friends; in September, in France, he inaugurated the Gold Dust Twins Firing Team of Boone and Boyer. Those two loved to fly together and had entertained us all. Now their blithe spirits were gone. The 20mm cannon of the ME-109 had been thorough. Death was instant and the Cub destroyed. The ambulance left and we returned to the radio car in silence.

I knew as I bounced through the dust to DIVARTY HQ that I'd ask for a couple of .50-caliber flak wagons of our own. We often ended up with only our single truck-mounted .50s as protection. Possibly the morning's attack would make our need a priority. General Sexton, with his connections in Washington, might be able to get special consideration. I asked for flak wagons immediately, while the need was painfully obvious.

On September 14, clouds once again clung to the horizon. The first rays of light broke through about 30 degrees above the earth. The masking of the sun's early rays acted as indirect lighting and gave the earth a warm glow. Each dawn had its unique entrance. Too bad we had to use that time to spot the muzzle flashes of German guns so we could destroy them and their crews. It was our last day at Vesoul. On the dawn mission I spotted three prospective fields, two within our new lines and the third just a valley beyond our lead tanks.

"I'll check the fields and lay out panels if I lose radio contact," I told Rosner when Stein and I left for the morning briefing by jeep. "Be prepared to move early afternoon."

"Bring back eggs," shouted Corporal Bill Burkhardt, our cook, as we drove past the kitchen area.

Once we got accustomed to finding fresh supplements for our canned rations, it was hard to subsist on just plain C-rations. Stein had brought the spare cases of ration and water with us, and we were all set for trading. For the invasion, my jeep had been equipped with a passenger-side pipe-mounted .30-caliber air-cooled machine gun. It would give us something to do if we were strafed, but it was mostly a psychological prop. It would be a puny response to the 20mm cannons of the ME-109s and FW-190s. As we left the DIVARTY area, I chambered a round and was ready to shoot. We drove up the road behind the infantry to check the fields. Stein pulled into a farmstead to complete our prime mission—find some eggs. Lucky for us, only a light tank sat in the yard. A small patrol had moved on through, so the barn could be regarded as virgin territory. Stein cleaned the place out and I got a report on the infantry movement. They'd met no opposition since dawn.

The first field we checked looked good. It had a gradual downhill slope to vineyards and low fruit trees on two sides. It could be a backup field if the advance stalled. The second pasture, although narrow, was long enough and had plenty of trees for hiding planes.

With the dogfaces lounging all around us in the dry road ditches, we moved forward to check out the pasture in the corridor ahead. The sounds of battle were only the distant rattle of small arms. The platoon leader had radio contact with the Sherman tanks well past the pasture I prized. Cattle were grazing in the field, a sure sign it was not mined. The closer we got to the pasture the better it looked, well grazed and smooth and parallel to the road. Small clumps of brush edged the far side. We topped a small rise in the road and I asked Stein to stop while I tried to get contact with our patrol plane. I'd just pressed the mike button when the SNAP–SNAP of small arms fire broke the morning calm.

My eyes darted to a clump of bushes in the far corner of the field and I jammed the trigger of the .30-caliber down as Stein backed off the rise at impossible speed. My finger froze to the trigger. My eyes were fascinated by the string of streaking tracers until they started digging dirt from the ditch beside us. Stein frantically turned the jeep around and sped back to report the action to the patrol leader. We'd had enough of checking out fields ahead of the infantry for today.

Long and narrow are not bad characteristics for a field, and with trees to hide the planes, the second site was a good choice. I walked the field and laid out the landing panels. The trip home was slowed by tanks and guns moving forward.

For the second time in a week, men were standing around the radio car, and that meant bad news. In a valley west of where I'd fired nearly a full box of .30-caliber slugs into the bushes, a 20mm German flak wagon had brought down the Ninth's second plane. Lieutenants James W. Carter and Joseph L. Bucholt, his observer, had been slightly wounded and had been evacuated. With great skill and presence of mind, Carter had squeezed his powerless craft into a small rocky field. If we could haul the plane out, replace the engine and patch the fuselage, it would fly in a couple of days.

From the mess tent where a crowd gathered, Stein waved his arms, motioning for me to come over. "Where did you learn to pack eggs?" Burkhardt asked with mock indignation as he showed me a handful of straw dripping with raw egg. "How can I make hot cakes with this?" he teased.

I'd always been secretly proud of the way Stein packed his foraged eggs. The C-ration cans had been moved to the ends of the wooden German ammunition box we'd lashed to our bumper. Packs of straw protected the eggs from the bottom and ends of the box, and as extra padding against jolts from pot holes in the road, handfuls of straw pressed the jewels in place as the lid closed. But that time Stein's work had been in vain!

"I risk my butt searching that barn and you let my work turn to mush, Captain," Stein chewed me out. His using the title of Captain threw me off guard because I didn't think officers' titles were in his vocabulary.

"You nearly get us killed, now look at this!" Stein continued. He was holding court, and his teasing provide relief from the despair and tension a week of casualties had brought to the Air Section. I had to play along.

"Ye Gods!" I exclaimed, as I peered deep into the box and saw the splinters. We'd been hit by a couple of bullets.

"See what Schultzie and I risk for you guys daily!" he reminded everybody within hearing distance. The expedition had been more than we'd bargained for. Both of us said a silent prayer of thanks for that narrow escape from an unseen foe.

Three strikes and you're out is the way baseball is played, and we'd had our third strike. We had to move. That particular field seemed to be cursed. The need for replacement planes was critical. I'd been unable to provide observation for all the missions called in for several days. The L-5, with its greater power, lost its advantage when it had to operate from postage-stamp fields. I needed L-4Bs, and I had to send someone to make two flyable machines from the four disabled airframes we had. I could do it. I'd done it for Devol in Sicily and Italy. If I had a long suit, aircraft repair was it, but I hated to let dispatching go to Rosner. Tanner could dispatch, but I'd sent him to fly for the Tenth FA as they supported the combat team.

The crashing thunder of enemy artillery heralded the dawn of September 15, indicating the full fury of a battalion or regimental-sized counterattack. Was it the enemy's last gasp or had they really dug in to halt our race to the Rhine? Our agenda for the day was set.

34 • *DEMOTION*

Third Division foot cavalry stormed ashore at St. Tropez and raced up the Rhone River Valley 100 miles to Montelimar, where we encircled two complete German divisions, destroying over 4,000 vehicles and taking 23,000 prisoners. Escaping our trap, the 11th Panzer Division and the 198th Reserve Division were fleeing ahead of us for the Vosges Mountains. Division reconnaissance units were in hot pursuit, for we did not want to give the Germans time to dig in.

Infantry FM radios were not well-suited for operation in the valleys of the Vosges because their range was limited to two or three miles and line of sight. To rectify that problem in fast-moving situations, L-4Bs would go ahead to establish radio relay links or visually identify forward positions and report on conditions. As our reconnaissance units moved farther and farther into the hills and valleys, chasing the Germans back to their homeland, more of our flights involved radio relay links.

Impossible landing conditions were destroying the substance of my air section, both in planes and pilots. Infantry commanders used our planes as air jeeps to leapfrog ahead to the advance points of their troops and recon units. We landed knowing full well that we'd have to dismantle the plane's wings to get it to a road for takeoff. But despite the hardships, those were heady days. Everyone was humming "I'll be Home for Christmas," and we really felt we'd beaten the Germans. Nevertheless, I still wanted to bring our section up to full strength. We were down to one L-5 and four Cubs.

We were still five planes below strength the day I got an urgent call from Division staff. "Schultz, Major Scott's on his way to your airstrip. Be ready."

Scott had an urgent mission. Our four air-worthy Cubs, one of which was my *Janey,* were in the air, and the L-5 was on the ground. Scott would get to ride in the L-5, and since I was the only pilot available, I would fly him. Major Scott described his encounter with me and the L-5.

General O'Daniel said to me, "Scott, get up to the airstrip, get an artillery plane and go find the Third Recon. If they've got clear sailing, I want everybody moving."

So I went to the airstrip in my jeep and looked up Schultz, the chief observation pilot. I also looked at the airstrip with some puzzlement. It had a definite downhill list to it, with a 4-foot drop-off about halfway along. There was a brisk wind blowing down the hill.

"I think I can make it downhill," Schultz said. "I'm game if you are."

"No choice," I replied. "I have orders to find the Third Recon."

We climbed into the plane, an in-line two-seater called an L-5 and strapped ourselves in. Schultzie revved up the engine and started downhill.

We never got off the ground. At the far end of the field was an orchard, and we flew right into it with our wheels never leaving the sod. Schultzie was skillful enough to guide the plane between two trees, which neatly clipped off the wings, and the plane nosed over and plopped into the soft earth.

The Third Division Air Section was now down to four L-4Bs and the Germans had dug in their heels. Our advance might be held up long enough to haul a couple of planes out of small

fields and patch a couple more. Then we would be up to eight
flyable Cubs. We were without an L-5 until the Colmar Pocket,
when Operation Horsefly proved the L-5 invaluable for both Air
Force-Infantry support missions and general artillery work.

Storm clouds had gathered around my command, yet I was
unaware of their potential for damage. After all, I was a brave
young captain marching against the Germans with the Third Infantry Division, the Blue and White Devils, the fightingest,
toughest Division in the entire U.S. Army. I didn't have time to
concern myself with minor details like managing, delegating responsibility, and using the talents of my men more effectively.
After all, we were fighting a war, not running a business. Lessons
had always come hard for me, and during the slugging match
against the Germans in the Vosges Mountains, I was forced to
acknowledge that I had neglected to learn from lessons offered
and to reflect on their full meaning.

We were in the foothills of the mountains and had at last
caught up with the retreating German troops. My air section was
widely scattered. Four of the ten planes were down, their carcasses being guarded against scavengers by our ground crews.
Two other planes had been knocked out of the sky. One pilot
and his observer were still considered missing in action because
their bodies had not been recovered and we had not received
notice of capture from the Red Cross.

Twice in the last two days I'd been unable to provide a
plane for a mission. I had pilots but no planes. Planes were a
function of Supply and not under my control. That morning I'd
asked the 41st FA Battalion to allow Captain Tanner to return to
DIVARTY control. Tanner had been flying L-5s and L-4Bs for
the Fifth Army for several months. For the invasion of France he
had been placed in charge of the artillery planes that were ferried
to Corsica and arrived at the beachhead on D-day plus three. I
requested two replacement pilots. Tanner was the first to arrive. I
sent him to help the 41st, which was fighting in a remote sector.

Lieutenant Rosner was looking for a forward field, or at
least something better than the uphill, downhill, gully-ridden

rock patch we were using. Lieutenant Richards took over operations while waiting for Tanner to fly in with his precious fourth plane. I was bleeding from a one-inch cut above my eye, probably caused by loose flares flying around the cabin of the L-5 as Major Scott and I flipped over. I wasn't really hurt, but the bleeding wouldn't stop. Holding a bandage to it did no good, for adrenaline was coursing though my veins and I couldn't sit still. I couldn't spend the rest of the day holding a bloody patch to my eye. "Stein! Get the jeep and take me to the aid station," I reluctantly ordered. "Bill, take over till Rosner gets back. I'll be at Division Aid," I shouted as we left the area.

Fighting was light and, fortunately, no casualties were coming in, so I was the only patient that afternoon. The medic sewed me up quickly and suggested that I lie down for a short time while they filled out the Purple Heart data. Proudly and foolishly I announced, "No Purple Heart for me. This is not a wound. I could have scraped my head getting out of the plane in a hurry." But I was asleep before my head hit the pillow.

When I arrived back at the Air Section a few hours later, Tanner was there waiting to take the next mission. I had to report to HQ, so after a brief check on the situation, Stein and I were on the road, hoping for a good meal and word of new planes.

Recently-promoted Lieutenant Colonel Chris Coyne motioned to me as we drove into the narrow boulder-strewn ravine sheltering the Headquarters trailers and radio cars. I went directly to him and saluted, then we walked past the Headquarters shelter to the yellowing folding camp chairs that had always marked his location since the early camps in the cork forest near Rabat, Morocco.

"Sit down, Schultz. Are you badly hurt?" he asked. I assured him that only my pride was hurt and, now that the bleeding had stopped, I'd fly in the morning.

"Schultz, we're placing Tanner in charge of the DIVARTY Air Section. I feel you've let it get beyond your control by not using all the capabilities you had at your disposal." Without more than a short pause for breath, he continued. "You're a good officer, but young. You need to serve in the executive capacity and learn to delegate. I'll recommend you to a Higher Headquarters, as an executive officer. You've served your time with line troops.

"In a Corps or Army Headquarters, in an executive capacity, you will eventually be in line for promotion to major," he continued. "However, Tanner and I would like to have you stay with us. You'd be a great help to Tanner. Think it over for a couple days." He rose to his feet.

I knew it, the Army system got me! I could tell the minute I saw Tanner that he was not only older, but he out-ranked me, and in the army, rank means everything. Norman G. Tanner had been commissioned in the spring of 1937 and had been a captain for more than three years. My commission was dated June of 1942 and I'd only been a captain for three months. No matter what they say, rank will get you sooner or later.

The GI grapevine is extremely efficient. Stein knew the reason for my visit and respected my silence as we drove back to the airstrip. Soon everyone would know. During the last several days, with the loss of my air sections' substance, I'd grown irritable with the men, barked orders, and groused over minor matters. Would they celebrate, now that Schultz had been sacked?

I didn't want to stop at the radio car. Two hours before, it had been *my* radio car, but stop we must. "Any messages, Glenn?" was my guarded question.

"No." Geist replied. "Tanner's still up. How's your head?"

Chitchat was normal as we fished our warm cans of C-ration from the cooling water and washed down the boring food with the ever-present coffee. Tanner was on a long mission, so I went to my tent. I needed to be alone. Tanner was flying *Janey*, my plane. Was he going to take over everything? A second cot and bedroll were now in my tent. Well, it was a two-man tent. What did I expect?

My eyes were wet, but I stretched out to rest. I was dozing when Tanner came in to set up his cot and lay out his bedroll. Our first words were awkward and guarded, but we shook hands and he repeated Coyne's words, that I could be of great help to him and the whole outfit if I'd help salvage the planes we had left behind. Tanner knew that replacement planes would not arrive soon. I was flattered and said yes. I volunteered to fly my usual dawn mission and spot the wrecks and see if I could consolidate them. Tanner stated that my jeep was still my jeep and Stein was still my driver, and with a twinkle in his eye he mentioned that Stein wanted it that way, and after all, who could defy Stein?

Sleep was fitful with all sorts of plans filling my mind. If I transferred to Army it would seem a promotion. Army would be better than Corps command, and after all, flying for Army would mean all sorts of trips to Paris. My half-dream thoughts returned to the cut over my eye and the Purple Heart. Why hadn't I asked for the Purple Heart form? I wanted that medal. In fact I wanted any medal. I decided to report the wound when I went to get the stitches out. Air Medals were OK, but I got one every twenty-five missions. A Purple Heart required the flow of blood, and I had bled profusely.

There was no enemy action on the dawn mission. As I spotted the crashed planes' locations I found that we could consolidate the wreckage near a group of barns not too far back that would provide us a good field and shelter for fabric repair and repainting. It wouldn't be such a tough job. I'd get it done and then be off to Paris and Army Headquarters. The crash roundup went well, and our skilled mechanics and ground crews soon had two of the four planes in flying condition.

I flew one plane back to the operations field and then drove two pilots to our repair site to pick up the other two planes. By visiting with the 36th Division's Air Officer, I was able to salvage enough parts from one of their downed planes to put the third plane in the air. Rain and fog closed in and grounded us for a day.

When I went to the medic with my cut eyebrow, he said there would be only a slight scar. But without a scar how could I claim a medal, especially a medal that honored the backbone of the Third Division, the front-line dogface?

The dawn mission was still mine and *Janey*'s. It gave me the chance to look for advance fields and I prized the early morning quiet and the colorful light show that ushered in most days. My nagging concern was *Janey*. She was being flown in the regular rotation, and my only claim to her was the morning mission.

My reputation of being able to repair and test planes and select fields grew. I was the embodiment of a Fort Sill training maxim: There are old pilots and there are bold pilots, but there are no old, bold pilots. If Schultzie picked the field, it was flyable. As we entered the Vosges Mountains, however, the valleys became marshy, narrower, dominated by small lakes. Good fields near roads were harder to find, and we feared the pockets of Germans we often bypassed might still be full of fight. Since September 15, the German counterattacks had become nearly a daily occurrence. The enemy could be likened to a coiled snake ready to strike and slither away. When I reported a new strip, the burning question was, "Who's beside us?" We wanted company to share the nightly guard duty.

DIVARTY and Division had not acted on my request for our own .50-caliber flak wagons, which disappointed Tanner. He vowed that he'd use his special relationship with General Sexton, our new DIVARTY commander, to remedy the situation. General "Mud," however, entered the war again, and since the Germans were relying on horse power, they had a distinct advantage. Our heavy gas-powered multi-wheeled vehicles and tanks were tearing up the light-duty French roads. We often had to bypass a blown bridge by fording rain-swollen streams that flowed through sticky red-mud banks, providing the Germans a good choke point on which to concentrate heavy weapons fire.

As the divisional fronts narrowed, air space became constricted and flying out of the path of our own artillery became more difficult. Many replacement pilots didn't believe the tales of our losses on Anzio and didn't keep their flying maps marked with new artillery positions. Sadly, two pilots and two observers from other divisions in our sector were blown from the sky before the lesson sank in: Know your sector's guns.

The local French people seemed to have special insight into the German mind and capabilities. Certain that the Germans would not be back for a return engagement, they were ready with a city-wide victory picnic after we took Rimermont in late September. I'd selected a landing strip in a city park where the Moselette and Moselle Rivers joined. The field was larger than two football fields, close to a good road and surrounded by trees —perfect. The liberation party was to be held about a quarter mile from our field.

Young French boys and girls, exuberant with pride and energy, swarmed our field, waving small tricolor flags. Fortunately or unfortunately, *Janey* and I were in the air working a radio relay and scouting for a new field. As I swept low over the rivers' junction, I saw a growing crowd of children and adults swarming to the north end of our strip. I changed my landing pattern and landed downwind, away from the crowd. As I pulled toward the sheltering trees, Stein followed me with his jeep— something was wrong!

Tanner's new L-5, that General Sexton had requisitioned with his personal intervention, wasn't around. "We've just killed a girl. It's a mess!" Stein shouted, shattering all possibility of a festive reception. "She ran from the crowd into the plane we had propped. We only had a couple of guys holding back the crowd. There wasn't a problem until she ran out."

"Is Richards around?" I asked, with dread in my voice. I didn't want to face an angry, grieving crowd of French people. My French was embarrassingly poor.

"Yes, he's there and doing a good job with the mother. She just came with a local doctor." The girl's death had obviously jolted Stein.

Lieutenant Richards came forward, blocking my view of the crowd as he reached up to straighten my shirt collar so my captain's bars would clearly and properly show. "You need your cap, or your helmet." he said. "You've got to look like a Commandant." Stein, as usual, quickly grasped the situation and retrieved my steel helmet with its two painted silver bars from the plane. I put it on and followed Bill to the crowd. It was the type of déjà vu that I didn't look forward to seeing. I instantly remembered the crowd around the little Italian boy who had lost his foot to the German mine.

Richards was masterful. He first introduced me to the girl's mother and family, then to the city elders in order of importance. Bill's fluency in French allowed him to carry the conversation. A Catholic priest arrived and ushered Bill and me away from the crowd. In broken yet understandable English the priest said: "You are not to blame. It is the war. But please leave. The longer you stay, the more bitter the memory."

Fortunately, the corridor in the Vosges Mountains broadened to the north and west in the direction of Epinal, our next objective. A satisfactory pasture with grazing animals lay about three miles ahead and two miles behind the lead tanks. The priest's request was reasonable, but it was tough to leave the celebratory picnic and the food it promised.

Rosner was in the air, so I told Bill to take over. "Stein and I will be at a new field inside an hour," I said. "We'll do as the priest suggests. I'll stop by DIVARTY and get clearance and we'll move." The priest understood the message. He shook my hand more than the five pumps dictated by French courtesy, and Stein and I were off.

Colonel Coyne approved the move and sent a staff officer in full dress uniform back to the scene to give the accident the proper ambiance for the French family. It was a thoughtful act, both for the family and for the Air Section.

Stein and I moved easily through the traffic because proper spacing of vehicles was now enforced both by order and as a practical matter of self-preservation. Almost-daily raids by the Luftwaffe brought home the lesson that during a strafing by one plane or many, our best protection was many well-spaced guns firing together for mutual protection.

Cattle and goats grazed in the pasture of the new airfield I selected, and the 40 mm AA pompom guns of the 441st had been set up along the road. The rough pasture resembled a shallow serving platter, making landings seem prolonged and floating.

The first field north of Remiremont spoiled us, for now as the dogfaces clawed their way toward St. Die and eventually to Strasbourg, finding airstrips near roads became increasingly difficult. The clear autumn air, saturated with moisture from frequent rain squalls, turned the early morning mists into sparkling white blankets that set the valleys aglow.

Each bend in the road erupted into a fire fight, and each stream flowed red with blood before we were able to cross it safely. It was slow going, but the infantrymen paid the price and moved ahead. As pilots and observers, our part in the action held a minimum of danger as long as we paid attention to our maps and kept a sharp lookout for bandits in the sky. Rest camps were announced, and Tanner sent me on the first rotation to Grenoble. Five days off the line, four days and three nights 200 miles from the sound of artillery was too good to be true.

My five days away from the unit had brought several changes. A 16-foot-wide wooden landing strip had been built on a mountainside. Tanner didn't like it and wanted me to check it out and test it by landing *Janey* there. He knew I wouldn't knowingly land *Janey* in an unsafe location. I easily brought *Janey* down on the wooden strip. Trees sheltered the plank runway from crosswinds and the landing was not too difficult if the pilots kept their tails high until the very last moment. At the moment the tail wheel touched the ground, the pilot had to shift his eyes from looking straight ahead to looking to the right or left side of the engine cowling. A pilot over 6 feet tall had an advantage in that he could see over the engine, but most of us had to maintain a straight landing path to the thumping rhythm of the 16-foot-wide plank runway. Landings on roads and grassy fields don't make noise, and I was glad when we got off the wooden runway a couple of days later.

35 · *TROPHIES— AND POWER*

Ed Hill and I saw tanks rolling down the main roads into Strasbourg, and from above, the airport looked abandoned, except for the few burning planes obviously torched as the Luftwaffe retreated. It would be a perfect place to spend the night, replacing the barns and roofless houses in which we had been camping. After circling the field several times and not drawing any fire or seeing any great damage to the runways, we radioed the coordinates, which clearly identified the airfield.

I landed *Janey*, and after taxiing tail up on the hard-surfaced runway, we halted in front of what appeared to be the base operation building. No one was around and yet a German Imperial battle flag flew from the flag pole. "That's mine," I told Ed. "If I can find someone to lower it." I remembered stories of booby traps and friends lost by reaching for a war trophy.

"I'll tend the radio, you explore," Ed suggested cautiously.

I left *Janey*'s engine slowly idling and walked toward the open doorway of the glass-walled building. My .45 was cocked and in my hand. Around the corner of the doorway, a white table cloth waved and three elderly men in blue workman's coveralls emerged. Had they just changed out of their German uniforms and now wanted to be known as civilians?

"Germans gone. Welcome!" was the message they gave in a combination of French and German, a language typical of the Strasbourg area. I brandished my .45, making it plain that I wanted the flag, and they stumbled over themselves to run to the flagpole and lower it for me. This strengthened my confidence in the safety of the area, but I was still cautious about booby traps. No one else came forward, but after the tenacity displayed by the Germans for the last two months, I truly felt the only good German was a dead German. One false move and I'd have pulled the trigger. A recon jeep raced down the runway toward us, followed by a couple of weapons carriers loaded with troops. Hallelujah! We were safe, and I had a prize trophy to take home.

The battle was moving fast and the recon troops had loot and food in mind. Hill and I gave them first crack at the goodies as well as a chance to disarm any mines or booby traps the Germans may have left for us. In an hour the men were gone and the base Gasthaus was stripped of food and booze. Our Air Section would be here before dusk to occupy this dream location.

Our only action on the field came at dusk on our first night. A lone FW-190 came sputtering over the rooftops with its wheels down. Our cook, not necessarily known for his alertness, opened fire with the ring-mounted .50-caliber on the kitchen truck. The pyrotechnic colors of the tracer's bullets lit the evening sky as they harmlessly followed the coughing plane over the horizon to the Rhine. "Cookie" claimed a victory, and wanted a swastika painted on the kitchen truck, but since no one saw an actual explosion or fire, it didn't count.

If the war had ended that day, we had the perfect location to spend years of occupation duties. We were set. The official word was: "We're out of the line." French civilians soon came forward, speaking a mish-mash of languages. Linguists followed, to help us master them.

Tanner wasted no time in giving us the benefit of his years of Stateside training. On the second morning he led the entire Air Section in calisthenics, even though we could still hear the guns. All pilots were required to make at least twenty dead stick (power off) spot landings. There would be a fifth of booze for the winner of a spot-landing contest within the week. I kept my mouth shut, even though this was the type of Army I'd sworn to avoid. Fortunately the calisthenics became fun when the half-hour of drill was followed by a great breakfast.

Actually, Tanner's spot-landing contest was a stroke of pure genius. It gave the ground crews a chance for plane rides because, to be meaningful, the spot had to be hit with a passenger on board. The paved runways of the large airport gave us ample space to practice without the danger of engine failure when the throttle was reduced to minimum power. We all quickly forgot the minimum of twenty landings as we realized how long it had been since we'd made power-off landings. We used power to drag our planes to the edge of the field, then cut power. We'd abandoned the vital ingredient of flying—knowing the feel of our planes in an emergency.

In five days the Air Section looked great. We had shaved, showered and put on clean uniforms, but our luck didn't last long. Early afternoon of the fifth day we were entrucked and moving to the woods. The Air Force evicted us from our airport.

We had traversed the rugged Vosges Mountains from the west in early winter, making us the first army to accomplish such a feat in recorded military history. By mid-December we were moving back to the cold and snow to replace our weary battle companions in the 36th Infantry and to serve under the First French Army to liberate Colmar. Through Red Cross channels we received word in late September that Second Lieutenant Paul Alpert had been pulled from the wreckage of *Sad Sack III,* and while still suffering a concussion, had been hidden by the French Resistance until the American dogfaces drove the Germans out of Besancon. Boucher's fate was still unknown. The fluid situation, the rapid shift in Division objectives, plus the difficulty in translation made it impossible to locate and examine the wreckage. All we knew for certain was that the plane had burned and no body was found in the wreckage. The immediate burial of casualties, a common practice of the Germans, made it impossible to classify Boucher other than missing. But on the second day that we were out of action in Strasbourg, November 30, 1944, the Red Cross officer attached to the Third Infantry informed us that Boucher was alive and a prisoner somewhere in southern Germany. A round-robin letter circulated. We wanted to send a note of cheer to the free-spirited Boucher to repay him for the many hours of hilarious conversation he'd sparked with his tales explaining why he bore the title of the most-crashed pilot flying. We let him know that if he could escape, we'd find him a *Sad Sack IV* to fly, even though it was an unlucky name.

Sergeant Glenn Geist wore many hats in December of 1944. In addition to being chief of the radio section, he was our advisor on all things electrical. As custodians of four searchlight generators we found at the Strasbourg Airport, we possessed assets of inestimable value. Geist had come to me earlier on the second day we occupied the quaint mountain hamlet of La Vancel and said, "Schultz, there's no electricity in town. The Krauts stole their generators. I can cut the two hotels we're using free from the power lines and use our generators to give us light." Of course I agreed, even though I wasn't in charge.

Major Tanner was now in command of the Third Division Air Section. With my envy and congratulations, he had received his golden oak leaves on December 15. The day after his promotion Tanner told me that he was going to fly General Sexton to several Higher Headquarters to visit the General's Stateside buddies. From the way it sounded, he'd be gone several days.

Once again, I'd be the Air Section's decision maker, but only as executive officer. The prime responsibility was Tanner's. I truly enjoyed my lower-stress position as executive officer. Geist's request to tamper with the main power lines in the village was above my comprehension. It wasn't covered by Tanner's instructions, but it sounded like a great idea. I sent Stein to find Bill Richards to translate. "Don't cut anything until we get the nod from the locals," I instructed.

To prevent being outranked on prime loot such as generators, Glenn had hidden the booty, four complete units, plus parts from several damaged units, in the area where we were guarding the wreckage of a downed plane. On the day Strasbourg fell, there must have been sixteen to twenty complete AA batteries, with searchlight units, at the airport. Grabbing four units didn't seem too greedy, for naturally we would share them since the generators make valuable trading stock. The mechanics of the 39th flight crew, whose plane we were guarding, knew that somewhere in the deal they would receive a cut.

Before lighting the hotels, I wanted to discuss it with the village officials. Richards, Geist, and I, with Stein following in the rear, started walking to the village hall. It wasn't long before we saw Mayor M. Font and a few villagers on their way to meet us. Our attitudes toward the French had swung 180 degrees since the mid-August invasion of southern France. The early fighting around the first inland village of La Londe had left us baffled. Frantic Frenchmen were shouting *Feldgrau* and wildly gesturing and pointing and pushing us toward woods or isolated houses. We had expected the French to speak French, not shout at us in German. The animosity of the twin factions of FFI (French Forces Interior), and Maquis (Underground), who were always screaming at each other, complicated our understanding of our allies. But the French gave us vital information, gathered at great danger and often suffering, to make our invasion as bloodless as possible. We understood and appreciated their valiant efforts.

Preservation of French life and property was a great concern of the American troops. We wouldn't hesitate to bombard a French building sheltering Germans, but risking French lives was against our rules. Knowing we would be in La Vancel for at least a couple of weeks made it doubly important to not upset the local populace. I wanted to be certain that cutting the power lines and hooking up a direct-current generator would not risk fire damage or any other hazard.

"Mayor M. Font," Richards began. "We wish to connect our generators to your hotel and the hotel of M. Grosse. Will it present any problems?"

"Bill," I interrupted, "Explain that the generators are direct current."

"M. Font, the captain says the generators are direct current.

That's important," was Bill's embarrassed and hasty correction.

"I don't know about direct current. I'll send Frank to get the power-plant operator. He will know," Richards translated.

"Lights again for Christmas. We would enjoy that very much. Could you light the whole village?" the mayor asked. "We would be very careful of blackout." It was apparent from the smiles on the growing group of people around the mayor that Richards's translation was both speedy and accurate. We had expected about ten Frenchmen to show up for the meeting, but we had a crowd. Candles and oil lamps had been their only evening lights for over a year. The prospect of electricity was pure bliss.

Slowly up the narrow, cobbled lane that served as La Vancel's main street came a gray-haired man, the power-plant operator. He walked with a pronounced limp, possibly the saving grace that spared him from forced labor in some distant factory. M. Kirk was the power plant superintendent or had been until the Germans took away their generator.

M. Kirk was briefed by a companion who walked beside him, and when they approached our group M. Kirk asked, "Is it true you have generators?"

"Yes," replied Bill. "But they are direct current searchlight generators."

"No matter. How big?" M. Kirk asked.

Geist looked blankly at Bill. It seemed we were at an impasse. We did not have an answer for the question.

"I'll get one and have it back before dark," Geist offered. Stein, without instruction, hurried off to get a truck. He didn't want to be left out of the adventure.

"OK," I instructed Geist. "You make the run with M. Kirk, and if it'll work, bring one back. Stein's already getting a truck."

Richards was busy keeping the mayor abreast of our conversation. With nods and additional gestures, they decided that two other men from the village would go with Stein and Geist to check on the precious generator. They were back long before dark but not with beaming faces. The generators were small.

Stein had used his invaluable Yiddish along the way and was able to explain that without the complicated converters, the direct-current machines would light only a few bulbs. Word spread rapidly, but the village took the news with good heart.

The power couldn't be transported very far. It would be one hotel per generator, and above all, we couldn't touch the main power line. M. Kirk wanted to do all the hotel installation and look after the machines. In return, we had to let the village use a generator for one day during their Christmas celebration.

"Schultz, why don't I bring three generators back here and leave the fourth one with the 39th as their part of the deal?" offered Geist. "After all, they painted them olive drab, and the guys in the 39th have their necks stuck out. They've even faked Third Division markings on the bumpers. If it wasn't for the Krauts' four-lug wheels, you couldn't tell the generator from official Government Issue."

"Work it out and get those lights going!" I said, adding, "Store the third generator at the city hall." The words were barely out of my mouth before Stein was translating them into Yiddish-French.

That night the officers' hotel enjoyed a few dim electric lights, as M. Kirk made the operational adjustments. It sure beat candles and lanterns. The additional generators were brought to La Vancel, along with the salvageable parts of the wrecked plane. The second hotel was brought on line and the city hall had lights too. Gas for the city hall generator was a local problem. We couldn't spare them gas.

Two days later, after the lights were on in the three locations, the mayor contacted Richards. He wanted a meeting. With great ceremony the mayor spoke directly to me. "Mon Capitan," Bill translated as he spoke. "Our village wants to entertain the officers and soldiers at a Christmas party in the city hall in appreciation for your bringing light to our village. Will you accept?"

I hurriedly extended my hand. "*Oui, oui. Merci beaucoups,*" I said in my best French, causing everybody to laugh. It was going to be a great Christmas, unless the Germans got skittish. We most certainly would have a few days of peace, for we were under the direct control of the French Army and they weren't about to degrade the Noël with combat.

Stein showed up grinning like the Cheshire cat. "Schultz," he said, "how about a three-day pass? If I can get to Army supply, I'll bring back a truckload of goodies. I can get bayonets, but they're not worth a damn one day back," he explained. "It'll take three days to make them valuable. I'll bring back goodies for my boys and a bottle Scotch for you." With that kind of a sales pitch, who could say no?

Word of the coming party and of Stein's special mission spread fast. Hopes were high, winds were mild, and *Janey* was flying at her best. The dreaded Germans were quiet on our front and, we hoped the war was called for the Christmas season. We prayed that we would soon have "peace on earth, good will toward men."

As I landed from my dawn mission, a sergeant and a corporal from the 41st Air Section walked toward me to help park *Janey*. "Schultz, are the niggers from the antiaircraft gun section coming to the party?" they asked.

"Yes, of course," I replied.

"Then we won't," they stated, awaiting my answer.

"Suit yourselves," I said. What else could I say? We were all in the same army fighting the same enemy. Christmas is a time for brotherhood and although we were involved in an un-Christian activity, I wouldn't compound it by failing to recognize the brotherhood of man. The corporal and sergeant had walked away. I could call them back, but they must be suffering enough with their decision. It had taken a warped sort of courage to confront me. As I rolled *Janey* into the woods by myself, I wondered what the hell we were fighting and dying for.

36 · *CHRISTMAS, 1944*

Private First Class Stein, with a signed pass of doubtful va-
lidity, moved out at dawn. His jeep was piled high with aircraft
parts of dubious value: a stripped engine block, a bent rudder
with Third Division insignia proudly displayed, and a box of
official-looking electrical gear. His mission was to get goodies for
the Christmas celebration his boys were planning. His problem
was passing through Division Military Police to the rear supply
area. The visible load of scrap aircraft parts should validate the
pass to the Air Force supply field, somewhere in the rear.

Tanner was flying Sexton to a round of parties. Sexton,
who had been a full colonel Pentagon officer on General George
Marshall's Staff, had joined us just before the invasion to get
combat experience and qualify for a one-star promotion. Naturally, now that he had a Star in a Regular Army Combat Division, he would show it off to his friends at Higher Headquarters.

Christmas was coming early for the generals. The Wehrmacht's death-throes counter-offensive had been stopped and our
Air Force was turning German equipment to scrap iron. The end
of the war seemed only a matter of days away. The Third
Division, when it replaced the battle-weary 36th, became part of
the First French Army under the direct command of the French
Second Tank Corps; therefore, we inherited several untaken objectives from the 36th plus a good supply of ammunition. Seizing
high ground and registering artillery were our first priorities.
Within ten days, driven by the newly-promoted Lieutenant
Colonel Kerwin, we completed the tasks and awaited orders from

the French commander. The Germans, however, attacked north-ward from Colmar to recapture Strasbourg. Their offensive was timed with the major December 16 drive in Belgium and France known as the Battle of the Bulge.

Kerwin's preparation paid off. It reminded us of our hold-ing action on Anzio, only this time we had more guns and closer contact with the Air Force. We stopped the Germans dead in their tracks. By raking their rear assembly areas with constant fire, we prevented them from reaching our outpost lines even in squad (8-man) strength. Every possible protected ground feature was targeted to receive a steady rain of searing metal shards and liquid fire. If battle can be beautiful, that battle filled the bill. The prearranged concentrations, fired in a seemingly random pattern, roved over the flood plains of Colmar. The sleeping countryside erupted with blue-gray and brown dirt geysers, highlighted by soaring yellow flames and crowned with billowing white smoke. Overhead, flights of four Air Force dive bombers, each carrying eight 500-pound bombs, circled in search for prey. As the dust from our barrages settled, the Air Force P-47 Thunderbolts dived, strafing and bombing. Our artillery shells weighed 100 pounds, while those big bombs weighed 500 pounds. The earth trembled as the powerful blasts smacked the ground, making our artillery dirt geysers look like feeble puffs of dust. Our 105s and 155s allowed us to keep up a staccato snare-drum beat, and the Air Force bombs were the bass drums, as we vented our wrath and unleashed chaos on the shell-shocked enemy.

I was ashamed at how much I enjoyed watching the car-nage, yet I felt a real joy in seeing Willie Lang's death avenged. Corporal Lang had been a constant morale builder and his tales of Wisconsin fishing, both legal and illegal, made many a gathering roar with laughter. He had heroically made the famous critical connection for the donkeys that were attempting to mate during the Anzio breakout. A single 170mm shell had hit his tent. We hadn't found his body at the tent, so we thought he was safe down by the planes. Five hours later, however, Sergeant Kastler found Lang's broken body draped over a fallen log, 30 yards from the impact point. We prayed his death had been swift.

On my second flight of December 22, our troops weren't visible and the guns were quiet. Red Cross banners dotted the still-smoldering German attack route. I dared not push my luck by flying too close, but plainly the Germans were abandoning their outpost line and picking up the dead and dying. The German tanks had not ventured from hiding and by midday their retreat would have become a rout if the French had ordered us to attack. The French, we found, had no intention of attacking during Noël. Without an attack by the Germans, a peaceful and merry Christmas seemed a certainty. We began making preparations for a memorable celebration.

The day after we moved to La Vancel, Bill Richards told me of M. La Due and his bakery. It was small, but M. La Due assured us he could turn our sacks of flour and tins of shortening into mouth-watering French bread, and with sugar and chocolate bars, he could even produce cookies. So many good things were being produced in La Vancel that we feared Higher Headquarters might discover our Camelot.

I knew I had to contact Hook. Croal went to get the process started. Sergeant Joe "Hook" Casanova and I had been trading partners since my days in Palermo as Patton's pilot. American troops were to have turkey for Christmas, plus a supply of such Yuletide goodies as cranberries and sweet potatoes. That kind of operation presented Hook with a great opportunity to use his unique skills. He liked having a hidden source or supply of something special. He promised to keep our village baker a secret and not glut the market. Snafus are always present in the Army supply system, and by our providing Hook with special trade goods, he might find us wood stoves for our field tents. It's the way the Army works.

Light fluffy snow dusted the broad Rhine River Valley. To the east of Colmar, the Rhine flood plain extended 8 to 10 miles to the broad river. The palisades of the Rhine's east bank were interspersed with steep wooded hillsides running down to narrow shelves along the river. Those hillsides gave the Germans good observation to the west, over the ground we had to capture. North of Colmar, the valley broadened to 14 miles and was intersected with small villages, streams, low stone walls, short wooded fence lines—ideal county to defend if we could cover it with observed artillery.

Each new snowfall hid more of the terrain. Small streams and the stubble in the fields became solid white. Only the early morning and late afternoon shadows gave contour to the land-scape. The dark stone walls and tree lines became more visible, but through *Janey's* steamy plastic windows, air observation became guesswork. When we had a mission, off went the cabin heat, for we had to open the door panels to get a clear firing view. Flights were cold, windy and miserable. Air observation became almost impossible. The infantry began using the white sides of their reversible coats. All major weapons and vehicles were painted white. German, French and American men and equipment were all the same color. Thankfully the fighting had died down to nightly patrols to capture German prisoners, many of whom were more than willing to be captured.

The Wehrmacht still could sting, but their offensive power existed only when the troops were driven by the officer corps, and many officers would surrender whenever possible, now that they knew the German's mid-December drive had failed.

Soft, moist snows covered the scars of the battlefield each night and camouflaged the low stone walls. Tanks gouged deep ugly scrapes in the frozen soil as the vehicles skidded their treads to turn. Neither side wanted to give away its position, so tank movement halted. Excessive foot traffic revealed a darkened path, so everyone seemed content to delay any offensive action. A truly merry Christmas would precede 1945.

Our wooded hillside became picture-perfect as the cottony soft snow accumulated on the pine boughs. Bright moonlight on the clear December evenings turned La Vancel into a winter wonderland of burnished silver. The only thing marring this tranquillity was the knowledge that deep pro-German sentiment existed in the area because generations of Alsatians had considered Germany the Fatherland. The treaty after the Franco-Prussian war of 1870 had made Alsace a part of Bismarck's Germany. People of both ancestries had lived in harmony, so it would be prudent to post guards and observe blackout. We made every effort to treat the villagers with respect and courtesy. Their smiles and nods as we passed in the lanes indicated that our presence didn't weigh heavily upon them. I prayed the Germans wouldn't fire on the village or pursue our Cubs.

Richards and Hill, with their above-average abilities to understand and speak French, kept me informed of French moods and wants. At the mayor's request, we brought two truckloads of cut firewood from a remote forest to the village commons. We maintained a congenial relationship with the local people. Information from the Division's morning briefings indicated the French Second Corps didn't intend to launch our offensive until mid-January of 1945.

A dark cloud, however, hung over our magic little kingdom. We hadn't explained to the local officials why we were so insistent that village children be kept off our strip. The decapitation of the nine-year-old girl in Remiremont by the idling prop of a Cub was fact. Although it had happened forty-five days before and 200 miles back, it remained fresh in our minds. We hoped the story wouldn't reach La Vancel.

Christmas for the Air Sections and the flak-wagon crews, including the standard GI turkey dinner, was to be held at the officers' hotel on Christmas Eve. We'd open gifts from home, and maybe Stein would bring some extra surprises. I had saved a package from my sisters, which I hoped were leather gloves. Our chaplain, with permission from the mayor, would hold a non-denominational service in the village's Catholic Church on Christmas morning. The villagers were welcome, which seemed right, for they had invited us to attend their Christmas Mass, to be held late Christmas afternoon when the circuit Catholic priest came. After Mass the villagers would have a party for every-one—a real French Christmas!

Ribbons, candles and pine boughs festooned the village hall.

Tables and chairs appeared from somewhere. We were in wine country and by the sly smiles on the French faces, we knew the best of their hidden bottles would be served. We gave M. LaDue the flour and baking supplies he requested, and he filled the air in the entire village with the enticing aroma of freshly-baked breads and cookies and pastries. We were anticipating the first normal Christmas for the French since 1939. Stein and the presents for his boys hadn't arrived yet. I hoped he wasn't in a military stockade somewhere for not saluting a Garritrooper lieutenant.

Still no word from Tanner, and Colonel Coyne, the DIVARTY Executive Officer, didn't anticipate Sexton's return soon, so the Air Section's responsibilities still rested with me. I called meetings to check out potential trouble spots. Word of my brief verbal exchange with the ground crew of the 41st Battalion Air Section about the integrated Christmas party hadn't spread. In fact, it seemed to have totally fizzled.

What a change twenty-four months had made. Christmas of 1942, I had slept on the ground in the Sultan of Morocco's cork forest in a one-man tent. Christmas of 1943, I was the new Division air officer and had shared a six-man pyramid tent with seven other pilots. We were outside Pietralamara, 20 miles north of Naples, in a rain-soaked area of southern Italy. I had slept on shell boxes above muddy ground carpeted with flattened cardboard from ration cases. I would spend Christmas of 1944 in La Vancel, in a private room in a resort hotel, sleeping in a feather bed between cotton sheets. This was certainly an improvement.

The wonder and tranquillity of our location kept our spirits high as we awaited the coming of Christmas. The lights of Koenigsbourg Haut, a modernized fifteenth-century castle, glistened like an enormous Christmas tree atop the prominent mountain six miles to the south. From its perch nearly 3,000 feet above the valley floor, it dominated the entire Colmar Valley. The French Army always used only the best facilities available for headquarters, so naturally the castle was theirs and they were daring the Germans to fire on it.

The guns—French, German, and American—stayed silent on December 23. We flew patrol missions but saw no targets. The guns stayed silent on December 24 as well. I landed *Janey* at dusk, making fresh tracks in the lightly-falling snow as I taxied to the tree line. I dreaded performing the cold-weather maintenance routine, but on the 25th *Janey* had to fly at dawn.

In extremely cold weather I always drained the oil from *Janey*'s engine and threw blankets over her still-warm engine to keep the electrical system dry. An hour before dawn, the cook heated the engine oil, adding some new to the old, and I carried the warm oil to the field in an old marmite insulated food container. Pouring the heated oil into *Janey*'s engine in the predawn darkness always resulted in a few messy spills, but it never failed to warm her engine so she would start. I liked the dawn missions but not the hot-oil treatments. Warming a Cub's engine was actually the ground crew's job, but since the observer and I were already up, we usually performed the task for *Janey*, allowing the men a little more sack time in their new feather sleeping bags.

Several French villagers attended the nondenominational Christmas Eve service conducted by our chaplain, but the village service on Christmas Day was packed. As an Episcopalian I felt at home during the service although it was in the French. The rhythm of the phrases had a familiarity that made the service meaningful. After the service, it was time to celebrate Christ's birth, and the party held something for everyone.

Stein had shown up and, to his eternal credit, had listened to what the villagers needed. He brought spices and condiments in large quantities to be divided and shared; needles, thread, and buttons; sugar, sugar, sugar; and pounds and pounds of coffee. From summer C-rations, we had packets of lemonade, cocoa, and instant coffee. He must have robbed the Army supply dump. The villagers hadn't seen such abundance since the prewar days. Stein received hugs and kisses from young and old alike. He truly played the part of Saint Nicholas.

Unfortunately, I had to leave the party early. I had a date with *Janey* at dawn the next day.

37 • *THE DRAGONS' TEETH*

As the snow and cold of the Colmar Plain gave way to spring, small bypassed pockets of German stragglers surrendered to us rather than risk being cornered by the FFI. In addition to processing prisoners, spring became a time of training, refitting and assimilating replacements. Rumors were rampant, ranging from our going to the Pacific, to being stationed Stateside as trainers, to the reality that we'd soon be in the line again.

We received two brand-new planes and two rebuilts. The new pilots all had excellent training and two even had experience on snow-ski-equipped planes, but spring was coming and the snow was gone. The quality of our rations improved, and the new equipment, particularly the feather-filled sleeping bags, gave the entire Division a lift in morale and the feeling that it could and would tackle anyone, anything, anywhere just to get the war over.

Major Tanner turned the daily operation of the Air Section totally back to me because he was now the full-time chauffeur for General Sexton. He flew the general to and from high-level victory parties and planning conferences. General O'Daniel was my constant passenger. He wanted to personally observe and share in the directing of the companies, battalions, and regiments as they marched into the German homeland in parade formation. We didn't have to wait long for that chance. On March 15, we attacked the dragons' teeth of the dreaded Siegfried Line.

The German-built dragons' teeth were pyramid-shaped concrete blocks about the size of pup tents, arranged in tight rows about 20- to 40-yards wide. Slave laborers had dug an elaborate series of trenches immediately ahead of and behind the concrete teeth, and behind the rear trenches loomed dense woodlands. It was impossible for our tanks to charge over the teeth, and the teeth were too well-embedded to blast holes through the rows. There was only one way to extract the dragons' teeth. Dogfaces had to take them out one by one with satchel charges, while crawling through minefields. Well-concealed pillboxes and machine-gun nests stood ready to cut our boys down, and German infantrymen were waiting to engage them at close range.

General "Iron Mike" O'Daniel had me fly low over the troops, and with *Janey's* side door removed, I cut the power almost to a glide so he could shout out orders and encouragement to the soldiers below. I flew at only 50 to 100 feet, within easy range of small arms fire, while our other planes directed smoke and High Explosive shells at the concrete pillboxes and fortified trench junctions. O'Daniel frantically yelled encouragement to the living, the dying, and the walking wounded, and he pointed to the parts of the dragons' teeth that were crumbling.

The distance was short, but we paid for that real estate in blood and suffering. Bitter man-to-man and squad-to-squad fighting dispelled the notion that the Germans had wasted all their resources at Bastogne. The Siegfried Line was well supplied. Shells rained in on us as if the Germans had an endless supply. Their 88s, from a distance beyond the range of our guns, showered shrapnel on the GIs who were trying to blast a workable path through the teeth and clear the mines. The enemy mortars, which dispensed death at closer ranges, had to be wiped out by wantonly spending lives, and progress came in jerks. Our tanks and tank destroyers, under German fire the entire time, stood ready to exploit the first path through the teeth.

It was an honor to be O'Daniel's charioteer. When I flew *Janey* low over the battlefield, my principal danger came from .30-caliber machine guns. But any prolonged elevated firing on the Germans' part would alert the dogfaces—and they'd make the machine gunners pay. German 20mm flak wagons were giving close support to their infantry, but past experience gave us faith that if we flew below 150 feet and 500 feet behind our lines, we had a safe zone. The Germans protected their flak wagons from our infantry mortar rounds by hiding them in gullies or by digging the flak wagons down into fields to gun-barrel height. Unless the operators parked the flak wagons at ground level on a battlefield, they couldn't depress the guns to rake the sky below 100 to 150 feet. Once the wagons were out in the open, our tanks, artillery, mortars and tank destroyers made mincemeat of them. Once *Janey* or one of the other Cubs was above 100 to 150 feet, however, flak wagons were deadly. Seeing a flak wagon broken and on fire was a cause for every Cub pilot to rejoice.

For three days we watched the dogfaces crawl through the concrete teeth and blunt them with explosive charges. It was a slow process, but we were cutting paths for our troops and vehicles. By the morning of the fourth day, they had cleared three paths through the teeth and were mopping up the German stragglers. It was the same story as in southern France. Once the Wehrmacht noncoms were gone, the privates lost their will to fight.

My three days of exhilaration were over. Each time I landed *Janey* after flying Iron Mike on his chariot rides, I felt 10 feet tall. The waves and cheers, though we couldn't actually hear them, made me feel that as the General's pilot I'd had a vital part in breaking through the Siegfried Line. Bleeding and dying, however, weren't over for the Division yet. The skies were clearing, so our Air Force could patrol, strafe and bomb, but now we artillery pilots had to worry once again about the stray ME-109s and FW-190s that still wanted to sneak in and take our scalps. We'd breached the wall and crossed the Rhine. Now the heartland lay open to us. Stiff resistance would meet us on our way to Berlin, and our little Piper Cubs had to hunt out the targets from the air.

Spring's warmth as well as its chill were in the March 1945 air. We were the conquering army moving into Germany, and we were going to live off the fat of the land just as their army had done when they marched into France. I routinely gave homeowners an hour to get out of homes that were adjacent to our new airstrip. In broken German I told them, "Open all doors or they will be kicked in." I meant it, for we could not control the conduct of our American soldiers in German homes. It was German soldiers who had killed their American buddies.

Stares of hatred burned from the Germans' eyes and made me think twice about my order, but why should we sleep inside a dirty barn or out in the cold rain while they enjoyed a clean, dry home? If our field was far away from houses, we used the closest weather-tight barn. The Army's golden rule was: Use what you need, eat what's available, and leave it as clean as when you arrived.

The food improved day by day because the German countryside yielded hidden stores we would not have taken from the French. The last couple of days had brought cool evening showers that produced heavy ground mist. As I walked the lonely road one March night, returning from a meeting at headquarters, the mist seemed as thick as fog and my conscience nagged at me. I had forced several families into the woods so that our men could use their houses and barns for shelter. The civilians' pleadings had left me cold. The atrocities I had witnessed and the memories of my dead friends left no room for pity. We had fought the good fight and deserved a roof over our heads. Might was Right. Right?

At the last outpost before the roadside barn where I would sleep, I checked my compass and asked the sentry, "How far to the next barn?"

" 'Bout a quarter mile," he answered. "Better hurry. Looks like rain. I can nearly feel it now. Good luck," he said as he doused his light so I could pass through the double blackout door draped with layers of GI blankets.

I didn't whistle as I walked. I didn't want to reveal my presence to those I'd evicted. The sentry was right. A light rain began to fall, and off in the distance I heard a strange sound. It was like someone was dragging a roller skate that had come loose from his foot with the strap still looped to his ankle. The sound was in front of me and it came closer. I kept walking. I didn't want to stray off the cobblestone road. It was my only guide back to the barn. I couldn't see a thing in the pitch-black soup. Hesitantly, I drew my .45 from my shoulder holster and held it cocked in my now-wet right hand. The butt of the gun was warm and dry because it had been protected under my leather flight jacket, next to my left armpit. The metallic dragging sound was nearly upon me.

"*Hande Hoch!*" I shouted, holding the .45 at hip level, but the sound continued. Suddenly, something about the size of a hundred-pound sack of flour and twice my size swung at me and knocked me to the ground. The thing kept going and faded into the mist, leaving behind it the beautiful aroma of horse manure. I lay on the muddy stones and laughed and cried. I'd been nearly scared to death by a horse with a loose shoe. As the sound faded away in the distance, the .45 was still in my hand, cocked. Luckily I hadn't squeezed the trigger. I'd already killed enough horses in the Montelimar Massacre.

Fred, also known as "Crash," Boucher had *Sad Sack III* ready to tangle with German AA guns. Boucher was captured and spent the last months of the war as a German P.O.W.
—*W. H. Boucher*

38 · *BREAKFAST OVER NUREMBERG*

Once we breached the Siegfried Line and started moving northeast toward the industrial center of Schweinfurt, the late March weather became our ally. The ground was firm and the temperatures pleasant. Flying *Janey* in daily missions once again settled into a familiar pattern. From the air, shades of green emerged, creating a fresh, clean countryside, except where both armies were churning out ugly paths of destruction. Fighting flared and subsided daily, and then again the dogfaces met strong delaying resistance from the Airman's Graveyard, the heavy 88 AA batteries that protected Schweinfurt, the Third Reich's aircraft industry center. Massed artillery and thousands of mines and booby traps were overcome yard by yard and piece by piece. Then we veered southeast to Nuremberg, the capital city of the Nazi Party. The destruction of Nuremberg was Biblical in scale. Not one stone remained upon another. Viewed from an altitude of 800 feet and 8 to 10 miles off in the distance, it looked like a gigantic splotch of mud-spattered laundry spread on a green lawn. I'd seen small Italian villages pulverized, but nothing like that. Huge areas of Nuremberg were totally destroyed. The closer I flew, the more I wanted to see, yet the German snake, coiled and waiting below, might sting with its 20mm fangs.

Janey and I flew Major Hugh Scott over Nuremberg to distribute surrender leaflets. He described the flight:

> Nuremberg turned out to be a hard rock itself.
> This was the spiritual home of the Nazi party, and

its defenders obviously had orders to hold it to the last man. The Third Division was assigned to take the northern third of the city by direct assault; two other divisions hit it from the east and west. The nearer to the much bombed center of the city we got, the harder the fighting became.

I was awakened early one morning when the fighting had reached the hand-to-hand, bayonet-to-grenade, house-to-house stage, and told to report to General O'Daniel.

"Scott," he said when I reached his trailer, "the krauts are holding out in the old fort in the city center. They're surrounded on all sides and can't possibly save themselves. I want you to get up in a Cub plane and drop surrender leaflets on them as soon as you can."

This was about 7 a.m. Within an hour, I had drafted a leaflet, had it translated into German, mimeographed in 2,000 half-sheet copies and tied into small bundles. I had alerted Captain Schultz (the same guy who had crashed me in Southern France) and told him to get a Cub warmed up. He was ready to take off when I reached the artillery air strip.

We climbed quickly over Nuremberg, and within minutes were circling over the burning center of the city. Schultz had told me there was a fairly brisk west wind blowing, so he circled to the west of the target area and gave me an OK sign with index finger and thumb when he thought the spot was right. The first batch of leaflets dropped out and fluttered earthward with agonizing slowness. They were soon dispersed by the breeze and it was difficult to tell where they were landing.

We made a second pass, and a third, until all

the leaflets were gone. About this time, I had had all the looking down while circling in a plane that I could stand, and I lost the light breakfast I had eaten while waiting for the pamphlets to be mimeographed.

When I got back to the CP, I reported to General O'Daniel, "I'm not sure whether all the leaflets landed on target, but I sure hit the krauts with my breakfast."

Whether they were hit by anything except rifle, machine gun, tank and artillery fire, I'm not sure, but the Germans gave up in the old citadel about noon.

I think it was the following day, April 20 —Adolf Hitler's birthday—that the Third Division rubbed it in with a little pomp and ceremony in the town square, trooping the colors while a small pickup military band played.

Also, at my suggestion, Iron Mike had the Tenth Engineers wire the huge Nazi swastika at the Nuremberg stadium with dynamite and blow it into a thousand bits. About an hour later, we got a TWX from General Patton instructing the division to place a guard on the swastika, as he wanted it crated and sent back to the United States as a souvenir. All General O'Daniel could do was to report the results of our demolition, with a figurative "Sorry about that" ending.

Hitler's birthday present for April 20, 1945, was that he no longer had to defend Nuremberg. The Allies had taken it. While the Third cleared Nuremberg, the 12th Armored exploited a breakthrough across the Danube River, the last major natural obstacle on the road to Munich. It was a reprise of our race through southern France. The 15th Regiment, entrucked, passed through the 12th and took up a blocking position to ensure rapid exploitation and communication.

Ammunition wasn't a problem for the Germans. The supply lines were short and the multi-purpose 88s that had defended the industrial centers against Allied bombers could now be used against ground troops. The barrages were deafening; the targets easy to spot. The 88s were in prepared positions, fortified and supplied over the last five years. Only a direct hit would silence them.

My air observers wanted more and more flights. We had so many visible targets that we were splitting batteries so that two guns instead of the normal four were assigned to individual ground-level gun positions. Saturating the air with smoke and whistling shrapnel made us proud when we saw the bursts close to the targets, but moments later the Germans fired again. With dogface blood, the infantry moved into their own mortar and grenade range, and with sheer guts, blasted each enemy gun position into silence.

Munich emerged as a second Nuremberg. As I flew *Janey* safely behind our lead elements and above the dust storm of battle, I saw total destruction in the heart of the city and every outlying cluster of homes. As our tanks started around the southwestern Autobahn bypass of Munich, the destruction assumed a different form. From 400 to 500 feet, what had appeared to be blocks of rubble turned out to be painted factory roofs with large nets and trees placed on them to fool the eye. Parts of Munich's urban area had been camouflaged to look like a rural area. Becoming bolder, I flew *Janey* closer to the airport and the inner city. Vast damage was evident, but, again, clever camouflaging had spared many industrial areas. The southwestern airport had a few real craters, but the main landing strips were intact and hiding under camouflage paint.

The Third Division Air Section and *Janey* were getting a free ride. The Luftwaffe and Wehrmacht were out of fuel. If a vehicle couldn't be pulled by horse or by man, the Germans abandoned it. From my ringside seat in the sky, the sight of our Division deployed in hot pursuit of the Germans was like the end of a cowboy-and-Indian movie when the cavalry at last rides over the horizon to save the day. It made the futile last-ditch German efforts look ridiculous, yet they continued to cost us American lives.

On a gray day in early April, I was flying a routine mission in *Janey*. The Germans had pulled back and were using only squad- and platoon-sized forces to establish roadblocks along the walled or hedged country lanes. Captain Dick Bently, an intelligence officer with the Seventh Infantry Regiment, wanted to see for himself the lay of the lush and undulating land. We had followed a small patrol of light tanks through a forty-house, one-church village where they had held up near one tier of homes before proceeding into the countryside. There wasn't a tank channel in my radio set, and the Seventh Regiment couldn't establish a relay for us. We heard neither incoming nor outgoing artillery, so it appeared they had a clear road ahead.

Just past the last house-barn combination in the village, a paved road snaked around the hamlet. Bently tapped me on the shoulder and indicated he wanted to fly over the road. I took *Janey* down to about 100 feet and started to circle. Just below us in the ditch was a German trying to flatten himself beside his bicycle. Was he a messenger attempting to deliver vital information to his *kameraden* ahead, or just a straggler separated from his unit? Whichever, he was fair game. I opened the throttle to gain airspeed, and after pulling *Janey* around in a sharp 360-degree turn, I drew the .45 from my shoulder holster and dived straight for him. Right over his head, I leaned out the open door and fired two shots into the roadway. Whether he was a soldier delivery man, I don't know, but he hopped to his feet, hands over his head, and started walking down the road toward the closest farmstead. *Janey* and I herded our German prisoner down the road to our troops.

"Hey Schultz, does this happen often?" Bently barked over the roar of *Janey*'s engine.

"Naw," I said with a shrug of my shoulders. The less I said, the better the resulting story would be.

39 • "DEAD" GERMANS

When each dawn mission was completed and *Janey* was safely parked, I went to Headquarters to get the briefing for the day's planned action against the enemy. Then I would take one more patrol flight. That second flight always ended with a reconnaissance for an advance landing strip for the next day's activity or someplace we could spend the night.

This April day had been a typical day. We were one day closer to going home, and one day closer to the climactic battle of the Redoubt, which we then believed was inevitable. On my second flight, in midafternoon, I'd found an especially satisfactory airfield—the lawn of a grand, palatial estate. I flew *Janey* low over the well-manicured lawn, then swooped back over it even lower, touching it gingerly with her wheels to check its smoothness. It was perfect, so I called the radio car and our flak wagon. As soon they arrived at the estate, I landed *Janey*, walked up to the house, and spoke to the man there, who perhaps had been a high-ranking German officer. We could have taken him prisoner but didn't. The occupation government was just a few miles behind us, and they handled such matters.

Since we needed shelter for the night, without hesitation I told him we'd give him an hour to leave the house. He didn't speak English, but he understood. I told him specifically that I wanted all the *schliessels*, the house keys. "Any locked door will be kicked down," I warned him. "I'll be bringing 60 men into this house. If you give me the keys, we'll open the doors and take what we want, but we won't damage your property."

He nodded in agreement and motioned for me to follow him to the basement. There, he showed me the most fantastic wine cellar I have ever seen. He was proud of his wines and made it clear they should be treated with respect. In addition to wine, there was a wide variety of hard liquors and case after case of Cook's Imperial Champagne, which from my college days I recognized as one of America's finest brands. The basement concealed a smokehouse, too, with cheeses, sausages, hams and other delicacies.

The man and his family and staff vacated the house, taking what they needed and going to the barn. Shortly, two of the housemaids came back. One was the cook. She agreed to prepare the evening meal for us, and we paid her in GI coffee, the one item the German man had asked for. The other woman was the maid. She was there to make certain everything stayed clean. Since we'd been wearing dirty clothes for weeks, we asked if she would wash our clothes. She nodded yes, and I gave her all my clothes, including the uniform off my back. All I could find to put on was a pair of Air Force coveralls.

As Division air officer, I pulled rank and took the master bedroom as my own. When I opened the bedroom closet, I knew for certain that the man we'd driven from the house was a high-ranking officer. I was unfamiliar with German military ranks, but the uniforms hanging in the closet were very impressive. There were several of them and they were elaborately decorated. I could still have had him arrested, but why? We didn't want prisoners. We were busy. His cook was preparing a feast. We wanted to relax and eat sausages and drink champagne. We were in paradise that afternoon, so I proceeded to let go of my reserve and joined in some serious drinking. At about 6 o'clock in came a call from General O'Daniel, "Schultz, go up and establish contact with the Third Recon. We've lost them."

I wasn't surprised. Establishing radio contact was a routine request for Cub pilots, especially when we were in fast-moving situations and in mountainous terrain. Our radios would only reach two to five miles, and we were now in the foothills of the

Austrian Alps. It was just another routine mission. I'd go up and fire a purple flare, which meant to change to Channel One, or I would fire a green flare to change to Channel Two. We had only two channels, so we changed the flare colors daily to confuse the enemy.

Soon *Janey* and I were airborne and over the Third Recon. They were spread out in a long column on a secondary road that ran through a rather narrow valley, and they were meeting no real resistance. I fired purple, and contact was established on Channel One. I reported the results to Division. The next step was to find a ground link. We were in constant fear that the Germans were listening to our radio broadcasts. To ensure privacy and to be certain that there was a clearly-understandable two-way message, wire was the desired method of communication. When I broadcast from *Janey*, it was like shooting out an umbrella of radio waves that went far and wide. When the infantry broadcast from their set in the valley, their radio waves were like an inverted ice cream cone shot into the air, and those waves required a more direct link. For that reason, the L-4Bs were valuable tools in establishing radio links and re-directing messages.

After being airborne for only 15 to 20 minutes, my mission was accomplished and I was ready to return to the party. Another Cub was up doing the evening patrol, so *Janey* and I were free. I had sipped several glasses of champagne back at the estate, and I badly needed to take a leak. By this time I no longer carried a funnel or a tin can for such a purpose. Tin cans had come in handy when we were calling air strikes and couldn't find a landing field quickly, but now it was just as easy to land the airplane, step outside and relieve ourselves as to trying to hit a tin can or similar receptacle while airborne.

I looked around for a place to land. Army tanks were all around, and up ahead was a field that looked really good for landing. I dragged the field to be sure. In making my last pass over the field, I saw a couple of Germans lying in the ditch by a bridge, their weapons beside them. I assumed they'd been killed during a short fire fight. I landed *Janey*, took a leak, and decided to relax and smoke my pipe. I reached in my pocket, and damn it, I didn't have any matches. I'd stopped carrying my Zippo lighter because when I filled it with gas from the jeep, I invariably overfilled it and the outside of the lighter would be wet with gas. My pants pocket got soaked with gas, and when my pants rubbed against the side of my leg, it caused a burn. I'd done this so many times that the skin of my right leg was hypersensitive, and I was now trying to give it a rest.

Being without matches wasn't a real problem, however. The dead Germans lying by the drainage ditch were apt to have matches in their pockets. Fleecing Germans was not the most admirable of activities, but we sometimes did it to get souvenirs, good German food, or cash. German soldiers carried their cash in the sweat bands of their helmets. We fished it out and used it in poker games, where credit was never allowed. German rations were a special prize. Their canned pork and gravy was wonderful over bread or even over K-ration biscuits, which were actually vitamin-packed grease blocks. Tins of sardines were such a treasure that we'd charge a German machine gun if we knew they had a supply on board. Swiss chocolate was ambrosia, and when we found brandy, the day was complete.

I cannot date the first time I searched a dead German, but as barbaric as it was, I did it. I was not a great poker player and I often ran short of cash because much of my pay was going into Stateside bonds. If I wanted to be pumped up and play, I had to shake down Germans, dead or alive, and use their cash. We never fleeced our own dead, at least I didn't. I wouldn't touch a dead American soldier.

I knew the Germans lying dead in the ditch were apt to have matches, and as long as they were there, I might as well fleece them. I reached down to go through one soldier's pack but decided to pull off his hat first. He was wearing a field hat, not a helmet. Suddenly he looked up at me. He'd been playing dead. I knew how to use a German rifle, and I figured I'd better use it before he did. I grabbed his rifle and yelled, "*Hande Hoch!*"

Then I realized he had something odd on the end of his rifle. It was a grenade launcher. I didn't know how to use the damn thing and my .45 was back in *Janey*, waiting in its shoulder holster. About that time the other German came to life.

Both Germans put their hands up and walked eagerly with me back to the plane. I got my pistol out of the back seat and there I was, the captor of two Germans. I presumed the two young men were supposed to hide under the bridge and engage the American tanks as they rolled by. How they were going to stop tanks with a rifle grenade? They were happy to surrender. I had saved their lives.

Each man had a small bottle of brandy in his pack, so naturally I had to have a taste to see how good it was. A liberated Rolliflex camera lay in *Janey*'s back seat, so I took a picture of the two men standing beside *Janey* to commemorate the first prisoners I had taken by myself.

I couldn't fly the two out of there, but since the Army tanks were just down the road, we went back to the bridge and waited for the tanks to come by. Small-arms fire crackled in the distance. Pretty soon the tanks came down the road and when they got closer I could see they had their hatches closed. That scared me. There I was with two Germans, and I wasn't even wearing my uniform. It was being washed and pressed back at the estate. I had on coveralls, and they had no insignia whatsoever on them. The two young Germans were wearing field caps. I hoped that the men in the tanks were battle-wise and would know that these two kids were not real soldiers, although they were wearing the Wehrmacht uniform.

The tanks were about 100 yards away when the hatch cover raised. I knew then they weren't going to shoot. At least not right away. I yelled and somebody yelled back. It was a newspaper reporter for the *Stars and Stripes*. He'd been riding in the lead tank so he could see some actual combat and report on it. They'd been ambushed a short distance back and taken some prisoners. I gave them my two and went back to *Janey*. It was starting to get dark now. But the estate had a big lawn that was easy to land on, so I went back to the party.

40 • *THE STORCH*

Crouched below me like a giant dark green grasshopper ready to spring skyward was a Fiesler Storch, our most feared, yet admired, enemy. What had been a relaxed flight to find our forward landing strip for the evening would soon become a tale of love, joy, despair and intrigue.

A Fiesler Storch was a dream come true or a nightmare —depending on who was flying it. A Fiesler Storch was the symbol of an aggressive and glamorous German Panzer commander. It became associated with Rommel and blitzkrieg because it had proved itself in artillery reconnaissance and in directing the dive bombing in Poland. The idea of his blitzkrieg, rapid encirclements and bypassing enemy strong points, was to save lives, not to spend them. Rommel felt that by striking disorganized enemy troops there was more of a chance to avoid casualties than getting into prolonged defensive positions. He couldn't direct a blitzkrieg from the comfort of a rear-echelon command post. He had to be everywhere on the front. Without a Storch, he couldn't have achieved that omnipresence.

Patton tried to out-Rommel Rommel, and Patton wasn't bashful about admitting it. Patton used an L-4B or other light aircraft to fly to and from the front. He would ride to the battle line in his command car, and then fly back to the rear in an L-4B. He believed that it would be bad for the combat troops' morale to see their commander heading for the rear in a car.

From Licata on the south coast of Sicily, to Cassino, midway up the boot of Italy, while we provided constant air surveillance, enemy groundfire was our main problem. I had no challenges from Storches. Even from Anzio to Rome, the Storch failed to put in an appearance. I was curious, but not disappointed!

In southern France I began to see Storch silhouettes in the distance, but I never saw our feared enemy in close proximity. If I had seen one within the danger zone, I would have spun or side-slipped *Janey* down to the deck. But even seeing the Storches far away was discomforting. Because our tanks and recon units raced into southern Germany with the Wehrmacht in retreat, there was always the chance of running into some die-hard SS units or other big guys in reserve. Some of those outfits might have had Storches.

We were unaware at the time that the gods of war had intervened on our behalf in the form of bad decisions by Goering and the Allied bombing of industrial areas in Germany. The Luftwaffe had farmed out production of the Storch to France and Czechoslovakia, not only to conserve aluminum but also because they needed the production facilities in Germany to build ME-109s, FW 190s, and later ME-262 jets. Those fighters were a higher-priority item because Allied bomber streams were battering Germany on a daily basis. French Resistance tales claimed that the French workers building the Storches urinated in the glue pots, which caused early failure of the laminated plywood wings; thereafter, Storch production was shifted to Czechoslovakia only.

One late April day, as I watched the villagers flow into a field, I suddenly spotted the angular and ugly profile of a Storch on the ground. The stories of Patton's troops "tanking" Bitburg had spread through Germany. The local people now came out of the villages not to welcome us but to show that their community was unoccupied. They didn't want their village to suffer the bombardment Bitburg had suffered.

I fought off my primal fear long associated with the profile of the Storch. The Storch was not moving, so my feelings quickly turned to rapture. It appeared to be in perfect condition. I was going to capture a Storch of my very own! I immediately called my ground crew to bring up troops. I intended to land and seize that prize. As I rolled to a stop on the pasture and the villagers edged forward, a self-appointed spokesman explained in fair English that the plane had landed hours ago and that no soldiers were in the village.

Our Third Division flack half-track raced down the field, followed by our radio car. It was understood that all personnel in our Air Section would share whatever benefits our prizes and booty brought. In the case of an enemy aircraft, that usually meant rides, trips, and booze.

I became extremely cautious in the last days of the fighting. I was now the only original pilot still flying out of the 34 pilots that had been assigned to the Third Division, and *Janey* was the only original L-4B still flying. We both would make it through the war if we survived the next few days. The dread of a battle in the Redoubt filled our waking hours and our dreams. Would there be an early end to the noise, dust and stench of fighting, or a long and bloody slugfest with diehard Nazi fanatics? The Austrian Alps were visible in the distance. Was this the Redoubt area that was to be held to the last man? We didn't know that Hitler had left his fortress to personally conduct the defense of Berlin.

I was also in constant fear of booby traps. The last FW-190 I had seen down was in mint condition, but I didn't go after its gun camera. Back in Munich a couple of Focke-Wulfs were booby-trapped and somebody had been blown to pieces. Combat-wise front-line soldiers knew that every German fighter plane had a camera, either a movie camera or a Robot camera with a motor drive. Nice mementos. But I wasn't going to take any chances with a Focke-Wulf, and I certainly wasn't going to take any chances with the grounded Storch. I asked the villagers to push the plane around, and I stood back. A villager who claimed to be a mechanic started the engine and fiddled with the controls. No surprises so far. I took the controls and taxiied the mechanic around the pasture, but to take the Storch into the air would have been suicide. An American gunner might have mistaken me for the enemy.

No men were around to guard the Storch, so keeping the German prize safe was a problem. Luckily an old friend of mine, Major Murray, showed up and we became partners in liberating the plane. We made elaborate plans. The next morning, Murray would drive in with a truck that was supposedly under repair and cart the dismantled Storch to his area for safe keeping. We'd find an airfield to fix it up on and paint it with our Division colors. To put the icing on the cake, the German mechanic agreed to go with the plane.

Murray offered to trade me my Storch for an Opel convertible, but I was hesitant, scared to death I'd never see the Storch again let alone fly it. I trusted Murray as a friend and thought long and hard about a trade.

The Salzburg airport, the last stronghold of the Luftwaffe, was soon ours, and Murray and I delivered the Storch to the airfield. We found some Germans out of uniform who helped us maintain the plane. It was in their best interest to do so. After all, the Russians weren't far away, and we had food. We wasted no time in getting the Storch airborne. In the two weeks we had the Storch, all our pilots had several chances to fly it, and our ground crews and flak gunners were eager passengers. We confined our flying to straight and level flights.

It wasn't until I took General O'Daniel up in my prize, to get his official permission to keep it, that a suggestion was made regarding the Storch's ultimate fate. I needed his permission to keep the plane and to have it painted with the Division's colors. O'Daniel took one flight, then told me to trade off the plane.

"Schultz," he said. "I'm only two-star. The minute we go down to Corps they're going to take it away from us." Even two-star generals, with earlier ranks than O'Daniel's, could take the Storch once the war was over and West Point rules were reinstated. Date of rank meant everything to West Pointers. General Dwight Eisenhower had been given a Storch, probably a French or Czech-made version. It was presented to him by the French as a trophy. I'm not sure if Eisenhower ever used it, but there was a strong possibility that some other senior general might requisition ours.

We spent a couple of days lamenting our bad luck, but we had great respect for the words of General O'Daniel and followed his suggestion. Major Murray, who had had only a few flights in the Storch, was informed of the prospect, and together we decided to dismantle the plane and declare it unsafe. We closed our eyes and bade farewell to the Storch. An Opel convertible was left in its place when the Storch was removed. Third Division markings were painted on the Opel and our authorization for a Mercedes kitchen truck was tucked in the glove compartment. Lieutenant Richards hopped into the Opel and headed for Grenoble, France, the Division's rest area. The Opel wouldn't fly, but it would be a lot of fun on leave. Little did I know that I would never enjoy its use.

The two Germans I captured in the field. They played dead when I landed *Janey* nearby. After photographing them and taking a taste of their brandy, I turned them over to a US Army tank column. *--Alfred W. Schultz*

41 · *THE GRAY LADY*

Being able to land on the smooth concrete Autobahn would have been ideal as we advanced east toward Salzburg and a link with the Russians. German Autobahns had broad grassy shoulders, gentle curves and a gradual slope. However, two years of combat experience had taught me it was nearly impossible to get military vehicles to separate long enough to give us a safe landing space. We had to forget landing on paved surfaces or roadways and settle for cropland or pastures, and the risk of mines and booby traps.

Out of respect for their fellow Germans, we thought the die-hard SS troops would stop using antipersonnel mines and booby traps in a cause that even the most fanatical Nazi must realize was lost. It was a bitter irony of war that in the final days, the SS would be killing and maiming their own people.

In the fast-moving situation we now enjoyed, the ideal landing strips were pastures along the Autobahn. Such fields were easy for the wire crews to make their connections, close to supply, and with enough traffic going by, only a minimum guard would be required. Theft of supplies had not been a problem since Italy and Africa; we were posting guards now because we wanted to be on the alert for any SS infiltrators who might be planning a death charge, fanatical *Volksturm* soldiers, young or old, and the displaced hungry drifters wanting to surrender to Americans rather than to the Russians.

In the closing days of the war, Major Tanner reiterated my three jobs: take charge when he was flying General Sexton, fly the dawn mission, and locate and move the Air Section to advance fields. Today, while watching the sun peek over the distant snow-clad mountains and burn the mist from our valley, I'd spotted a couple of lush green landing fields a couple miles ahead; in Iowa we'd call the crop winter wheat.

Both fields would be ideal if they were half as good as the slanting sun's rays made them appear from the air. I had to be patient if I wanted to find out just how good they really were, and the only sure answer came from ground inspection, which was my job.

Flights of fancy took possession when the ground below looked like a two-dimensional air photo, and the observer didn't have a target to check. My mind often explored each passing patch of ground as if I were looking for a bride on a beach full of beautiful girls.

Any field is beautiful to a Cub pilot when it has a smooth surface, is 300 to 400 feet long and clear of obstructions at both ends, provided it's at least 60 feet wide. And, too, the fantasy field should have a slight tilt into the wind and its long dimension should run parallel with the wind. The higher the side obstructions, the wider the field must be to minimize the effect of a crosswind, the dreaded enemy of all aircraft.

A nice level square would have been ideal, but that was rare. Instead, we learned to deal with our constant companion, the crosswind. With practice, a pilot can master the crab approach to the longest landing path and then with more resolve, try to go smoothly from the crab position to straight running on the strip, but the moment of truth happens so fast that if a puff of wayward wind lifts a wing, a-looping you can go. That's why when landing between obstructions that create the wayward swirls, a pilot must be right on or be prepared to handle a ground loop without panic.

My job required selecting fields that were good for aircraft operation and also provided creature comfort and safety for twenty-five to forty men. Each day brought new challenges as the terrain shifted from flood plain to valley to hillside and pilots brought to us their unique skills and shortfalls. Planes were hard to come by, weather controlled repair capabilities, so it was a shame whenever a Cub became a casualty to a bad airfield.

Those of us who flew L-4Bs had enough trouble from the Germans, who were trying to collect the bounty on our heads—so why make it harder by choosing a difficult field? Pilots have gigantic egos and they know each takeoff is being watched by nearly everyone on the field. Did I hold it down long enough? How many bounces before airborne? Did I establish a uniform and sensible rate of climb?

Tired after an hour and forty-five minutes of our enemy-fooling, ack-ack-dodging ballet, we landed with our kidneys about to burst as we tried to grease a landing in a gusty cross-wind with mechanics, cooks, drivers, observers and other pilots making book on how many bounces it took before we finally got settled and how much of the field we used. To endure that routine three or four times a day and suffer in stoic silence without bopping someone when they awarded us a trophy for the highest bounce of the day or the all-time multi-bounce record, took a man who was at peace with himself and knew damn well he was the finest pilot in the air. My job was to provide all players a level field, so I wouldn't be killed by an irate award winner.

A battery of the Ninth FA Battalion was displacing forward, so Stein and I joined their section of the convoy. Once in convoy, vehicles stayed in line unless there was an urgent reason to drop out. I was doing my job, so the slow-paced convoy was a welcome opportunity to enjoy Bavaria's spring weather, even though we had to endure the start-stop-start-crawl around the blown Autobahn bridge spans and cater to the whims of the often ill-humored MPs.

Enemy resistance had nearly evaporated, yet we still feared that the coiled Nazi snake might strike. Our ring-mounted .50-caliber and pedestal-mounted .30-caliber machine guns were manned and pointed skyward, waiting for the

Luftwaffe to make a pass. New replacements wanted some action before the battles ended. Many wanted the thrill of firing their guns in anger and the chance to build up a stock of war stories for children yet unborn and to match the tales of World War I veterans when they gathered in smoky bars back home.

Stein and I were pleasantly trapped among friends, swapping lies and enjoying the balmy spring day with its faint bouquet of flowers and musty smell of freshly-turned earth. Wildflowers and fruit trees blossomed along the ditches and stone walls of this small rural wagon road. Partially hidden from view between a fruit tree almost ready to burst forth in white and pink petals and a low gray stone wall veiled by still-bare vines, a bundle of gray cloth seemed wedged. It wasn't the discarded field-gray uniform of a German soldier. It looked more like a bulky peasant skirt. As we inched ahead and stopped again, I saw that it was a body clad in a gray wool gown. As we moved again, the peasant woman became forever etched in my mind.

Silver hair covered her head and flowed onto the fine amber netting of her shawl, which blended into a voluminous gray skirt. A full view revealed a large, brown cowpie-colored, cowpie-shaped blob where her face had been. I looked away, hoping we'd lurch forward again, but we stalled momentarily. Drawn like a magnet, I looked again. Sadly, my first glance had seen it all. The horror was too real. The farm wife might have been caught in the field when a fire fight erupted. Perhaps in panic she had hidden from the bullets behind the wall or under the tree planted by her family decades ago. Had she been forced into the *Volksturm* to snipe at our dogfaces as they marched east to join the Russians and to extinguish the death ovens, which were still roaring at full blast?

My mind took off on wild flights of fancy as to whoever or whatever was waiting around the next corner. We were so close, yet there was still time on the game clock before the final whistle blew.

Janey's engine had coughed a day or two ago when I

reduced power for a landing. I wouldn't do that again. From now on, I'd always make power-on landings. My .45 hadn't been cleaned since that night in early September 1944, when flush with victories, the cooks had made apple cobbler and we'd received gun-cleaning supplies and went on a cleaning binge. Four of the men who had fastidiously cleaned their .45s were no longer with us. I didn't want to be the fifth missing gun cleaner.

Still etched in my mind was the image of Boone. After eating the apple cobbler we'd saved for him, he'd sat cleaning his gun while whistling "Paper Doll." He and Boyer lost their lives the next day to an ME-109, two days before Boone would have received confirmation of the Silver Star I'd recommended for his heroism on Anzio. Despite a gas tank that contained only fumes, he and *Janey* had stayed in the air within reach of enemy weapons in order to direct the Big Guns on a column of Tiger tanks. Boone and *Janey* had prevented a disaster on Anzio.

The bureaucratic delay in announcing the award made me bitter at first, then on reflection I realized that the thorough examination was a credit to the Third Division. It ensured that each medal awarded was deserved and not a numbers game played to please the Press.

Each night before sleep, each dawn when I awoke, I prayed, first to thank God for my being alive and then to ask Him to grant me another day. I refused to clean my .45, and I insisted on flying the dawn missions. The superstitious baggage I nurtured couldn't be shared with anyone, for it would destroy the self-image of the macho dashing captain I wanted to project. When I relaxed, spooks from the past marched by as if passing in review at a parade, and now the slow convoy had forced me to digest one more grisly sight. I hoped one of the fields up ahead had animals grazing on it so I could be certain it was free of mines.

42 • *MOON OVER THE AUTOBAHN*

"Schultzie, O'Daniel is coming. He wants two planes!" Sergeant Vince Romeo called from the radio car. Victory was in the air. Perhaps we'd fly forward to take the German surrender. What a great picture it would be for *Life* magazine: O'Daniel, Schultz and a couple of German generals ending the war. I hadn't fired a shot in anger since Munich, so I too was eager for some last-minute action, even a surrender.

I gulped my coffee and yelled across the field to Richards. "Bill, bring your plane over! We've got a mission and we don't want to keep the general waiting."

Four jeeps raced cross-country off the Autobahn directly to *Janey*. Iron Mike O'Daniel was in one of them. "Get me another plane for my interpreter," he ordered as he jumped out of his jeep. I'd flown O'Daniel for two years and I'd never seen him so agitated. "Let's get going. They can follow," he barked, and off we went.

Croal had *Janey*'s motor humming with a single spin of the propeller. After a short warm-up and a quick magneto check, I eased *Janey*'s throttle full forward and started our roll down the green carpet. Tender young stalks of grain cushioned our path, and soon *Janey*'s wheels lost contact with the earth. We were airborne three minutes after the General's arrival. Bill climbed right behind us with the General's interpreter in his plane. The smooth takeoff into the clear spring air of this beautiful, broad sunlit mountain valley surrounded by distant snow-covered peaks made the war and its memories seem like a bad dream.

"Follow the Autobahn. Land where you see a couple of French command cars," O'Daniel ordered in the deep gravelly voice that I knew so well. We flew about five miles east over the jammed Autobahn. The westbound lanes carried an orderly stream of happy Wehrmacht soldiers organized in company-sized groups (250 men) marching to the safety and the good food of our American POW cages. For them the war was over. The east-bound lanes were crowded to the shoulders with a hodgepodge of French 20th Armored, Rangers and Third Division vehicles. General Patton would have taken O'Daniel's scalp if he'd seen that mess. But O'Daniel didn't care. As soon as he spotted the French delegation, he tapped my shoulder, indicating that this was the spot. Landing, however, seemed impossible. Military vehicles rarely yielded to aircraft. But as I swooped *Janey* down low, the traffic separated like the parting of the Red Sea. O'Daniel's aide had placed a 6-by-16-inch red placard with two white stars in *Janey*'s rear window. I landed on the Autobahn and pulled the plane to the shoulder. Richards and the interpreter landed right behind us.

Accompanied by screaming tank sirens, the French Commanding General and his party followed us in. A spirited discussion took place, with Iron Mike throwing up his hands in gestures of desperation. Something was going on, and it was obvious the French didn't like it. The sirens sounded again, and O'Daniel, his interpreter, and the French generals drove off to the east.

As Richards and I stood by our planes watching the troops herd their prisoners down the road, a jeep stopped across the way and out jumped a small, scrappy-looking Ranger with a jaunty swagger in his stride. The man waved frantically to us, so Bill and I began to walk in his direction. I suspected this was the same jolly Ranger I had first met outside my dugout in Anzio, the one who had said "Sam's boy reporting;" the one who gave me a snappy British Army open-hand salute; the bombardier who sat in *Janey*'s back seat tossing out 81mm mortar shells during a night-time sneak attack on Cisterna; the very same Ranger who had claimed my German cousins would always spare my life. Yes, it was Keith Rozen! And now he was Captain Keith Rozen.

When we were about 20 yards apart, with a great flourish, he dropped his drawers, turned, and pointed to the cheek of his ass to show where he'd been sliced by shrapnel on the fourth day of the Anzio breakout. Luckily we were far enough from the Grand Conference of Generals that our reunion went unnoticed by the Brass, or Grease, as the French call their generals.

The dogfaces in the Third Infantry probably thought it was just another one of those damn-fool things their officers did for amusement, further proof that without corporals and sergeants we'd be losing the war. But Keith's display had a very different effect on our captives. Like a wave racing along a sandy beach, the first German to see the dropped drawers nudged the next, who nudged the next, and so on. Nudge by nudge, smile by smile, and laugh by laugh Keith Rozen again broke the tension of our deadly game of War. Some of the Germans probably regarded this display as some sort of juvenile pantomime, but we will always refer to it as the "Mooning of the Wehrmacht." Hitler and Goebbels would have had fits had they known that a Jewish Ranger captain was mooning their master-race Aryans, who were now being marched into captivity.

The mooning lasted only seconds. The vanquished continued to move west to safety, and the victors moved east to the Redoubt area, where we feared SS troops were preparing for a fight to the death. Sirens sounded again and French Tricolors slapped the command-car's fenders as it drove into sight. Rozen buckled his belt and continued shepherding his prisoners, and I was standing by *Janey* when O'Daniel returned. We left behind a shining moment in the annals of warfare.

As the general climbed into *Janey* for the ride home, he grinned like the cat who had eaten the canary, feathers and all. I started west to our Division strip, but O'Daniel tapped me on the shoulder and pointed east to Salzburg. Moments later we were over the junction of the Saalach and Salzach Rivers. I circled the Schloss Klessheim (Hitler's guest house for foreign dignitaries) and just beyond, spread like giant tapestry, lay the Salzburg Airport. It was a picture out of a storybook or from a Hollywood war movie. Planes of all descriptions and markings were parked helter-skelter on the field and peeked out of the woods surrounding the grassy landing spaces and runways. Bomb craters were painted in brown and gray on the concrete, tarmac, and grass. From two miles away it looked like a scene of total destruction, yet at 800 feet, it was an abundance of usable space.

A few plumes of smoke rose in the still air of the broad mountain corridor, but we didn't see any signs of troops. I asked the General if he'd like to land, but he motioned me back to base. Iron Mike climbed from *Janey* smiling like Jolly Saint Nick, then he literally jumped into his jeep, which had trailed us down the landing path. Something Big was up and I knew not what it was.

Later the story circulated throughout the entire Division. O'Daniel, rather than let the French pass directly through our Division as decreed by Higher Headquarters, was to have the solo honor of humiliating Hitler by capturing his home, the Berghof. O'Daniel had saved the honor for the Third's Seventh Regiment, so the Stars and Stripes would fly there first. How had Iron Mike saved that honor for his Blue and White Devils? Without disobeying orders, he had allowed Third Division units to move forward, causing a gigantic traffic jam on the only road that bypassed a major demolished Autobahn bridge. The French could either construct their own bypass or take turns with the Third's vehicles while the Third's MPs set the tempo.

The French had to be satisfied with a repeat flag-raising ceremony the following day for the Press and posterity. A French Army color guard raised the French Tricolor to fly beside the Stars and Stripes on poles of equal height.

As soon as Iron Mike O'Daniel was clear of *Janey*, I taxied over to Bill's plane and without cutting power shouted, "Bill, tell Rosner we're going for a check ride! I've got something to show you!"

I wanted to get going before all the planes I'd seen at Salzburg were torched. Once airborne I checked with Geist. "Stand by, need you soon, have a field."

"Loud and clear," Geist responded. We had good contact, and I hoped we could keep it. Within minutes Bill and I were flying awe-stuck over Salzburg's green paved runways decorated with painted bomb craters. Below, in and out of the surrounding woods, lay an array of American and British planes, in mint condition, sporting their original markings, and several others bearing the German Cross and Swastika. The only planes being destroyed were those queer-looking airframes without propellers, the ME-262 jet fighters.

I gave Geist a final call. "Over, out. Landing."

"Roger, moving," Glenn answered just as *Janey*'s wheels touched the smooth grass where moments before I'd seen an American truck traveling parallel to a paved road that circled the field. Land mines always scared me. I made it standard practice to land in the tracks of other vehicles or on the dogfaces' marching routes.

Rumors spread that the war would be over in hours, or tomorrow at the maximum. The Germans had made us pay dearly for each mile we had traveled in their country. Augsburg, Nuremberg and Munich had all been costly battles.

I had neglected to remove O'Daniel's two-star placard from *Janey*'s rear window and decided to leave it showing while Bill and I explored the field. The two white stars on the red background would give *Janey* two-star protection.

Bill and I knew enough to keep our hands in our pockets and let others explore and de-mine the enemy's war machines. Just three days before at the Munich airport, an overeager soldier had tried to pry a gun camera from the wing of an FW-190. He lost both hands, and was lucky to be alive. As we walked around the planes, we made a 30-foot circle, and even this safety buffer seemed daring.

Across the road stood a two-story barn. The mottled stucco building was surrounded by a shoulder-high stone wall. The wide main entrance led to a courtyard bordered by tall pines. A smaller opening in the stone wall was filled by an ornamental steel grille sporting the Luftwaffe's flying eagle in the center. The site looked good, and I wanted to explore it. Bill and I were pondering how to get someone else to enter and poke around when the answer emerged from a doorway. A huge, coarse man wearing the loose gray uniform of a German POW started toward us. My damp hand tightened its hold on the checkered grip of my .45. After my experience with the two *Hitlerjugen* playing dead a week ago, I always carried my .45 on me whenever I was away from *Janey* on enemy soil, and my gun hand always sweated.

In very broken German the giant spoke in a deep rumbly voice. "*Nien Soldat! Nien Soldat! Nien Soldat—Yugo!*" He raised his arms high over his head, and his face beamed with joy. His joy became contagious, and I relaxed my gun arm.

"*Nien Soldat—Yugo! Yugo!*" he repeated as he slowly lowered one arm and twisted his body to point to the faded white POW letters stenciled on his back. He was telling us he was a Yugoslavian, not a soldier.

"Ya, ya," I responded.

"*Oui, oui,*" Bill called out, to see if his French might strike a common bond. Yugo only smiled, revealing a row of stumpy teeth capped with a dull silver-type metal.

"*Yugo—Kooken, Kooken. Gut kooken,*" he said next and accompanied the announcement of his job qualifications with animated motions. He moved his hands as if he were mixing cake batter and then pretended to wash and dry his hands. Last, he flexed his biceps and smiled broadly enough to split his face. We knew we had a winner. We engaged him on the spot. He gave us a tour of the building and grounds while the general's two stars protected *Janey*.

In the past the building was probably a country inn or a school. The ground floor was a combination kitchen, dining hall, and bar. The second floor was partitioned into a lounge and eight sleeping rooms. An exterior addition had served as a combination privy and bathroom. It wasn't the movie-set Officers' Club in an old castle we'd always hoped for, but it was far better quarters than we'd had day in and day out for the last three years. I secured the building for the Air Section. It took only a good bluff and a piece of chalk. I wrote "CP, 3rd Div. Air Section, Maj. Tanner, CO" on a door facing the street.

The sooner I could get Geist and our radio car parked in the yard with some bodies hanging around, the safer I'd feel. Possession is far more important than rank when it comes to finding combat housing, and I wanted this rough-cut gem. The significance of the sign wasn't lost on Yugo. He smiled again, revealing years of neglected dental hygiene. The grove of pines surrounding the compound sheltered dozens of Wehrmacht and civilian vehicles. Once de-mined, the collection of mobile equipment would provide hours of enjoyment for our mechanics.

Within an hour, the first plane landed and in it were the clothes to transform Yugo into a Yankee soldier. The former prisoner of war wedged his huge feet into our largest combat boots, barely squeezed into the pants, and stretched the extra-large sweater to the limit, but he looked like a GI. Not long after that, six lieutenants were lounging on the doorstep of the new command post and three L-4Bs were parked across the road. By early evening Geist's radio car was parked behind the stone-wall entrance and our kitchen truck partially blocked the large gate to the inner courtyard. For effect, the driver let the air out of one of the truck's front tires.

The *chunk-chunk* of American Tommy guns and the burp of German Schmeissers could still be heard in the distant hills, but the frequency and duration of those fire fights indicated they were oozing to a close, like the cooling of lava flowing from a volcano. The fire in the crater must be nearly out and maybe tomorrow all could be quiet. Below us, the Germans marched west in orderly ranks, while a hodge-podge of American vehicles and captured German trucks, moved east. The hoods, cab tops and doors of the liberated German trucks were now emblazoned with our 3-foot white stars. Everyone wanted to ride, and who could blame them?

On April 29, outside Munich, we had registered the Big Bangers for the last time. On May 3, with the rumor of Marshall Albert Kesselring's armistice commission gathering somewhere near Salzburg, we were able to leave the counterattack protection of the infantry to the self-propelled 105s.

By May 5, our country inn was registered with both Division Headquarters and DIVARTY. Wire connected us to the communications network and the official unit sign proclaimed our location. The general's two-star placard lay face down inside the trunk of Geist's radio car. No one had questioned the stars displayed in our window.

Major Tanner returned briefly on May 6 to service his L-5. Almost immediately, General Sexton received another call for a high-level staff meeting, so Tanner again left me charge. I wanted the war to be over and when I got into bed, I prayed, "Please God, end it tonight." But my prayer wasn't answered. We still had to make potential combat flights for one more day.

On the morning of May 8, 1945, right after first light, Geist shouted from the radio car the news we'd been expecting for days. The war was officially over. Geist and Romeo started dancing for joy and jeep and truck horns everywhere started blowing. The Third Infantry Division had fought for twenty-two months and paid nearly 35,000 battle casualties for this news flash. *Janey* and I didn't have to fly the morning patrol.

43 • *JOY RIDES*

The Air Force, naturally, took over the Salzburg Airport, but Yugo and the little inn on the far side of the field was ours. Thanks to Sergeant Joe "Hook" Casanova and his far-reaching trade network, Yugo was now properly fitted with extra-large boots and regulation olive-drab pants, shirt and sweater. He looked like a bona fide member of the Air Section, and no garritroopers or "pink pants" would be likely to spot him.

One day I was watching the usual steady flow of war prisoners straggle past our inn. A German officer sat in the back of an American jeep stuck in the traffic. He wore a rumpled uniform with a bright burst of silver and jewels under his chin where one might expect a bow tie. I walked over to closely inspect his medal. Dressed in my GI shirt and pants and adorned only with my captain's bars and wings, I was boringly plain in comparison.

"*Vas ist Das?*" I asked in German.

"Many would have worn these if we'd had more time," he responded in English and the jeep drove on.

Years later I saw a picture of the man and realized I had spoken to Inspector General Adolf Galland, one of Germany's greatest aces and the head of the Luftwaffe. Because of his hundreds of victories, the medal around his neck was the Knight's Cross of the Iron Cross with Cross Swords, Oak Leaves and Diamonds, Germany's highest award for Valor, the World War II version of a Blue Max.

Not long after VE Day, the Army's old peacetime chicken rules were reinstated—morning calisthenics, repeated inspections, and seemingly-pointless tasks to keep the troops busy. I was a chauffeur again and *Janey* was my limo. We flew Brass to meetings and conferences and back again. Whenever General O'Daniel called for a plane, naturally I'd be his pilot.

Iron Mike greeted me with a broad smile as he arrived at the strip one particularly clear, sunny day. "Schultz, today let's take a joy ride!" he ordered in the hoarse, gravelly voice I had become so accustomed to. "We'll soon be leaving this area. I'd like to get a look at King Ludwig's fairyland castle from the air. And while we're at it, let's fly down and circle Hitler's Eagle's Nest. After all, we took the place just ahead of the French."

It was a perfect day for flying. The long grassy pasture on the valley floor gave us a smooth takeoff and soon I had *Janey* circling the storybook castle. How such a magnificent structure could have been built in that rugged area defied imagination. On the third circle, O'Daniel tapped my shoulder and I headed *Janey* southeast to Berchtesgaden and the Eagle's Nest.

I had estimated from my large-scale map of the area that I'd need to gain an additional 3,000 feet to give us a good overview and to safely clear a set of high-powered electric lines. The lines stretched between the mountains that guarded the approaches to Hitler's hilltop retreat. Altitude is a precious commodity when you're flying close to your plane's service ceiling, which in a Cub is 12,000 feet. I had used 60 to 70 percent of the *Janey*'s potential in getting above Ludwig's castle. My flight plan called for a minimum climb of 3,000 feet above the ridge to clear the high-power lines by about 2,000 feet, and be a few hundred feet above the Eagle's Nest. The plan gave me a 20-percent safety factor. It seemed logical until we flew over the swinging cables and started an uncontrolled free fall in a downdraft I hadn't planned for.

Milliseconds became hours as my mind spun with tales I'd heard in hangars of mountain crashes, flat spins, and downdraft evasion. I imagined the smirks of future pilots who might confirm pilot error as the cause of death for General "Iron Mike" O'Daniel, the Conqueror of Kesselring, the Avenger of Anzio, and the Scourge of the Siegfried Line.

The seat belt pressed against the top of my legs. We were in a free fall, headed for the bottom of a gorge cut by a rapid rushing stream 6,000 feet below, if we didn't hit the four giant power cables and get barbecued first. Instead of a control stick, I held a handful of mush. *Janey*'s throttle was wide open, and I didn't have an iota of feel on the control surfaces. We had no forward movement; Mother Nature was in control. I gingerly held the stick in a slight forward position, fearful of exerting any pressure that might cause a wing to drop and start a deadly spin. The force of gravity assisted the downdraft and both were sucking us to our fate. I was floating above my seat as the cables raced up to meet us.

The altimeter spun backwards. O'Daniel could easily see over my right shoulder as our air cushion of support and safety spun away. He and I had shared many adventures since I'd flown him on that first reconnaissance flight over Anzio. Now we'd share our last adventure together. I felt a surge of inner peace. It was over. My mistake had been in trying to fly over the cables. Only prayer could help now as those cables rushed up to ensnare us. Slowly I settled into the seat, then bounced up and settled back again with only a slight pressure from the seat belt. My hand felt a welcome pressure on the stick. I saw *Janey*'s airspeed increase and the cables pass below me. We'd lost nearly 1,400 feet, but we were past the cables and still above the stream as *Janey*'s airspeed continued to increase. *Janey* was still aloft, and we would continue our spring joy ride. Was it a miracle, or was it a simple and sudden shifting of convection currents?

I started a slow climb to regain the altitude we'd need to properly view Hitler's pride and joy. I rubbed the sweat from my hands onto my pants and hoped the stench of my underarms hadn't enveloped the whole cabin. O'Daniel gave no indication he'd been aware of our near-death experience. After two circles of the mountain top and a few slow, scenic passes over the complex known as Berchtesgaden we headed home. I held *Janey* to the low route, about 2,000 feet below the cables. As we approached the broad green landing pasture, it looked like a mother's arms outstretched to welcome us home safely.

"Good flight," O'Daniel said. "I'll be down in the morning to fly to Freiburg for a staff meeting."

Right: **Yugo, after his transformation from a German P.O.W. to a happy, oversized cook for our Air Section.**
—*Alfred W. Schultz*

Bottom: **Major General John "Iron Mike" O'Daniel, commander of the Third Infantry Division posed with *Janey*. *Janey* and I had flown him above battlefields from February 1944 in southern Italy right through to the end of the war in Germany.**
—*Alfred W. Schultz*

44 • *THE FINAL FLIGHT*

June wore into July, and I developed a toothache from an impacted molar. An old friend who happened to be a dentist, Captain "Dee" DeMartini, examined me and said, "Six months ago I'd have given you several slugs of Scotch and blasted the bugger out while you screamed to high heaven. But now I recommend you go to a base hospital in Paris so you can be treated properly. I just don't have the equipment to do a proper job."

"To minimize the pain until the paperwork comes through," Dee continued, "gargle with saltwater every hour or so. Drink two shots of booze in the evening to help you sleep." Then he added with a broad smile, "Doctor's orders."

I didn't have to wait long for my Paris trip. Tanner had a new set of orders for me that very same day. "You'll never believe this, Schultz." Tanner said with a grin. "You get to fly *Janey* to Orly and report to Captain Mike Strok, Air Force Supply. You're on special duty for the next ninety days."

Lucky? Ninety days? Mike Strok's experiments and gadgetry had nearly killed me at Cassino. He had me performing reckless stunts, dropping rations to the knife-happy French Moroccans and attempting to lay wire for the Pack Artillery. His modifications to *Janey* and the devices he'd dreamed up had nearly resulted in spreading *Janey* and myself over the mountainsides. What new experiments did Mike have in mind? The war was over. I wasn't a test pilot. I hadn't come this far to perish because of some Rube Goldberg contraption.

"What's the mission?" I asked, holding back a strong urge to refuse to go.

"Something about a victory exhibit of aircraft under the Eiffel Tower," Tanner answered. "Whatever it is, you'll be in Paris for three months. You can take one of your crew with you. Who'll it be?"

"Croal," I responded immediately. "Chuck and I have been together the longest. He's my first choice, if that's OK." The memories of all the places and experiences Chuck and I had shared made it an easy decision. "How soon do they want us?" I asked.

"As soon as possible. Check it over with Croal and I'll get the paper work going. You deserve this, Schultzie. Have fun and send us a postcard."

My tooth didn't bother me any more that day. In fact, in the excitement I nearly forget my gargle routine, but not quite. The saltwater gargle had definitely relieved the pain, but as a safety valve I went to see Dee again.

"Schultzie, the anger has gone out of your gums," he said, peering into my mouth. "If you gargle for a few more days, you might not have to have that molar out till you get home. Meanwhile, to make sure you get the saltwater where it belongs, take this old bulb syringe of mine. Squirt the saltwater between your teeth and along the gum line."

Even though Paris was four hours away, I had three days to make the trip. By dawn the next day I had packed most of my worldly goods into *Janey*'s rear seat, and we were airborne. Croal drove to Paris in a ¾-ton weapons carrier, courtesy of the Ninth Field Artillery Battalion Headquarters.

I flew *Janey* on a zigzag course to Paris and did plenty of gawking along the way. The weather was balmy, so I flew with the top-half of the door off. I squirted saltwater from Dee's syringe onto my aching gums, then I spit the saltwater out the open top of the door. The next day, streaks of salty residue were visible on *Janey*'s right side, like she'd been leaking white engine oil.

Croal bunked at Orly with the Air Force ground crews. I shared a room in a downtown Paris hotel with a P-38 pilot, Captain Jim Rogers from Delaware. He was not a full-blown ace with five kills but had plenty of assists and over forty missions. Our experiences were not exactly the same, but we both knew the nerve-shattering crack of ack-ack.

I could hardly believe my good luck. I was alive, un-scarred and stationed in Paris. Chuck and I busied ourselves by cleaning and polishing *Janey* and giving public-relations flights around Paris to Brass and to Chuck's new-found friends. But those flights ended with a BANG. An Air Force plane crashed in a Paris suburb, and all recreational flights were banned. Chuck and I then began living the life of Riley.

During the last week of July, 1945, *Janey*'s wings were removed and she was pulled tail-first through the streets of Paris to the Eiffel Tower. There she was re-winged and suspended over the Big Boys of the Air Force. The Victory Exhibition opened August 1, 1945, to huge crowds. *Janey* became a favorite due to stories in the Paris newspaper *Le Figaro* re-counting her work in Italy with the French and the Moroccan armies. Croal and I worked from 10 to 3 every day, answering visitors' questions about the famous Cub. It was easy duty, yet when I finally got a phone call from Division Artillery in Germany, I made an on-the-spot decision about my next posting.

"Schultz, you have the points to go home this weekend. Shall I keep your name on the list?" the major asked.

"Yes," I blurted without hesitation. It was over for me. The boys in the Air Section would understand. All the plans, obligations and commitments during the last three years didn't mean a thing now. Home beckoned. I didn't need to be asked twice. I just had to say goodbye to Croal and to my plane, then I'd let my family in Iowa know I was coming home.

Under the view of the Eiffel Tower, I said farewell to *Janey*. I stood under her suspended airframe and looked up, wishing I could touch her one last time. I imagined walking the short distance around her outspread wings, caressing the smoothness of her propeller, and running my hands over her patched, olive-drab skin. With imaginary fingers, I slowly traced her name on the engine cowling and remembered how carefully Croal had painted it there. I was sorry I couldn't sit one last time hard-assed in the pilot's seat soaring over the European countryside. I was proud of *Janey*. She had served longer than any other reconnaissance plane in Europe during the war. She was a part of history now—and a part of my soul.

Right: **Colonel Chris Coyne surveyed the results after Air Force bombers destroyed a German war machine fuel supply. Towards the end of the war, German tanks were powered by charcoal generated propane.**
—Charles Croal

Bottom: **We posed after being awarded Air Medals upon completion of the Colmar Campaign in February 1945.** *Top row, left to right:* **W. A. "Bill" Richards, Virgil H. Dahms, Edwin "Irv" Rosner, Norman H. Tanner.** *Bottom row, left to right:* **John J. Rodrigues, Alfred W. Schultz.**
—Third Division Signal Corps